FEMALE
SECRET
AGENTS

Also by Douglas Boyd

Histories:
April Queen, Eleanor of Aquitaine
Voices from the Dark Years
The French Foreign Legion
The Kremlin Conspiracy: 1,000 Years of Russian Expansionism
Normandy in the Time of Darkness:
Life and Death in the Channel Ports 1940–45
Blood in the Snow, Blood on the Grass:
Treachery and Massacre, France 1944
De Gaulle: The Man who Defied Six US Presidents
Lionheart: The True Story of England's Crusader King
The Other First World War: The Blood-Soaked
Russian Fronts 1914–22
Daughters of the KGB: Moscow's Cold War Spies,
Sleepers and Assassins

Novels:
The Eagle and the Snake
The Honour and the Glory
The Truth and the Lies
The Virgin and the Fool
The Fiddler and the Ferret
The Spirit and the Flesh

FEMALE SECRET AGENTS

DOUGLAS BOYD

Cover images, from left: secret aents Agnes Smedley, Andrée Borrel and Cynthia Murphy.

First published 2016 as *Agente: Female Secret Agents in World Wars, Cold Wars and Civil Wars*

This paperback edition published 2023

The History Press
97 St George's Place, Cheltenham,
Gloucestershire, GL50 3QB
www.thehistorypress.co.uk

British Library Cataloguing in Publication Data.
A catalogue record for this book is available from the British Library.

ISBN 978 1 80399 375 1

Typesetting and origination by The History Press
Printed and bound in Great Britain by TJ Books Limited, Padstow, Cornwall.

MIX
Paper from
responsible sources
FSC
www.fsc.org
FSC® C013056

Trees for LYfe

Contents

Introduction

What makes a woman volunteer to become a secret agent, knowing that, if caught by the enemy, she risks sexual violence in addition to the injuries, imprisonment and tortures that may be inflicted on male comrades? If she is a mother, she also may be putting her children at horrific risk. Yet some women are courageous enough to do that. Espionage has been described as 'the second oldest profession' and the anger of the men they outwitted has often had these courageous women labelled whores. It is an age-old sexist slur, sadly given modern currency by misogynist Islamic fundamentalists, but some were indeed whores. Three-and-a-half millennia before Mata Hari, the history of women agents goes back to the Old Testament Book of Joshua, which records how Rahab, a 'harlot of Jericho' – that most ancient of cities – risked her life to hide two Hebrew spies during Joshua's conquest of Canaan *c.* 1400 BCE.

If female agents have generally received less acclaim than their male counterparts, this is because spying is widely and wrongly treated in fact and fiction as 'a boys' game'. Even if those agents were also ladies of the night and used their feminine wiles and sexual favours to obtain information, or escape capture, is that wrong? If a woman beds several men in the course of her clandestine life, is that somehow reprehensible when a James Bond in fiction or a Sidney Riley in fact treated women as tools of the trade or toys for their pleasure, and are heroes?

This book is not just about women who spied and their motivations for doing so. It also looks at other clandestine work that is *better* done by women, partly because of their personal qualities and partly because, even today, her male enemies are still less suspicious of a woman apparently going about her daily business than of a man in the same place at the same time. A friend of the author who was a teenage girl during the German occupation of France recounted how, when transporting incriminating material in the basket of her bicycle, she talked her way through several checkpoints by flirting with the sentries checking her papers, to distract them. Polish countess Krystyna Skarbek, alias Special Operations Executive (SOE) agent Christine Granville, outwitted Germans troops hunting her in the Alps during 1944 by dressing as, and pretending to be, a simple Italian peasant girl. She also had the nerve to reveal her true identity to a Gestapo officer when bluffing him into releasing her boss and lover Francis Cammaerts, just hours before he was to be shot during the US–French invasion of southern France in August 1944.

Much has been written about the women agents of SOE. Yet, in a debate in the House of Lords on 6 June 2011, Baroness Crawley of Edgbaston urged the government to make a gesture commemorating all the women sent into France by SOE. Her speech included the following:

Apparently, they had each been told when recruited that there was only a 50 per cent chance of personal survival. Yet, to their eternal credit, off they went. Some were already mothers; some just out of their teens. In France, they often had to travel hundreds of miles by bike and train, protected only by forged papers and, as they went about their frequently exhausting work they were under constant danger of arrest by the Gestapo. Some were even exposed to betrayal by double agents and turncoats. The story of what happened to those women is often unreadable and, in twenty-first century Britain, is perhaps too easily under-remembered.[1]

One hundred years before the Second World War, during the American Civil War, 17-year-old Belle Boyd (no known relation of the author) and Rose Greenhow flirted with Union officers and reported their plans to Confederate general 'Stonewall' Jackson after a fast ride on horseback through the battle lines. Known as *la belle rebelle*, Boyd was arrested six times before escaping to Britain. In the same conflict, Quaker-educated anti-slavery activist Elizabeth van Lew spied *for* the Union.

During the Algerian war of independence French communists known as *les porteurs de valises* literally carried suitcases full of money across the Mediterranean to finance the Armée de Libération Nationale fighting the French armed forces. When several of these couriers were caught, tortured and killed by their compatriots in uniform fighting a dirty war with the ALN, female comrades volunteered to replace them, thinking they were less likely to be detected. They too were tortured and killed. After suffering multiple rapes, their bodies were dropped from helicopters into the sea.

Hiding wounded combatants from those who would kill them, running an underground railway to help Allied soldiers or black slaves to freedom, or caring for children whose parents have been arrested by an occupying army are just a few of the clandestine acts better done by women. Communist Litzi Kohlman married Kim Philby to save her life in strife-torn Vienna, but went on with Austrian-born photographer Edith Taylor-Hart to talent spot British traitors for Stalin. Berlin-born GRU colonel Ursula Kuczynski was ordered by Moscow to divorce her Soviet husband and marry British communist Len Beurton as cover. She later said that the nappies on her washing line and a pram in the garden threw MI5 officers completely off her scent during the period when she was transmitting *thousands* of messages to Moscow from Soviet agents in the UK, including Tube Alloys atomic bomb project spy Klaus Fuchs, recruited by her brother. Also spying at Tube Alloys was Lithuanian-born Melita Norwood – dubbed 'the Red Granny' when blown by renegade KGB archivist Vasili Mitrokhin in 1989. Croatian–American Frieda Truhar spent the 1930s travelling the world as a Communist International (Comintern) courier, carrying huge sums of Moscow's cash stitched into her corselette. She risked arrest by the British police in Shanghai hunting communist agents, but her most pressing problem was an American male comrade who thought her body was common property.

This book explores why female agents from all social backgrounds and many different countries volunteered over the centuries for this dangerous life, how effective they were and what training, if any, they were given. Were the odds against them in the field better or worse than for men, given that some were apparently regarded as disposable assets by male spymasters? Some of these regarded them as inherently unreliable because they might fail to kill when necessary or were prone to form emotional attachments in the field, and even change allegiance for a lover.

In fact, the list of achievements of these courageous women is long and their many motivations fascinating: political or religious belief, love, patriotism, revenge, anger and compassion. Their achievements deserve not to be forgotten because, as Mathilde Carré, who betrayed her Resistance comrades to the Gestapo, said at her post-war trial, 'It is different for the women.'

1

The Perfect Cover for the Perfect Spy

In May 1907 a daughter was born to economist Robert Kuczynski and his artist wife Berta, who moved shortly afterwards to the pleasantly wooded suburb of Schlachtensee, south-west of Berlin, near the Havel lake. Named Ursula Ruth, this girl attended the prestigious Lycée Français and afterwards served a two-year apprenticeship as a bookseller, which was a respectable profession for the daughter of a middle class intellectual Jewish family. Already at the age of 17, her politics were far left, as were those of her parents. Whereas they hid their sympathies, she did not, joining the Allgemeiner Freier Angestelltenbund, or Union of Free Employees, and the Kommunistischer Jugendverband Deutschlands, which was the German Young Communist League. She was also appointed leader of the Propaganda Section of the Kommunistische Partei Deutschlands (KPD), after which time her political activities took up so much time that her 'day job' with the major publishing house Ullstein Verlag was lost for lack of application.[2]

With her father Robert and older brother Jürgen – both already working as agents of Soviet military intelligence Glavnoe Razvedyvatelnoe Upravlenie (GRU) – Ursula moved to New York in 1926, using the cover of her father's work as an economist. While there, she seems to have worked in a bookshop for some months before returning to Berlin and marrying Rudolf, or Rolf, Hamburger, who was a qualified architect and also a GRU agent. In July 1930 the couple moved to China, where Rudolf had been offered a job with the Municipal Council of Shanghai, a city then enjoying a construction boom. His salary, augmented by the funds supplied by GRU, enabled them to mix with the prosperous foreigners of the international settlements. The city was a hive of espionage with several high-ranking Comintern agents, including Elise and Arthur Ewert, whose paradoxical brief at the time was to muzzle the Chinese communists because Stalin then wanted Kuomintang leader Chiang Kai-shek as his ally.[3] Within a few months of the Hamburgers' arrival, their son, Michael, was born. By that time, Ursula had already been introduced by US journalist and Comintern agent Agnes Smedley to German expat Richard Sorge, a senior agent of GRU, and was using the name of Sonya[4] Hamburger, to dissociate herself from her overt political work as Ursula Kuscynski in Germany. For two years – whether or not with Rudolf's knowledge – she and Sorge had an affair under the cover of his training her in espionage techniques. Smedley, too, played an important part in her life, coaching her in journalism for the worldwide communist press.

In late 1933 Sonya was ordered to Moscow for seven months' training in tradecraft, microphotography, Morse code, cryptography and the building, operating and repairing of radio transmitters. During this time, her son was sent to live with his paternal grandparents in Czechoslovakia, so that he did not happen to pick up any Russian words and blurt them out afterwards. She was then posted to Mukden – modern Shenyang – in north-east China, which was an important centre of Japanese expansion. Her official job there was working for an American book publisher, but this was just cover for her activities as a channel between GRU in Moscow and the Chinese partisans fighting the Japanese in Manchuria. Shortly after arriving in Mukden, she became pregnant by a top Soviet agent, cover name 'Ernst', who may have been US diplomat Noel Field.[5] In August 1935 she was ordered to leave China after the arrest in Shanghai of Sorge's replacement there. Since the prosecution of communist agents was one of the few areas where the Western police forces in the international settlements collaborated with the Chinese police – the latter using torture routinely – Moscow's fear was that he might disclose details of other agents while undergoing interrogation.

She departed with Rudolf, using his contractual entitlement to home leave, for London, where Sonya's father was living under the cover of lecturing at the London School of Economics, having taken advantage of the influx of Jewish immigrants after Hitler came to power in Germany in 1933. Also staying with Sonya's parents was her old nursemaid, Olga Muth, who took charge of Michael and Nina, the daughter of Ernst, when Sonya and Rudolf were assigned to Poland by the GRU. In June 1937 Sonya was recalled to Moscow, where so many of her fellow agents had been liquidated in Stalin's purges for real or imagined failings, or simply to keep them from talking about their work. In her case, it was to be invested with the Order of the Red Banner and promoted, which makes it clear that she had already accomplished important clandestine tasks.

The purges had killed off the main players in the GRU network in Switzerland, which Sonya was now appointed to

rebuild, settling with Muth and her two children in a mountain
village near Montreux in September 1938. It was during this
period that Rudolf had had enough of their relationship and
was posted at his own request back to China, his place in Sonya's
bed being taken by Alexander Foote, a British veteran of the
Spanish Civil War, recruited as her clandestine radio operator by Sonya's sister, Brigitte, living in London. When Foote
arrived in Switzerland, to take up his GRU duties, life for him
and Sonya was very comfortable thanks to money supplied from
Moscow, laundered through the Irving Bank in New York and
passed on to them by Swiss lawyer Dr Jean Vincent, who had
been working for the Comintern in China.[6] Although Sonya
was regarded as the head of the new Swiss network, she claimed
to have been ordered in December 1939 – this was during the
phoney war – by her Russian superior Maria Polyakova to
hand her network over to Alexander Rado, head of the Lucy
network, also called 'the Red Orchestra'. Whatever blow this
might have dealt to her professional ego was salved by her sister
Brigitte, acting as a GRU talent spotter in London, sending out
another British survivor of the International Brigades in Spain
named Len Beurton,[7] who replaced Foote in her bed and affec-
tions from his first night in Switzerland.[8]

In fact, the apparent demotion was part of a convoluted
GRU plot to move Sonya into position for even more important work without the knowledge of any of her current GRU
and Comintern comrades. Many loyal Party members all over
the world, who had believed they were fighting fascism in all
its forms, were deeply disillusioned that the Nazi–Soviet Non-
Aggression Treaty signed by Molotov and von Ribbentrop in
the previous August had allied the Soviet Union with the most
extreme fascist government in Europe. Thousands tore up their
Party membership cards. It was therefore quite credible when

Sonya began complaining that the Treaty had shattered her belief in Stalin and communism, also that she was afraid Hitler would shortly invade Switzerland and liquidate her and her children, together with all the other Jews in the country. As a result, she said, she wanted out of her clandestine life before it was too late.

The truth was that the GRU was playing a very long-term game, in which she was required for a deep cover operation in Britain, which needed her to obtain British nationality by divorcing Rudolf Hamburger and marrying Foote. Unworried by this order from Moscow, Sonya chose instead to marry Beurton and received a British passport as his wife. The fly in the ointment of this neat arrangement was the nursemaid Muth who, being German, would have been an embarrassment in Britain at war. Distraught at the prospect of losing all contact with the two children whom she loved, Muth headed for the British consul in Montreux to denounce Sonya as a Soviet agent.[9] What action he took, if any, is unknown, but the news apparently never reached London.

Travel in Europe was already complicated in late 1940 with many people stranded in countries they wanted to leave, but Sonya was more than equal to this. She and her children managed to reach Lisbon and take a ship for Liverpool, where they arrived in mid-February 1941, leaving Len behind in Switzerland to avoid him being called up in Britain. Playing the part of a distressed Jewish refugee, Sonya was invited to stay in a vicarage near Blenheim Palace, to which much of the British counter-espionage organisation MI5 had been evacuated from bomb-damaged London. It was in Blenheim Palace that her first agent was working, so she rented a bungalow in nearby Kidlington and commenced clandestine radio communications with Moscow. This agent may have been Roger Hollis, later director-general of MI5, who had been a freelance reporter in Shanghai at the same time at Agnes Smedley and was often seen there in her company. Since both were journalists, their association may have been entirely innocent but it is a coincidence that he lived in the same village, less than a mile from Sonia and her father, both of whom lived within easy distance of a dead letter drop in the graveyard of St Sepulchre's cemetery. Hollis was also in charge of an MI5 section charged with watching Soviet and other spies in Britain. When Sonya's deeply encrypted messages were picked up by the Radio Security Service operating under MI5 section MI8c, it was up to Hollis to decide whether or not to use direction-finding vans to track down the transmitter. He decided not to.[10]

With Sonya's brother, father and sister all working for GRU, Britain thus had accepted as refugees four GRU agents from one family working for the USSR, an ally of the Axis enemy. She bought a bicycle for apparently innocent rides through the countryside in this time of severe petrol rationing; her motive was not fitness but visiting this and other dead drops serviced by her agent in Blenheim Palace to collect his or her material for transmission to Moscow. Len Beurton was finally ordered by the GRU to join her in Britain in July 1942 and was drafted, some months later, into the RAF, where his time was not wasted. He obtained and gave to Sonya copies of technical drawings of the latest British aircraft and, in various postings, contacted men who had been communists before the war, and now had specialist military or political knowledge, whom he enlisted as additional sources. Technical drawings, whether from Len or Fuchs, presented a problem, which was solved by Sonya passing them to a man in London, whom she knew only as 'Sergei' – presumably via a dead letter drop.[11] This was Simon D. Kremer, a member of the military attaché's staff at the Soviet Embassy in London, who was also a GRU officer.

The far-sightedness of the GRU's move in bringing Sonya to Britain was clear when Hitler launched Operation Barbarossa on 22 June 1941, with Stalin unwilling for several days to believe this was more than a local incursion despite clear warnings from Churchill and Sorge, working under cover in the German embassy in Tokyo until he was arrested and garroted in a Japanese prison. It was Sonya's transmitter that sent the top level news to Moscow that the British War Cabinet did not intend to supply materiel to the USSR because it considered the Soviet defences would collapse in a matter of weeks, such was the initially rapid progress of the Axis onslaught. Her source for this intelligence was most probably her father, who was frequently consulted as an economist by Marxist politician and former ambassador to Moscow, Stafford Cripps, a member of the War Cabinet.

In late 1941 Sonya's brother, Jürgen, was approached by the socially inadequate but intellectually brilliant theoretical physicist Klaus Fuchs, another of the 400-odd KPD members living as refugees in Britain.[12] Employed on British nuclear research, which was still in its early stages, Fuchs offered to pass top secret material to Jürgen, for him to send on to Moscow. Jürgen handed Fuchs over to Kremer, who was known to Fuchs only as 'Alexander'. They had four meetings over a period of six months in a safe house near Hyde Park, with Kremer trying and failing to instil the rudiments of tradecraft, and was understandably alarmed when Fuchs called openly at the embassy to make sure 'Alexander' was genuine! Starting in autumn 1942, Fuchs was instructed to pass material to Sonya or leave it in a dead letter drop near her home in Oxfordshire when visiting his refugee parents, who had moved there from London – ostensibly as evacuees but perhaps as accessories. To begin with, Fuchs handed over only his own research, feeling that he should not 'betray' his colleagues by stealing theirs, but this qualm of conscience was eventually overcome by Marxist 'logic', leaving him free to pass over everything to which he had access.[13]

In late summer 1943 a son was born to Sonya and Len Beurton, whom they named Peter. The 'happy event' did not long interrupt her clandestine work, transmitting to Moscow material from several agents including Fuchs and Lithuanian-born Melita Norwood, working as a secretary at Tube Alloys – a lowly position that nevertheless enabled her to read top secret material passing through her office. Working with Jürgen in London was another top flight GRU agent, who had been allowed to enter Britain as a German refugee from Nazi Germany's anti-Semitic laws. This was Spanish Civil War veteran Erich Henschke, using the cover name Karl Kastro, whose penetration of the fledgling American Office of Strategic Services (OSS), created in June 1942, ensured that many of the émigré Germans parachuted as agents behind the battle lines into the Third Reich during the war – in an OSS operation code-named Faust in reference to Goethe's character who was avid for all knowledge – were more loyal to Moscow than to Washington. Handling material from all these sources, Sonya was the most important GRU asset in Britain, beautifully concealed from suspicion by her role as a housewife and mother. With two young children playing beside Peter's pram in the front garden and a row of nappies on the washing line, who could suspect her? This was a cover identity no man could have equalled.

It was through Fuchs that she was able to pass on to Moscow in 1943 news of the UK–USA agreement to pool nuclear research. When he was transferred to work on the Manhattan Project in the USA, she handed Fuchs over to USSR consul-general Anatoli Yatsov, also using the name Anatoli Yakovlev, who was the senior GRU officer in the United States.[14] Although Fuchs' traffic no longer went through Sonya, her

transmissions to Moscow of material from other sources continued; in November 1944 'Sergei' conveyed the appreciation
of GRU Moscow Centre and handed her a more efficient and
smaller transmitter, after which she dismantled the one she
had built, keeping the parts as standby in case of need.[15] After
the atomic bombs were dropped on Hiroshima and Nagasaki in
August 1945, Fuchs returned to Britain to occupy an important
post in Harwell nuclear research station, from where he continued to feed highly secret information to Moscow via Sonya. At
the end of the war, Sonya, Len and the children moved to Great
Rollright in Oxfordshire, which became the family home, so to
speak, with both Sonya's parents eventually buried in the local
churchyard. It was here in 1947 that she was twice visited by MI5
officers and admitted her communist sympathies, while denying
that she had ever been a spy. Also living in the house at Great
Rollright was an English couple named Greathead. Madeline,
the wife, afterwards recalled that Sonya asked her to help with
the housework while she spent hours each day at her typewriter,
carefully burning every page at the end of the day. A photograph Madeline took of Sonya shows a laughing young mum
apparently without a care in the world except for mumps and
whooping cough. Madeline was also asked to look after Sonya's
children during their mother's frequent visits to London, but
she and her husband were not allowed to use the cellar, where
Sonya's transmitter was concealed.

The Western world was staggered by the explosion on
29 August 1949 at the Semipalatinsk testing ground in Central
Asia of the USSR's first nuclear bomb, which was not surprisingly a near copy of the Fat Man bomb dropped on Nagasaki.
This was several years earlier than the USSR would have been
able to produce a nuclear device without the material from
Fuchs and other Soviet spies working on the Manhattan Project.

To prevent further leaks, the FBI in America and MI5 in Britain made it a top priority to identify by whom and how the top secret documentation and samples of plutonium had been passed to Moscow. Fuchs' eventual undoing came through the Venona programme of decryption of encoded spy traffic from the USA to Moscow, conducted by the male and female code-breakers of the US Army's Signals Intelligence Service at Arlington Hall in Virginia. This led to his arrest in January 1950, shortly after which Sonya decamped with the three children to Soviet-controlled eastern Germany, newly constituted as the German Democratic Republic, telling them that they were going on holiday. It was a great disappointment for the children when they discovered they were never going home to Great Rollright again and were stuck in a grim, war-damaged country whose language they could not speak. Len had recently broken a leg and followed as soon as he was fit to travel. It is thought by some people in the Intelligence community that Sonya may have been warned by none other than Roger Hollis, then a rising star inside MI5, of the risk of her being implicated in the Fuchs investigation.

Put on trial in January 1950, Fuchs confessed to his espionage activities in Britain and the USA. In November, having given her plenty of time to escape, he named Sonya as his GRU contact. Her cover now blown internationally, Sonya resigned from the GRU or was 'let go' but left at liberty, unlike so many of her fellow spies, who were 'pensioned off' in a Gulag camp or shot so that they could never talk about what they had done. Immersing herself in the life of a civil servant in the rigidly controlled society of the GDR,[16] she was at one point fired from the State Information Office, so it may well be that her new life was deeply unsatisfying to this woman who had spent so many years controlling important agents and outwitting the best counter-espionage brains of the free world – which could have made her a very difficult subordinate. Len, meanwhile, was working for the GDR news agency ADN. In 1956, after some intermittent journalism, Sonya published the first of her several books, which was the last time she used the name Sonya Beurton. More volumes followed from various GDR state publishing houses, some for children, but all in her new name, Ruth Werner. In 1977 her book *Sonjas Rapport* was a highly sanitised account of her espionage activities without mention of any colleagues who were still alive.[17]

This extraordinary woman, who had been twice awarded the Order of the Red Banner[18] and numerous other Soviet and GDR honours, denied that she had been a spy, let alone a major spymaster, claiming, *'Ich arbeitete bloss als Kurier.'* I was only a courier. She remained an implacable apologist for Stalin and his discredited brand of Soviet communism, even after Nikita Khrushchev's denunciations of the former dictator at the 20th Congress of the Communist Party of the USSR on 25 February 1956, listing among other crimes Stalin's murder of ninety-eight of the 139 members of the Central Committee of the Communist Party of the Soviet Union in 1937–38. Nor was she moved by the fate of Rudolf Hamburger and Sandór Rado, among other loyal comrades with whom she had worked who were sent to the Gulag after years of devoted service to the cause of Soviet communism. She simply said, 'They must have made errors.' When the Berlin Wall came down in 1989 and 99 per cent of East Germans rejoiced in their new liberties, Ruth Werner pleaded publicly for the continuation of what she called 'socialism with a human face' – which is not how many people would have described the harshly repressive regime of the GDR.

Her source, Klaus Fuchs, was released from prison after serving nine years of his fourteen-year sentence, and also moved to the GDR. Sonya's other source inside Tube Alloys, Melita

Norwood[19] was publicly outed in 1999, although MI5 had become aware of her espionage activities even before they were revealed by KGB archivist Vasily Mitrokhin in 1992. After a long struggle with Parkinson's disease, Len Beurton died in Berlin in October 1997, followed nine months later by his wife. They were survived by three children, five grandchildren and three of the Kuczynski sisters.

2

Handmaidens of the Red God

The Cold War is often said to have started in 1945 as a consequence of the Second World War. This is wrong. It began a quarter-century earlier. The Communist International, its title generally abbreviated to 'Comintern', was founded in Moscow in March 1919 as a tool to subvert foreign, i.e. non-Soviet, trade unions, disseminate Soviet propaganda, finance civil and industrial unrest worldwide and exploit all the weaknesses of the so-called 'bourgeois democracies', to achieve a worldwide quasi-communist revolution *controlled by Moscow*. With all the double-talk and glib promises pared away, it was a subtle way of expanding the Russian Empire – which already reached from the Baltic to the Pacific and from the White Sea to the Black Sea – to place the whole world under Soviet hegemony.

The thousands of Comintern agents despatched into the West on these missions included many nationals of the target countries, especially women, who were in those days far less subject than their male comrades to surveillance by counter-espionage organisations such as MI5 in Britain. No one knows exactly how many non-Soviet women were devoted servants of the Comintern. What follows illustrates some of the many different ways in which they served.

Edith Suschitzky, more famous as a photographer under her married name of Tudor-Hart, was born on 28 August 1908 in Vienna, then the twin capital with Budapest of the Austro–Hungarian Empire. Her father owned a bookshop, which was a natural meeting place for academics and intellectuals, and the family had sufficient funds to send Edith to the Bauhaus in Dessau and for her to train as a Montessori kindergarten teacher. Like many other Central European Jews, the Suschitsky family was pro-communist, and Edith used her camera technique to photograph social injustice, mixing in a milieu that inevitably included Bolsheviks and other revolutionary socialists.

The capital was a fertile ground for her kind of photography, since Austria had lost both the war and its empire. Refugees, war wounded men and blind and deaf people begged openly on the streets or busked for coins if they could play an instrument. Her photographs showing adults and children in rags, some with no shoes and no access to clean water or heating in winter, remain a harrowing social document. According to historian Nigel West, in addition to being a known member of the banned Austrian Communist Party, she had been commissioned on occasion by TASS, the Soviet news agency, and undertook clandestine missions to Paris and London for the Comintern in 1929.

Aged 18, she met a British communist named Alex Tudor-Hart, who was studying orthopaedic surgery in Vienna. He had been married before and Edith was a liberated young woman. After a seven-year relationship that included the birth of an autistic son in 1927, the couple married at the British consulate in 1933 when Edith was released from jail after arrest as a highly visible left-wing agitator. The wedding enabled Alex to bring her to Britain, where she had won respect on a previous visit as an inspiring teacher of young children. With the coming to power of Hitler's NSDAP in neighbouring Germany and growing police violence against left-wing demonstrations in Austria too, it was a good time for a woman who advocated birth control and sex education for children – and was also Jewish – to be leaving Vienna.

Edith was already working for the Comintern, having been recruited by agent runner Arnold Deutsch.[20] After three years as a general practitioner in the depressed mining areas of the Rhondda Valley, Alex went to Spain, working as a surgeon for the International Brigades fighting Franco's fascist troops in the civil war, while Edith continued her photographic career in Britain, exposing the plight of working class families in industrial areas and receiving commissions from several respected British magazines, of which the best known was the iconic *Picture Post*. Although 35mm cameras were cutting edge for photo-reportage, thanks mainly to the cinema industry producing vast quantities of that gauge of film very cheaply, Edith preferred using a bulkier 2¼ in square Rolleiflex both because the definition was better and because it was held at waist level, leaving her face visible to her subjects, which she thought important.

Edith's work for the Comintern at this stage is hard to evaluate. Vivacious and extravert, she did not keep the low profile of a trained agent, but played an active part in politically committed exhibitions, making no secret of where her sympathies lay. She did not even take the elementary precaution of using a code name, but was known to comrades in the Communist Party of Great Britain (CPGB) under her own name. As another example of her imprudence, in March 1938, a Leica camera belonging to her was found during a police raid on the home of a CPGB member called Percy Glading, subsequently convicted of organising the Woolwich Arsenal spy ring for Moscow. Presumably, she had lent it to him for photographing documents illicitly borrowed from the arsenal but, when questioned by Special Branch detectives, Edith denied knowing how it came to be there. She was not charged with any offence, despite being under intermittent watch by MI5 ever since she came to Britain with her husband.

However, she did show great flair as a talent spotter for the Comintern, concentrating especially on privileged students at Oxford and Cambridge. The most famous of her finds was Kim Philby, who had married Litzi Friedman – an Austrian Jewess very active in the left struggle there – in Vienna so that she could emigrate to safety in Britain as his wife. In 1934 the two women recommended Philby to Edith's own handler, Arnold Deutsch, then living in Britain, ostensibly as a post-graduate student of psychology.[21] At a meeting in Regents Park on 1 July 1934 the two men met. Deutsch approved the choice of Philby, who had had – to put it mildly – a complicated upbringing, with his anti-British father living in Saudi Arabia with a slave-wife, given to him as a present by Ibn Saud, and his British wife in Britain kept perennially short of money. Their son's natural talent for deceit impressed Deutsch, who was also interested in Philby's ambitions for a career in diplomacy, journalism or the civil service. Deutsch's training in tradecraft of this recruit was to prove so watertight that Philby betrayed Britain for more than three decades, together with the other Cambridge spies. Among other future spies Edith spotted at Oxford were Arthur Wynn and Anthony Blunt.

Under the Nazi–Soviet Friendship Pact, the USSR was an ally of Hitler for the first twenty months of the war, so the Soviet Embassy in London had to be closed down in

February 1940, after which Edith acted as a go-between for the Comintern and its British agents. Later in the war, she had to give up her studio in Brixton and with it her career as a freelance photographer. After 1945 she found life increasingly difficult, with a handicapped son to bring up and a slow but steady decline in commercial interest for her kind of politically committed photography. The result was a nervous breakdown after the boy was taken into care. At one point she was employed as a housekeeper and did very little professional photography, although her pictures of children were praised, even by the Ministry of Education. In 1951, as the Cold War intensified, she took the difficult step of destroying most of her photos and negatives, from fear they would be used as evidence against her if she were prosecuted. Attempting to get back on her own feet, she opened a small antiques shop in Brighton and died in a hospice there on 12 May 1973 of stomach cancer.[22]

It is not easy in the second decade of the twenty-first century to understand the motivation of the thousands of women and men who volunteered through seven decades to spy on their own countries for the USSR, carry the Comintern's orders to foreign parties, clandestinely transport vast sums of money around the world to finance the worldwide revolution planned by Lenin and, on occasion, conduct industrial or marine sabotage. A critical role was played by the couriers who could pass as citizens of Western democracies, travelling on their own or false passports. They were thus mostly not Soviet citizens and, because women were less likely to be suspected in those days, many were female. These mysterious agents of the Comintern took very real risks of arrest, and worse, in many countries. They came from rich homes and poor ones, but all thought that they were 'making a better world' through the imposition of Marxism–Leninism after the destruction of the status quo.

Frieda Truhar was born in 1911 to Croatian immigrants who had settled in a grim Pennsylvanian steel town after migrating from the Balkans. She grew up witnessing her father and other men doing dangerous underpaid work in steel mills and mines, where hired thugs broke up strikes and armed police put men and women in jail for demanding improved working conditions or fair wages. Her first political steps were taken at the time of the October Revolution, when she was 7 years old, distributing leaflets during the 'Hands Off Russia' campaign and collecting coins for 'the starving children in Russia'. In 1919 the massive strike of United Steelworkers of America, the union to which her father belonged, closed down every steel plant in western Pennsylvania. Reprisal came swiftly in what were known as 'the Palmer raids'. On 2 January 1920 US Attorney-General Mitchell Palmer had 6,000 union activists jailed. After twenty-two union organisers were killed in the raids, all those not arrested went into hiding, many staying in the Truhar family home, used as a safe house for comrades on the run.

At the time of the Wall Street crash of 1929, Frieda was reading economics at the University of Pittsburgh, where she earned the reputation of an outspoken socialist and feminist. Collecting money for the families of striking textile workers in North Carolina imprisoned on charges of murdering strike-breaking thugs sworn in as deputy sheriffs, she was arrested and spent her first night in jail, singing *The Red Flag* to keep her spirits up. Her father being unemployed like millions of other men, she had to leave college and take a poorly paid job in an engineering factory, where she met an older Scottish activist named Pat Devine, who swiftly banished her feminist ideals. As she later realised, he wanted an impressionable communist virgin who would worship him and have no previous experience with which to compare his performance in bed, while she was in love with the political hero, not the man. Despite all the talk of sexual equality between socialist comrades, 'reality turned out to be making his meals, providing clean shirts and being available in bed when he wanted'.[23]

The far from feminist marriage was interrupted by Devine's arrest for illegal entry into the United States. While he was in jail, Frieda manned picket lines and organised welfare for families of the unemployed, but felt unable to cut loose from her husband, whose imprisonment made him a martyr for the cause. On release, he was deported back to his native Britain. The marriage had been a deep disappointment for 20-year-old Frieda, its lowest point coming when she had an abortion because Pat refused to let her bear his child. When she announced that she did not intend to follow him to Britain, Frieda's mother, who had always preached feminism, argued that a communist woman's place was with her husband – in proof of which she herself was going to accompany her husband to Russia, where he had signed on 'to build socialism' as a bricklayer in a new steel town on the Asiatic slopes of the Urals.

Bowing to this bourgeois–communist morality, Frieda skipped bail to rejoin Devine in Britain early in 1932. It was a lonely period. Apart from brief conjugal visits, he lived his own life as a travelling activist of the CPGB. He was in jail once again when Willie Gallagher, a founder member of the party, introduced her to its secretary-general Harry Pollitt, who gave Frieda work as a secretary in the CPGB's King Street headquarters. Before she had adjusted to life in Britain she was ordered by Devine to join him in Moscow, where he had been promoted to work at Comintern headquarters. She wrote later:

> My emotions as I disembarked in Leningrad might be compared with those of pilgrims to Mecca or Rome. The

briefest glimpse of the city as I drove to the station, drab
streets, unpainted buildings, gold-domed churches glistening
in the late afternoon sun, a sparkling river spanned by a beautiful bridge. Then the overnight train to Moscow.[24]

Lodged in the shabby Hotel Lux, overcrowded with other
ardent workers for worldwide revolution from many countries, who included her cousin Sophie, Frieda worked in the
Comintern typing pool near the Kremlin. The foreign comrades
had little contact with ordinary Russians, but she could not help
seeing malnourished men and women begging in the streets and
the starving *besprizorny* – homeless orphans with distended bel-
lies and desperate eyes, dressed in rags, pleading for food. Other
Soviet citizens spent hours each day queueing outside empty
stores, on the off-chance that anything might be delivered. In
contrast, the Comintern workers were allowed to use the *valyuta*
stores of the *nomenklatura*[25] to buy luxuries never seen in ordinary shops. Even there, things such as coffee, chocolate and
feminine hygiene articles were unobtainable, and were brought
in by comrades returning from missions in the West, to be shared
around. Occasionally, when a comrade returned from a dangerous illegal assignment abroad, there was a party with plenty to
drink, but never much to eat.[26]

The living conditions were so appalling that Frieda joined
other women in a naked protest against the inadequate and filthy
showers. The Comintern staff took their meals in the Lux canteen, which was run on the basis of Orwell's *Animal Farm*: all
animals are equal, but some are more equal than others. Sophie
and Pat were graded Class 1 employees of the Comintern and
had chicken plus extra food parcels while Frieda, a Class II
typist, received just one meatball for her supper. Defying their

unthinking acceptance of this privilege, she divided food equally and even shared hers with other girls in the typing pool.

Devine had no place in his selfish lifestyle for paternity. When she became pregnant again because he refused to use condoms, he was furious, accusing her of being responsible for the problem. Abortions in Russia were frequent because few Russian men would use contraceptives. Devine procured a rail ticket for Frieda to visit her parents, more than 1,000 miles to the east of Moscow, so that she could have the abortion where her mother could look after her. Instead, Frieda decided to have the child, which was still-born. Back in Moscow, she received no sympathy from Devine, but her post-natal depression lifted when she was invited to the Bolshoi Theatre and met, in the former royal box that was permanently reserved for the Comintern, its boss Georgi Dimitrov:

> All that evening I looked more at Dimitrov than at the performance of Othello. It was the most memorable moment of my young life and I was the envy of all my friends in the Lux.[27]

That meeting at the Bolshoi began Frieda's lonely and dangerous life as an illegal courier, using the British passport that marriage to Devine had given her. She knew it all: international train journeys carrying secret documents and considerable sums of money in her clothes; secret compartments in her luggage; furtive meetings in Paris, Amsterdam, Prague, Zurich, Basel and Hitler's swastika-bedecked Berlin with strangers who exchanged passwords and vanished into the shadows. Occasionally, she took a plane – a rare event in those days – to avoid passing through hostile countries carrying something of which the discovery would have been fatal for her. Then back to the sordid Hotel

Lux, to find that Pat was sleeping in her absence with other women there, all captivated by his political record.

With all the foreigners cooped up in the Lux that was common enough. But, although it was against all the rules, Frieda had fallen in love for the first time in her life with her contact in Vienna and was impatient to be sent back there. However, her successful European missions earned her an unwanted promotion. She was 23 years old in the autumn of 1934 when ordered to take funds to China, a country torn apart by the civil war between Chiang Kai-Shek's Kuomintang Army and Mao Tse-Tung's Red Army, fighting its way across several thousand miles of the war-torn land in the Long March.

At this point, Stalin was still thinking he would be able to control a China emerging from the chaos of the warlords and the civil war. With the Kuomintang preventing commercial bank transfers to their enemies, Frieda's mission was to smuggle in American banknotes worth US $100,000 – equivalent to more than $1.5 million today – to purchase arms for the Reds. She travelled to London, to obtain a new passport without all the giveaway European visas and was told by an older woman comrade to wear a full body corselette, in which to conceal the money. As the weather got hotter onboard ship in the Indian Ocean, it was an uncomfortable assignment.

In Shanghai, the squalid Chinese quarters contrasted with the luxury of the international settlement, where Chinese were admitted only as servants, and seemed to confirm her political beliefs. After handing over the cash, she was relieved at last to take off the sweaty corselette, but dismayed when ordered to remain in Shanghai and give the appearance of respectability to a safe apartment where an illegal transmitter was hidden. At the time she had no idea that the two Chinese radio operators of the Shanghai cell's link with Comintern Centre had recently been arrested and tortured into giving away the whereabouts of their transmitter. Her most pressing problem was not the British security police searching for her, but the American replacement radio operator, who expected Frieda to service his sexual needs on demand. After several months of jamming a chair under her bedroom door handle each night, to keep him out of her room, Frieda had to leave Shanghai hurriedly when her name was placed on a British arrest list. Since the savagely repressed 1927 communist uprising in Shanghai, the Chinese, French and inter-national settlement police forces collaborated on one thing only: hunting down communist agents. Of Frieda's Comintern com-rades, at least one had been assassinated by the Chinese police in collusion with British Military Intelligence.

Smuggled aboard a Soviet cargo ship with a suitcase in which were concealed highly incriminating documents, she endured a typhoon in which other ships were sunk nearby and entered Vladivostok harbour behind an ice-breaker. After a week on the Trans-Siberian railway, she was back in Moscow, handing over the documents and being debriefed. Expecting high praise for the risks she had run in China and the initiative she had shown, she was allocated a dirty bedroom at the Lux and awoke covered in lice, with the house doctor mocking her fears of typhus, from which one of her friends had died in Russia. Commuting again to European capitals, carrying money and compromising docu-ments, Frieda returned to Vienna, made more dangerous since the 1934 Austrian Nazis' attempted *coup d'état*, to find that her lover had been arrested and was probably dead.

Frieda's faith in the cause was still intact, but her mother's socialist dreams had melted like snow on the water in the remote Urals. Having prudently kept her American passport, she left the USSR after advising her daughter to do the same by applying to rejoin Pat, who had been sent to stoke the fires of revolution in Eamonn de Valera's Ireland, now independent of Britain. It was as well that she did, for very soon Comintern agents with Frieda's tradecraft and knowledge were not allowed to leave the USSR, but were shot or sent to the Gulag to keep their mouths shut. Frieda's disillusioned father, having Russian citizenship, was refused an exit visa, but Cousin Sophie's close relationship with Dimitrov procured an impressive-looking document covered in Comintern seals that frightened the frontier guards into letting him cross the border.

Joining Devine in Ireland, she found that her new enemies were not the local fascists, but priests who inveighed against communism as the Antichrist and granted absolution to their communicants wanting to throw Devine into the River Liffey. Retreating prudently from Ireland with him, Frieda settled down to life as wife and mother in Britain, doing occasional work for the CPGB including standing outside London's Victoria station surreptitiously handing rail tickets for Paris to British volunteers illegally heading for the Spanish Civil War. Later, as Europe headed into the Second World War, the CPGB toed an anti-Nazi line until ordered by the Comintern secretariat in Moscow to reverse its policy in accordance with the Nazi–Soviet Non-Aggression Pact. In London, Pollitt and others were incredulous that the CPGB was being ordered to support a fascist enemy, whose actions in Spain he had personally witnessed. Frieda was in the audience at a noisy meeting when party cards were torn up, with Pollitt and others made to eat crow. Later, she wrote:

> Depressed by it all, I sat still, my son quiet in my arms. I felt unable to grasp this, let alone get up and challenge it. Again, that phrase, which had been dinned into us, surfaced: 'Moscow knows best.'[28]

Divorced from Devine, Frieda married fellow-CPGB member Charlie Brewster and lived with him and her two children by Pat. Becoming less active in politics, but never abandoning her communist beliefs, she trained as a teacher and wrote her memoirs, entitled *A Long Journey*, in 1988. They were not published in her lifetime. By comparison with other internationally active Comintern agents, Frieda Truhar was extremely fortunate not to end her life labouring in the sub-zero Gulag or lying in a grave with a single 9mm bullet in the back of her skull.

One Comintern female agent who came from a different, middle class background was Margarete Thüring, whose father was a prosperous brewer in Potsdam, near Berlin. In the turmoil of post-First World War Germany, both of his daughters espoused socialism because it promised a better future than German women's traditional lot, summed up as: *Kuche, Kirche und Kinder* – kitchen, church and children. Margarete's first marriage to Rafael Buber, a member of Kommunistische Partei Deutschlands (KPD) ended in divorce, after which her ex-husband took their two daughters to live with him in Palestine, then under the British mandate. Seeking a purpose in life, she married Heinz Neumann, an MP representing the KPD, when she was 25 and he a year younger. From then on, she called herself Buber-Neumann. He edited the KPD newspaper *Die rote Fahne* (*Red Banner*), sat on the KPD Politburo and was a KPD delegate to the Comintern for the rare plenary meetings that Stalin allowed between long periods when the pretence of consultation was ignored and it was overtly controlled from Moscow in the clandestine war against the democracies.

Margarete first visited Moscow with Neumann in 1931. Like Frieda Truhar, she saw it as the Promised Land until faced with a crowd of *besprizorny* begging for crusts outside a bakery.

Although shocked to the core by this evidence that Soviet communism was a sham, she later wrote, 'The faithful Communist is unbelievably good at excusing negative aspects of Communism as temporary problems on the way to an all-justifying end.'[29]

In 1932 the Comintern ordered the KPD leadership to support the Nazis in overthrowing the Social-Democratic government of Prussia. With her husband, Margarete refused because this was bound to assist the rise to power of Hitler's openly anti-communist party. For this disobedience, Neumann was expelled from the KPD Politburo and deliberately assigned dangerous Comintern missions in Spain and Switzerland, while Margarete also undertook courier missions that occasionally allowed the couple to meet. When both eventually returned to Moscow, most of their old friends in the bug-ridden Hotel Lux avoided them in a climate of terror quite unlike the euphoria of 1931–32. Georgi Dimitrov, still general secretary of the Comintern, employed multilingual Heinz Neumann as a translator. Margarete and he were then sent to Brazil on Comintern business, but retribution for Neumann's disobedience followed when he was arrested on his return to Moscow. On 27 April 1937 he was tried in an NKVD court on a trumped up charge and shot the same day as just another statistic among the hundreds of thousands killed in Stalin's purges.

Margarete was not told that he was dead. Trying to find in which prison he was being kept, she took a food parcel every day to one jail after another, knowing that the guards would accept it only if the addressee was there. In July 1938 she too was arrested. From Moscow's grim Butirki prison she was transferred to a hard labour Gulag camp in Kazakhstan, where she would eventually have died from the work, the climate and malnutrition. From that fate she was 'saved' by the signing of the Nazi–Soviet Non-Aggression Treaty on 23 August 1939. One of its hidden clauses was Stalin's undertaking to deliver to Hitler any German communists who were in the USSR. Margarete was transported uncomfortably by rail to the women's concentration camp at Ravensbrück, known to French prisoners as *L'Enfer des Femmes* or Hell for Women. In the filth and terror of this camp where 50,000-plus women died from disease, starvation, over-work and ill-treatment, she survived five years of seeing fellow prisoners used for medical experiments, shot or killed by lethal injections or sent away to the gas chambers. As the Soviet armies approached, in early April 1945, the camp was evacuated and the last 24,500 female prisoners were herded without food on to the roads of the disintegrating Reich on a death march. Fortunately for Margarete, the guards released all the German prisoners, including her, just four days before the Red Army arrived, so that she narrowly escaped being returned to the Gulag, or worse. Instead, she began a new life at the age of 44, writing several books about her experiences, the most famous being *Als Gefangene bei Stalin und Hitler* (English title, *Under Two Dictators*). Her uncompromising hatred of *all* totalitarian dictatorships earned her constant vilification from her former comrades.[30]

In April 1944, 39-year-old Viktor A. Kravchenko, a Ukrainian who had witnessed the widespread starvation in his native country caused by Stalin's enforced collectivisation, defected from the Soviet trade mission in Washington. He was debriefed by the FBI and given a new identity to protect him from assassination by Smersh.[31] In 1949 his best-selling autobi-ography *I Chose Freedom* opened millions of people's eyes to the hypocrisy of communism and the total lack of liberty in the USSR. Moscow immediately launched a global smear campaign against Kravchenko, in which the French communist weekly *Les Lettres Françaises* alleged that the book was a tissue of lies, ghost-written by American intelligence officers. Kravchenko sued the magazine's publishers for defamation. When the case came to trial in Paris, Stalin had Kravchenko's former colleagues and his ex-wife flown in to testify that he was a sexual pervert, mentally sub-normal and a pathological liar. Kravchenko's lawyers asked Margarete Buber-Neumann to testify for the prosecution. In court, having herself been imprisoned both in the Gulag and in Nazi concentration camps thanks to Stalin's betrayal, she testified that there was no difference between Hitler's and Stalin's dictatorships. Kravchenko won the case.[32]

In 1951 the same party-line French magazine attacked David Rousset, a survivor of Neuengamme concentration camp, for writing about the Gulag, which was previously unknown to the general public. Margarete testified also in his defence against *Les Lettres Françaises*, which lost the case. She continued writing about her experiences, politics and knowing Franz Kafka, dying in Frankfurt am Main on 6 November 1989.

Neither Frieda Truhar nor Margarete gave anything away in their accounts of the Comintern episodes in their lives. Frieda never renouncing communism, that was understandable. But Margarete did see through the hypocrisy of the USSR, in whose service she had risked her life and which had murdered her husband Heinz. Yet, for reasons that have to be guessed, she too refrained from any indiscretion.

3

Born in Bessarabia,
Buried in Beijing

Liza Rosenschweig was born auspiciously on the first day of the twentieth century in the *shtetl* of Rzhaventsy – then in Bessarabia but now in western Ukraine. She was to use many names in her lifetime, most notably Elizaveta or Zoya Zarubina, Liza Gorskaya, Elizabeth Zubilin and Sara Herbert when she was travelling on an American passport in the West. As a teen-ager, she was active in the Bessarabian Komsomol, or communist youth organisation, following the October Revolution. Her studies of languages and philology at Czernowitz University in 1920 led to recruitment by Soviet intelligence, where she was employed in Feliks Dzherzhinsky's INO – an acronym of *inostranny otdel*, meaning the foreign department of the Cheka. This was a position dangerously close to the centre of power in such a paranoid organisation. Under the cover of continuing her studies, she attended the Sorbonne in Paris 1921–22 and Vienna University 1922–24, during which time she joined the Austrian Communist Party. These years left her fluent in Russian, French, English, German and her twin mother tongues, Yiddish and

Romanian. Such a prolonged and privileged period of study and travel was financed for this girl from a poor *shtetl* family by the INO, using wealth confiscated from the royal family and other bourgeois and noble 'enemies of the Bolshevik regime' who had fled Russia or been executed.[33]

In 1924 she was working as an illegal in the Soviet trade delegation in Vienna and graduated from there to work in the Vienna INO *rezidentura*, becoming a Soviet citizen in 1925. In 1929 she married fellow agent Yakov Blumkin for reasons similar to those which made Frieda Truhar marry Pat Devine: he was a hero of the Revolution, being the assassin who had murdered the German ambassador to Russia, Count Mirbach, in 1918. According to Pavel Sudoplatov, who was present at the wedding, her colleagues saw this as a true love match, after which husband and wife were posted together as illegal agents to Turkey – Russia's traditional enemy. To finance their espionage work there Blumkin sold on the black market valuable Hassidic manuscripts looted from Russian museums and synagogues. However, he also gave some of the money to Leon Trotsky, then living in exile on the Turkish island of Prinkipo after being banished by Stalin following their leadership struggle that would end in Trotsky's assassination. Zoya denounced her husband for this deviation from orders and two senior Chekists in Turkey arranged for Blumkin to be smuggled onboard a Soviet merchant ship bound for Russia. Immediately on arrival, Blumkin was arrested and shot.[34]

The 30-year-old widow – by her own hand, so to speak – swiftly married Vasily Zarubin, with whom she spied in Denmark, Germany, France and the United States over the following seven years, swapping false passports and aliases, sometimes as a Czechoslovakian couple in the textile industry or representatives of American film companies. In 1931 she gave birth to a son named Pyotr. One of their prime recruits was a mid-rank Gestapo officer named Willy Lehmann. The 1930s were a dangerous time for Soviet intelligence officers, during which she had seen many of her colleagues – especially those who had travelled abroad, as she had – executed in Stalin's insane purges. The fortunate ones were retired and given work far removed from any contact with the West. By 1941 Zoya had reached the rank of captain in Soviet intelligence, and was given a top priority assignment: penetration of the Manhattan Project, still in its early stages of creating the first nuclear weapons.[35] Zarubin had been promoted to the rank of general, and was designated *rezident* in the Soviet consulate in New York that autumn, whence Zoya travelled frequently to Los Angeles, to cultivate the family of Robert Oppenheimer, the so-called 'father of the bomb', convincing him and his wife, who had leftish sympathies, that Stalin had put a stop to the traditional Russian anti-Semitic prejudice throughout the USSR – which was the reverse of the truth, as she well knew. This lie removed Oppenheimer's reservations about passing information to Moscow which, after being Hitler's ally for the first twenty months of the Second World War, had become an ally of the Western Powers following the German invasion of the USSR in June 1941.

With her impeccable command of English, her sexy, dark Semitic beauty and relaxed manners – very unlike most people's idea of a Soviet female spy at the time – Zoya was the perfect choice for this work. Having gained the trust of Oppenheimer and his wife, she groomed them to stop making left-wing remarks or otherwise attract the attention of the FBI. Another of her brilliant coups was to set up a network of Polish–Jewish refugees in the US, some of whom had been in place as sleepers for a decade or more, and two of whom acted as her channel to Oppenheimer when direct contact became too dangerous.[36] Another important 'catch' was the secretary of nuclear physicist Leo Szilard, who handed over many top secret documents from his office. Not all Zoya's recruits had any love for the USSR or communism. In their cases, blackmail compelled their co-operation. Pavel Sudoplatov named George Gamov, a Russian-born physicist who had fled to the US in 1933, and who was 'persuaded' to suggest left-wing colleagues who were prepared to pass material by Zoya's threat that unpleasant things would happen to his relatives in the USSR, if he did not.[37] This was a standard NKVD/KGB ploy.

In the summer of 1943 Zoya and her husband moved to Washington, where Zarubin was given diplomatic cover as third secretary of the Soviet Embassy. Shortly afterwards, the FBI received an anonymous letter naming the Zarubins and nine other NKVD active spies in the US, who were all placed under surveillance. The sanity of the writer was made suspect by his allegations that Zoya was also working for Nazi Germany and Zarubin was a Japanese agent, but the FBI under J. Edgar Hoover was easily persuaded that the letter was genuine. It soon became apparent that the letter had been written by Lieutenant Colonel Vassily Mironov, a schizophrenic NKVD officer, who also reported to Stalin that Zarubin was an FBI informant. As a result of that, they were recalled to Moscow under suspicion, but the allegations were found to be false. Mironov was shot, although diagnosed as mad.

One of the couriers who took the material culled by agents inside the atomic research team to the NKVD *rezident* in New York, was Lona Cohen, who had been persuaded by her husband Morris that they were not committing treason, but working for peace. The first Soviet A-bomb, exploded on 29 August 1949, several years before this would have been possible without the theft of Western secrets, and code-named *pervaya molnya* or 'first lightning', was dubbed 'Joe 1' in the West, when detected by US analysis of high-altitude air samples. After fleeing to Moscow when Julius and Ethel Rosenberg were arrested as Soviet spies in 1950, Lona Cohen was later to become famous in the Portsmouth spy case.[38]

The Rosenbergs were executed in the electric chair on 19 June 1953. By then, Kremlin paranoia had suspended Zoya and her husband from all intelligence work or travel abroad, but she was allowed to take up an appointment as dean of the Moscow Institute of Foreign Languages. She also remained an important Party member, who took to playing the Party system and used her influence for many quid pro quos, in the Soviet way. So, it was – as NKVD/KGB sackings went – a very mild disgrace, in which her successes in the West allowed her to avoid a firing squad or long years in the Gulag. Yet the predominant paranoia meant that Mironov's schizophrenic allegations were allowed to taint the reputation of one of the NKVD's most successful agents and see her further potential in the Cold War written off. As do all intelligence officers' memoirs, Pavel Sudoplatov's book contains deliberate errors and omissions, but he does say that Zoya was recalled to duty in the renamed MGB under Beria, together with Zarubin.[39] According to Sudoplatov, he attended the Victory Day celebrations in Moscow on 9 May 1993 with Zoya Zarubina and 'our children and grandchildren'.[40] In fact, Zoya had died on 14 May 1987.

By early summer 1941 Moscow had received several reports of German preparations for an invasion of the USSR that had proven wrong. Even when Winston Churchill sent a personal warning through the British Ambassador in Moscow, Stalin's paranoia convinced him it was some kind of capitalist plot because he had convinced himself that Hitler would never repeat

Germany's error of 1914–18 by fighting a war on two fronts. No one dared point out to the *vozhd* that the ground war in the West was over, and Britain far too weak militarily to invade the German-occupied Continent. This was, in fact, exactly the moment when Hitler *had* to attack in the East.

The Comintern's most valuable agent at the time was in Tokyo. Richard Sorge set up a network of highly placed informants while employed as political adviser to the German ambassador. On 12 May 1941 he sent to Moscow a shattering report: *170 German divisions will attack on 20 June.*

> Still Stalin forbade any preparations, arguing that 149 Soviet divisions on the western frontiers were more than enough to hold any German attack. He refused to listen when told by General Zhukov that a German division was roughly twice as large as a Soviet one, as well as being far better equipped and combat-experienced.[41]

Sorge's mentor, American ex-schoolteacher Agnes Smedley, was 49 years old at the time and had led a double life for years – as a respected international correspondent, writing for *Frankfurter Allgemeine,* the *Manchester Guardian* and other newspapers and magazines, as author of several books and a spy for the Comintern. She had been married for six years to a fellow member of the Socialist Party of America, which in turn led to her involvement with the Indian independence movement. There she first came to the attention of British Intelligence investigating Berlin's attempt to exploit dissidents in the Raj during the First World War and this led to a liaison with Indian Communist Virendranath Chatopadhyaya, with whom she travelled to Germany after the war. He too was dumped by 1929, when she finished writing an autobiographical novel entitled

Daughter of Earth and moved to Shanghai for the Comintern, under the often-used cover of journalism, writing regular contributions for non-communist German and other newspapers.

It was during this period that she and Sorge became lovers as well as fellow agents for Moscow supporting the Chinese Communist Party, whose Red Army under Mao Tse-Tung was fighting a civil war against Chiang Kai-shek's Kuomintang Army. She once applied for membership of the Chinese Communist Party and could not believe that she was rejected because of 'independent thinking'. She introduced Sorge to Ozaki Hotzumi, correspondent of *Asahi Shimbun*, who was to play an important – and for him fatal – part in Sorge's spy ring in Japan. During the war, Smedley's knowledge of China saw her employed briefly as an advisor to the famous General 'Vinegar Joe' Stilwell. He was the American liaison officer with Chiang Kai-shek's forces, whom Agnes persuaded to send some supplies and materiel to the Reds, to assist in the fight against the Japanese Army in China. Returning to the US after the war, her activities were a mystery despite a team of FBI officers investigating her. Perhaps with an insider warning, Smedley travelled to Britain in 1950 just before she was subpoenaed to appear before the House Un-American Activities Committee. She died there in 1953 following an operation for a stomach ulcer, after which her ashes were transported to Beijing and spread in the cemetery for foreign comrades who had significantly helped the Chinese revolution of 1948.

4

The Women Who
Did Not Talk About It

Many young adults today have trouble listing the important European conflicts of the twentieth century. The Cold War, yes. The Second World War, just about. Then, they jump back to the so-called Great War, if indeed they get there. It seems that few have ever heard about the Spanish Civil War, which raged from 1936 to 1939 and cost a million lives in what is now the sunny paradise of North European retirees eating all-day breakfasts. Nine years after Mussolini's brand of fascism was installed in Italy in 1922 – and partly in reaction to that and the way things were heading in Germany – the Spanish people elected a strongly left-wing government in the Second Republic of December 1931. Spain, separated by the Pyrenees from the developed countries of the Continent, was then dominated by the Catholic Church, hereditary landowners and right-wing movements, of which the most important was the Falange. Those elements refused to accept the 'will of the majority', which they despised, and it was only a question of time until a cabal of generals commanding the Spanish Army, supported by the rich and the Church, rebelled against the legal government.

Although a number of books exist in English about the Spanish Civil War, most of them concentrate on the experiences of the 30,000-plus foreigners who, after Hitler came to power in Germany in 1933, went to fight for the Republican, or government, forces in the period 1936–39. Accounts by participants include Ernest Hemingway's work as photographer and reporter; George Orwell, Laurie Lee and many other men from the Western democracies volunteered for the various International Brigades in order to fight the spread of fascism, which had already taken over Italy and Germany. They witnessed first-hand the war for which they had come to Spain, but also the internecine in-fighting between socialists, communists and anarchists in the Republican ranks, which culminated in a week of full-scale street fighting in Barcelona during May of 1937. Among the International Brigades, the Comintern's Soviet commissars also regularly assassinated other communists who did not toe the Moscow party line. Working happily with them was the fanatical Caridad Mercader, personally responsible for murdering twenty or more Parti Obrer d'Unificació Marxista (POUM)[42] volunteers during the war. Her son, Ramón, assisted her and showed such promise in this bloody work that he was selected for special training in Russia that equipped him later to assassinate Leon Trotsky after seducing his target's loyal secretary, Sylvia Ageloff, through whom he gained access to Trotsky's heavily guarded villa in Mexico.

This was not a war where two professional armies faced each other with all the logistical and other support necessary for the conflict: brother fought brother, father fought son and massacres by both sides reached an estimated 50,000 civilians killed by the Reds and three times as many killed by Franco's troops. The comparatively well-equipped army of General Francisco Franco, transported from Morocco, where it had been used to suppress resistance to Spanish colonialism – in other words, to practise the ruthless repression of native tribes – looked set to usurp power from the elected left-wing government. Once landed on the Spanish mainland, it also forcibly conscripted civilians, no matter where their political sympathies lay.

The Republican forces were familiarly called *los Rojos* – the Reds. Franco's *nacionales* were often simply referred to as *los Azules* – the Blues. But the Reds, who were fighting to keep the elected government in power, included brigades of largely untrained workers, peasants and trade union members. Although mostly civilians, they had to confront not just Franco's professional army but also German and Italian aircraft, tanks and artillery after Hitler and Mussolini decided to use the conflict as a testing ground for their new weaponry and a training ground for their fighter and bomber pilots. Some ground and air support for the Republican forces arrived from the Soviet Union, but it was not decisive.

Many women did fight in the loosely organised workers' brigades on the Red side, and were known as *milicianas*. In the three-year siege of Madrid one entire Red brigade was composed of women in uniform, fighting successfully to hold at bay Franco's Blue forces. Julia Manzanal was a 17-year-old commissar tasked with political education in the Batallón Municipal de Madrid, who carried a rifle and .38 revolver, taking her turns in the front lines. On occasion, she also put on civilian clothes and crossed the lines to gather tactical intelligence. Another *miliciana* named Fernandéz de Vasco Pérez was wounded after eighteen months' front line service that included a bitter winter on the plateau de León, fighting in trenches filled with melted snow. Unfit to bear arms afterwards, she handed in her uniform and made a number of sorties through the lines in plain clothes, spying on the enemy's front line troops and officers at headquarters.

Yet, for the most part, women worked in support of their fighting menfolk. Their contribution as washerwomen, cooks, cobblers and carers for children orphaned by the struggle was vital, as was their function as nurses, replacing the nuns who had formerly monopolised hospital care in Spain. Dressmakers also turned their hands and skills to the production of uniforms in makeshift factories and hastily stitched the hessian sandbags that would save lives in hard-pressed defensive positions. Food production – of every hunk of bread, every egg and every can of soup – was also largely in women's hands. Many women who refused these traditionally feminine tasks put on uniforms and learned to use handguns, rifles, machine guns and mortars – only to find that they were also expected to scrub floors, wash clothes and cook for the men of the units to which they were posted.[43] Teachers and peasant women alike learned to make ammunition and mended weapons in workshops. In Villamayor's arms manufactory they were said to be harder working and more accurate than the men they had replaced. With Soviet-style flourish a current slogan of the Republicans was *Todas a engrosar las Brigadas de Choque. ¡Ni un solo brazo femenino inactive!*, meaning 'All women to the shock brigades. Not a single woman's arm to be idle'.

Organised around cells of the Partido Comunista Español (PCE) were the Agrupaciones Femeninas Obreras, which enlisted 1,200 women in Gijón alone. They joined in the belief that they were actively fighting not just fascism, but also for the right of women to paid work at reasonable rates after the conflict was over, instead of the pre-war half-pay for the same work. Such was the influence of the Church that previously only widows and single women had been supposed to work outside the home; all other decent women were charged with the sacred task of *hogar y niños* – looking after the home and children. In addition, women played their part as spies, carrying intelligence between the lines – in the course of which they were just as likely as their husbands, fathers and brothers to be arrested and imprisoned, or shot out of hand in some muddy ditch, often after suffering rape. Even today, nearly eight decades later, no one knows exactly how many thousands of women were put up against a wall alone or thrust into a huddle of victims in a cemetery and shot without trial. The known statistics are horrifying enough. It is reliably estimated that the remains of more than 100,000 men, women and children lie in unmarked mass graves all over Spain.

One of these female spies was simply known as 'le Blonde' – a curious *nom de guerre*, since 'le' is masculine and 'Blonde' feminine in French. Operating a clandestine radio in Republican Barcelona, she transmitted scores of messages in Morse code to Franco's headquarters in Burgos. For many years her identity and precise activities remained a secret, until a bored conscript sorting out old army records in 1964 in Madrid came across a file of the Servicio de Información y Policía Militar (SIPM) – Franco's intelligence service during the civil war.

The story begins in 1936 when this mysterious agent inside Republican-held Barcelona contacted SIPM in Burgos and offered to use a radio transmitter, to which she had access, to send useful intelligence on troop numbers, their deployment and the conditions in the Catalan capital. Having nothing to lose, Burgos accepted the offer. After a few trial transmissions in Morse code, 'le Blonde' sent useful information for several months. Then came a warning that the Reds were planning an attack to recover the important power station at Sórt in concert with a feint in the direction of the River Ebro. This was disinformation. The Reds' attack actually came on a 100km-wide front near Gandesa. Further misleading transmissions were received, so that by December 1938 SIPM came to the conclusion that 'le Blonde' had been detected by the Reds' own counter-espionage service Servicio de Información Militar (SIM) and either replaced at the transmitter by one of their own people or forced to transmit disinformation.

On 20 February 1979 a Catalan historian named Domènec Pastor Petit received a phone call from an elderly lady addressing him in the dialect of Barcelona. She said that she was the person who had called herself 'le Blonde' during the civil war, to give the impression that she was both male and French. She admitted that she had spied at first for Franco until her husband was killed in a bombing raid by Italian or German aircraft, when she changed sides. 'For love,' she said, 'not politics.'[44] In addition to naval bombardments from German ships, Barcelona suffered air raids by Hitler's Condor Legion and L'Aviazione Legionaria Italiana that cost at least 2,500 lives. In March 1938 forty-four tons of bombs were dropped on the city in twelve raids spread over two days and nights, so it may have been this raid that caused 'le Blonde' to change allegiance.

In the same way that men fought for one side or the other sometimes by conviction and sometimes by the chance of which side conscripted them, so women spied for both sides. Ibón Rosales is an investigative reporter who interviewed 93-year-old María José del Pino in June of 2013. Her clear memories of the civil war began during the nine months when Málaga held out against Franco's forces – to be exact, on the day when the Reds occupying the city beat up two of her neighbours for allegedly disseminating Nationalist propaganda and 'took them for a walk', which always ended with a bullet from a rifle in the chest or from a pistol in the back of the neck. The daily executions generated a universal paranoia throughout the city. With all the food in the house requisitioned by the Red occupation troops, María and her brothers scavenged the small pieces of fish left in fishermen's nets on the beach for their mother to cook in a soup. Each time aircraft flew over dropping bombs, the family took shelter in the house of some foreign friends, which had a Dutch flag on the roof.

María recalls her father listening with headphones to the Nationalists' radio – an offence that was punishable by firing squad if he had been caught. Hunted by the Red militia, a friend of his was hiding in an empty water butt, from which he could only safely emerge at night. María's job was to hide information on the Reds' movements and dispositions inside her bra and take it to the water butt each morning, to the accompaniment of the noise from firing squads executing those arrested during the night. What the man in the butt did with it afterwards, she did not know.

She also told Rosales that the policy of free love, much vaunted by the Reds as a rejection of bourgeois marriage, was a justification for Red soldiers kidnapping at gunpoint a girl they fancied and using her for sex. On one occasion during the siege of Málaga, while still a schoolgirl, she was on a tramcar when a militiaman started chatting her up with obvious intent. Terrified, she waited until the tram slowed down on a corner, jumped off without waiting for it to stop, and ran home as fast as she could without looking back.

After a broadcast by the Nationalist General Queipo de Llano announcing that his troops were at the gates of Málaga, María's whole family took shelter in the house of the Dutch neighbours, expecting a great battle, but for once there was no sound of shots or bombs falling. Then a strange grinding noise was heard in the street outside, with a loudspeaker calling, *'¡Viva España, malagueños salgan de sus casas!'* People of Málaga, come out of your houses! Franco's tanks had arrived and were hailed, by the del Pino family at least, as liberators.[45]

Perhaps the strangest woman spy in the civil war was a Swedish actress named Karin Tekla Maria Lannby. Her father died when she was 3, leaving her to be brought up by her mother Lilly, who was the Swedish representative of the Metro-Goldwyn-Meyer film empire and also a director of the Hotel Carlton in Stockholm. Karin grew up in considerable comfort, accompanying her mother on cruises and holidays abroad, yet by the age of 15 was already a member of the Swedish Communist Youth League. In 1936 at the age of 20, she was studying to become a nurse, but interrupted her course the next year to travel with the Swedish–Norwegian aid committee, working as a secretary and interpreter at its hospital in Republican-held Valencia and writing poetry, which was later published in Sweden.[46] In her spare time, she was also embroiled in Comintern activity, but returned to Sweden after a few months, where film director Luis Buñuel tracked her down with instructions to travel to Biarritz in south-west France and there spy on pro-Franco exile groups. Her reports were sent to Luis Araquistáin, the socialist ambassador in Paris, who forwarded them to the Republicans in Spain. At one point, Karin re-crossed the Spanish border, as a result of which she returned to Stockholm at the end of the civil war with a bullet lodged in her body. During the Second World War her strong anti-fascist convictions made her volunteer to work for the Swedish Defence Staff, reporting on German activities in the neutral capital while living with the young cinema director Ingmar Bergman and acting in several films. She was, in fact, a double agent, also reporting on the Germans to Moscow. After the war, Karin changed her name to Maria Cyliakus and moved to Paris, where she worked in journalism and films. She died there in 2007.

In Galicia, north-west Spain, the family of Consuelo Rodriguéz López lost both parents and four of their seven sons to Franco's Guardia Civil death squads hunting down Red sympathisers betrayed by neighbours. After the official end of the war, Consuelo took to the hills and joined a band of armed men and women living high in the mountains of Lugo, who continued the clandestine struggle as late as the 1950s under the banner of the Federación de Guerrillas León-Galicia. Occasonal forays of the Guardia included ambushes when the guerillas came down for food, during one of which clashes Consuelo's 'mountain husband' died in her arms. When interviewed by journalist Natalia Pugo in 2011, she voiced the opinion that life in the mountains was hardest for the women, especially in the bitter winter weather, with deep snowdrifts all around, when the shepherds' summer huts in which they sought shelter had few comforts. The only water this high was melted snow, the only food what they carried up from the plains.

To begin with, the women served as spies and couriers, carrying messages to and from the coastal plain, but also provisions and arms, and were thus more likely to be caught, tortured and sentenced to long prison terms or shot. To Franco's men emerging from their fortress-like barracks in the towns to conduct punitive raids, they were bandits. In their own eyes, they were warriors, refusing to knuckle under to Spain's fascist dictator. Other women, who remained in the family homes down on the coastal plains, were a vital source of food, maps, clothes, ammunition and information about the Guardia's movements and plans, but they too were in perpetual danger.

When the young Galician documentary producer Pablo Ces decided half a century later to make a film about this prolonged anti-Franco resistance, his research swiftly revealed that the history of the civil war in Spanish school books was a tissue of lies. But his mother's generation never spoke of what they had endured, which is why he called his film *As silenciadas* – the women who never talked about it. His film concentrated on the wives, sisters and mothers of the men who acted as their eyes and ears, but also provided everything from clothing to weapons. When summoned to the Guardia barracks, these women returned so badly beaten that their entire bodies were covered in painful bruises – if indeed they did return. One woman spent thirteen years in one of Franco's prisons, her daughters being sentenced to ten and eleven years for the same 'crime' of supporting male relatives in the mountains.[47] Clotilde Valle was the sister-in-law of a guerrilla fighter using the *nom de guerre* 'Bailarín' or Dancer. She told Pablo Ces how a summons to the Guardia barracks struck fear into every woman's heart because she never knew whether she would be allowed to leave, or be beaten to death. She recalled Clarisa Rodriguéz, a courier who was questioned, found to be pregnant, then raped and assassinated, her body dumped in a ditch as a mute warning to others.

As the history books tell it, the main confrontation ended in 1939, in time for Hitler to ask Franco in October 1940 at Hendaye on the French–Spanish border to repay the help he had received from Nazi Germany. He received a cautious promise of support, hedged around with many conditions impossible for Hitler to fulfil. Spain, with its ruined economy, was, whatever Franco's personal inclinations, in no condition to furnish troops for other people's wars. However, some RAF escapers who crossed the Pyrenees to arrive in Barcelona in 1942 and were incarcerated in the Montjuich prison regularly heard firing squads at work in the prison courtyard three years after the official end of hostilities. A British prisoner, violinist Mavis Bacca Dowden,[48] who was held in a women's prison for twenty months for the crime of helping in an underground railway network, also heard screaming during her detention and was told by other prisoners that the people being tortured were Reds. In 1945 there were still eight jails for female political prisoners in Madrid.[49] The establishment of Franco's dictatorial regime, which lasted until his death in November 1975, continued the hunting down and execution of 'internal enemies' under a veil of silence, in which *as silenciadas* conspired, fearful that careless talk would cost theirs, or other women's, liberty or lives.

5

Women Against Hitler

As the Second World War progressed towards the Western Allies' planned invasion of Normandy, a major problem for the planners was the lack of up-to-date intelligence from inside Germany and, to a lesser extent, German-occupied territory, due to the Gestapo's relentless and very efficient suppression of dissidents before and during the war. This was why the American Office of Strategic Services (OSS) set up an office in London, tasked in February 1942 with inserting agents inside Nazi Germany in liaison with British Intelligence. Within this set-up, the misleadingly titled Labor Desk was tasked with finding émigré anti-Nazi trades union members for Operation Faust – named for Goethe's character who was so avid for knowledge that he sold his own soul. It was thought that they could liaise with their former comrades still inside the Reich and possibly organise them as saboteurs when the time seemed ripe. The plan called for 200 suitable agents, who had to speak German fluently and have the accent and dialect of the area to which they were being sent. Recruited from the ranks of religious dissidents, Spanish Civil War veterans, political refugees and underground labour groups, they also had to have 'experience in underground activities in Germany and contacts with anti-Nazi groups'.[50] It was this last part of the brief that made it easy for Erich Henschke and Jürgen Kuczynski to infiltrate many communists among those selected for training at a country house not far from London.

Among them was Anne Ebbert,[51] born in June 1906 in the town of Bochum in the Ruhr area of Germany, where her father was a miner. Like many mining families at the time, when safety precautions underground were inadequate and men frequently died unnecessarily, the Ebberts were active in union affairs. At the age of 13 Anne joined the Sozialistische Arbeiter-Jugend socialist youth movement. Her ambition was to become a nurse but poor health forced her instead to train and work as a kindergarten teacher. Meeting her ardently Catholic future husband Jupp Kappius – two members of his family were priests – in her early 20s, she enlisted him in the Internazionale Sozialistische Kampfband (ISK) a strongly anti-fascist organisation. She took the name Ebbert-Kappius when the couple married in the late 1920s after agreeing not to have any children in order to be free to risk their own lives unencumbered in the fight against the rising tide of fascism in Germany. After the coming to power of Hitler in 1933, ISK became an illegal organisation; its members who painted anti-Hitler slogans on all the brand new bridges of the Reichsautobahn in the night before its official opening by Hitler on 19 May 1935 not only caused many editing problems for the propaganda film of the event, but they also risked long spells in Himmler's already brutal concentration camps, if caught.[52]

When the other German socialist and other anti-fascist political parties were harassed and closed down in the late 1930s, ISK survived because its cell structure prevented any one member from knowing more than a few others, all of whom were using cover names. To her comrades in the anti-Hitler struggle, Anne was known as Jutta. Nevertheless, placed on the Gestapo's wanted list in November 1937 under their true identities and charged with high treason, Anne and Jupp fled to Switzerland, leaving all their belongings behind to be confiscated by the Nazis. To survive, she took work as a domestic servant, continuing her clandestine work in her free time. From Switzerland, Jupp moved to Paris and later to London, where he had contacts in the Vanguard group of social revolutionaries, who were British allies of ISK. To earn a living there, he worked in a vegetarian restaurant. On 25 June 1940 Jupp was arrested in Sheffield during the nationwide round-up of enemy aliens and sent with long-term émigrés, Nazi sympathisers, anti-Nazis, Jews and other Germans and Austrians to 'the island of barbed wire', which was the wartime Isle of Man. From there, he was shipped to Australia, where he was incarcerated in camps from September 1940 to July 1942.

There are some agents who develop a taste for the adrenalin kick of the clandestine life; Anne was not one. Although she lived in terror of the long arm of the Gestapo, her conscience made her continue the fight against fascism. In August 1944, Supreme Headquarters Allied Expeditionary Force (SHAEF) was particularly concerned with the lack of current intelligence from within Germany, and ordered OSS in London to execute Operation Faust with an initial core of thirty selected agents drawn from anti-Nazi exiles living in the Hampstead area of London. In command was 29-year-old Lieutenant Joseph Gould, who had some union experience in the US film business behind him, but knew little of European politics.

Jupp fulfilled Gould's requirements exactly. Having been shipped back to the UK, in the late spring of 1944 he was given parachute training at Manchester's Ringway airport, together with two other male ISK comrades and a woman comrade named Anna Beyer, for his mission which involved parachuting back into the heavily bombed Ruhr. Further training was conducted in Scotland. Not the least important item was a visit to a clothing store of refugees' garments to find under- and outer-wear, every item of which had been made in Germany. Since this was the first operation of the kind, and Jupp the first Faust agent to be dropped into Nazi Germany, a reconnaissance was vital, to update contacts with ISK and other trades union members on the ground, to find who was still free and willing to continue the struggle, who had been arrested, who was under surveillance, and who was simply too terrified of the ubiquitous Gestapo presence to take any further action.

For this highly dangerous reconnaissance mission, the OSS office under Allen Dulles in Berne gave Anne the identity of a Red Cross nurse and false identity papers in April 1944 so that she could cross the loosely guarded so-called 'green frontier' between Switzerland and Germany, where there were no major towns, and travel to Berlin, Göttingen, Hamburg, Hannover and Kiel at a time when Allied carpet bombing was devastating German towns and cities. On the Eastern Front, the Soviet armies were pushing the Wehrmacht back from the Crimea and entering Ukraine, Romania and Poland. The Western Allies had invaded mainland Italy, and the German High Command was aware of the enormous build-up of US forces and materiel in Britain, which meant that a cross-Channel invasion was imminent. Inside Germany, therefore, the Gestapo was more vigilant than ever. If caught, Anne knew she would be tortured at length and finally beheaded by axe or guillotine, or killed in an even more painful way.

There had been talk between the ISK comrades and their OSS handlers about the RAF parachuting weapons drops to arm an anti-government socialist resistance movement inside Germany. It was the failure of the 20 July plot, which had enjoyed support at the very top of the German military machine – seven field marshals were hanged on meat hooks in Plötzensee prison for it – that put paid to the idea of arming socialist civilians. In any case, not only were the numbers in each ISK cell very small, but there was little chance of recruiting more after US President Franklin Roosevelt unilaterally imposed the principle of unconditional surrender at the Casablanca Conference. This effectively meant that, however the war ended, all Germans would be treated as equally guilty. At this point the ISK leadership resigned itself to the fact that the Nazi regime could only be overthrown by force of arms, i.e. by the Western Allies and Soviet forces.

On 1 September 1944, on a windless moonlit night, Operation Downend saw Jupp parachuted from an RAF aircraft into the Ruhr region.[53] Once on the ground, he buried his parachute and jumpsuit, but then understandably experienced an almost paralysing fear on realising that he had lost his identity disc in such a compromising place. After dozing until daylight, he forced himself to head for the nearest train station. First, however, he had to find out what was the conventional greeting, which could have been *Heil Hitler!* with right arm outstretched in the Nazi salute. Meeting the first people on the way, he made as if to say hallo, but waited until they had said *Guten Morgen!* before returning the traditional greeting. Surviving in this hostile Germany was to be a succession of such toes-in-the-water tests like that. Having been in exile for seven years, his second big error was to address the ticket collector on the train in English, but fortunately the man took no notice!

Jupp's brief from OSS was to:

> create an underground organization for the purpose of (1) promoting internal resistance to the Nazi regime; (2) committing acts of sabotage against the war effort; (3) encouraging subversion in all its forms.

It continued:

> ... you will cause rumors [sic] to be spread according to the following directions: (1) to create dissension between Wehrmacht troops and political formations, e.g. Waffen-SS, Gestapo, Hitler Jugend [and] (2) create panic on the German home front and among troops resulting in a run on the banks [and] (3) to encourage surrender or desertion.[54]

OSS seems to have been unaware that Jupp did not consider himself their agent, being so opposed to capitalism that he had refused any payment from the organisation apart from the sum of £5 per week for expenses.[55] He personally saw his mission in Germany as the reorganisation of underground socialists for political action after the Allies' defeat of the Nazi regime.

On the day after the landing, he arrived at the safe house in his home town of Bochum, which would be his base until January 1945. To obviate the risk of being recognised by old acquaintances in his home town, not all of whom would be friendly, he had to stay indoors during daylight and use his host to contact people. Soon after his return to Germany, Jupp realised that it was impossible even to build a meaningful network of anti-Hitler socialists, such was the intense surveillance of the civilian population by the Gestapo and the universal fear this engendered. He therefore confined himself to organising a cell

structure of seven men,[56] each of whom had contact with two
to five others, mostly former shop stewards or union organisers,
but including railway staff, a publisher, an important employee
of the Krupp metal works and directors of a mine company and
Deutsche Bank.

He also prepared extensive situation reports, covering bomb
damage in the Ruhr, industrial morale, which factories had been
bombed out of production, the state of electricity production
and transport – all of which was strategic information. Although
later German agents dropped back into the Reich were equipped
with directional VHF transmitters to communicate with Allied
bombers overhead without being monitored by German listening stations, these so-called Joan-Eleanor sets – hardly bigger
than a modern smart phone – were not available for Jupp.[57] To
overcome the problem, Anne was flown to Britain for training
and despatched, together with another ISK veteran of the struggle against the Nazis named Hilde Meisel – code name Crocus
– to Thonon-les-Bains on the shore of Lake Geneva. Hilde's
mission was, once in Germany, to travel to Vienna and organise
an espionage network among fellow anti-Nazi socialists there.
Their conducting officer, Lieutenant Anthony Turano, likened
these two committed, vegetarian activists in drab clothing to
secular nuns.[58]

There was nothing monkish, except his vegetarianism,
about Jupp. Through his contact at Krupp, he had the promise of 250 rifles and a local police commander had agreed to
hand over all his firearms for an uprising just before the Allied
troops arrived, to prevent last-minute Nazi execution squads
from doing their bloody work. Also on Jupp's list of priorities
was the frustration of the Nazis scorched earth policy, so that
there would be food and other vital supplies for people after the
fighting had passed on. To his surprise, a knock on the door of

his safe house at the end of September revealed Anne standing
on the doorstep, bringing him news from the ISK comrades in
Switzerland. In return, he gave her his reports for OSS and the
co-ordinates of a drop zone he considered safe for the RAF to
parachute additional firearms and ammunition. What the result
of such a small-scale uprising would have been, is impossible
to say, but it would likely have been wiped out to the last man
and woman. So it is perhaps fortunate that RAF photo reconnaissance revealed a searchlight unit and flak battery near the
suggested drop zone, after which the mission was aborted.[59]

A few days later Anne set out on the return journey with
Jupp's reports at risk of her life. Once across the frontier, she
handed them over at OSS headquarters in Bern, but also gave
copies to an association of socialist émigrés called 'Union
deutscher Sozialisten im Ausland', who in turn forwarded them
to Willi Eichler, head of ISK in London. On her journeys, Anne
also contacted other old comrades in the pre-war struggle against
Nazism, collecting intelligence from them, too. In addition to
the dangers inside the Reich, illicitly crossing the German–Swiss
frontier, although in a country area where guards were few, was
dangerous – as Hilde Meisel was to find out.

Shortly after Anne's departure, on 4 November Bochum
suffered its first heavy bombing raid, in which hundreds of
tons of incendiary and high-explosive bombs literally rocked
the earth beneath the streets for forty minutes. Jupp observed
this from above ground, unable to enter a shelter in case an old
acquaintance recognised him. Afterwards, whole streets were
flattened; food failed to appear in the shops; public transport
was non-existent; water supplies were irregular; with electricity unpredictable, candles became worth their weight in gold.
People packed suitcases and lived ready to flee at short notice,
but remained cowed by eleven years of repression, to the point

that Jupp realised it would be impossible to assemble enough fighters to mount even the smallest uprising.

At the end of December 1944 the Gestapo used a female agent to penetrate the ISK-affiliated women's groups in Hannover and Berlin, which Anne had visited shortly before. These cells were immediately rolled up, with all members arrested, interrogated at length under torture and sent to concentration camps or imprisoned.[60]

Fortunately the ISK members in Hamburg and the Ruhr were warned in time to go to ground because, from then on, Jupp was the sole contact for ISK in the whole Reich. In the chaos of the disintegrating Reich, Anna returned to Bochum for several weeks in January and February 1945. All radios capable of picking up foreign stations having been confiscated long since, she brought Jupp a radio receiver, on which he could listen for coded messages broadcast from London and the BBC's accurate war news, so different from Goebbels' distorted version on German state radio.

On 9 May 1945 – one day after the ceasefire – Jupp travelled to meet the nearest US troops and liaised with OSS officers there, to be extensively debriefed, but it soon became apparent that his hope of ISK being given some civil power in return for his bravery was not to be realised. Meanwhile, Anne in Switzerland organised food and medicine deliveries into the former Reich before rejoining Jupp in the heavily bomb-damaged industrial and mining region of the Ruhr, settling with him and some other party comrades in the city of Bochum within the British Zone of Occupation.

The disintegration of normal life at this period in Germany is hard to imagine. In a letter dated 30 October 1945 – five months after the end of hostilities in Europe – to comrades who had survived the Nazi years, she talked of the problems of growing food that could not be found in the shops, and expressed sadness that the USSR, to which socialists had looked before the war as an example, was imposing a brutal form of occupation on the satellite countries of central and eastern Europe and especially on the population of the Russian zones of occupied Germany and Austria, from which thousands of people were fleeing into the western zones every day. She also discussed the difficulties of organising self-help among the civilian population of the western zones, who for so long had been punished for showing any initiative or any private enterprise. In 1946, both she and Jupp joined the Social Democratic Party, which had to fight against a new enemy in the form of the Soviet-controlled Sozialistiche Einheitspartei, or Socialist Unity Party, based in East Berlin. Anne had long suffered from heart trouble exacerbated by the stress of her clandestine years. To this was added the loss of sight in one eye. She died in 1956, aged 50. [61]

To return to Anna Beyer, the woman who trained with Jupp in Scotland, means picking up her life story in 1933. She had formerly been an active member of the Allgemeine Deutsche Gewerkschaftsbund – similar to the British Trades Union Congress. When the Nazis came to power in Germany, she moved to Frankfurt and sold the ISK newspaper openly on the square in front of the Hauptwache building in the town centre. It was entitled *Der Funke*, an exact translation of the Marxist revolutionary publication *Iskra*, meaning 'spark'. She also adapted a suitcase so that when it was set down on the ground, an impregnated pad printed the slogan *Nieder mit Hitler* – Down with Hitler – on the pavement. To finance this and other anti-Nazi activity she left her job and opened a vegetarian restaurant in the centre of town. With a choice of kosher lunch menus, illegal materiel hidden in the kitchen and specially hollowed out legs of the tables, in which to secrete lists of members' addresses, the restaurant became the clandestine headquarters and meeting place for Frankfurt's ISK comrades, organised in cells of five members.

For three years, the restaurant HQ survived in the increasingly Nazified city, its exposure being eventually due to a comrade who had spent the night there, having been arrested by the Gestapo for refusing to perform military service. In the course of his interrogation, he spilled the vegetarian beans. After handing over the restaurant to a friend who had nothing to do with the Resistance, Anna went underground while the ISK cells in the Rhein–Main region were rolled up by the Gestapo which, however, missed the big fish, as Anna left Germany, travelling through Belgium to Paris. Although it sounds bizarre, while there she held an editorial role in the production of the monthly socialist revue *Warte*, meaning 'viewpoint', which was financed by profits of vegetarian restaurants in Germany, smuggled out for the purpose pasted inside calendars. In return, copies of *Warte* were printed on very thin paper and smuggled back into Germany. After the Munich Conference in 1938 the French police started cracking down on anti-Nazi émigrés, obliging Anna to move to Switzerland and, when her residence papers were not renewed, to Britain, where she supported herself by a series of jobs in domestic service and eventually work in the kitchen of a vegetarian restaurant in London.

It is sometimes said that no one in Germany could have foreseen what was going to happen to the Jews, yet between December 1938 and 1940 several thousand Jewish children under the age of 17 were allowed to enter Britain on 'temporary' travel documents after their parents saw good reason to send them away in a 'Kindertransporte' group. One of these boys was later at school with the author, and recounted how his mother put him, aged 4, on a train in Berlin, saying that he was going to the seaside, where she would join him the following week. Sadly, he has never forgiven her for that lie, without which he would have been gassed in Auschwitz with her and the rest of his family. Since most of the Kindertransporte children spoke no foreign language, German-speaking couriers were urgently needed to bring the children to Britain. Anna Beyer answered the call and took the risk of returning to Frankfurt in order to escort a group of children to Britain. Her political activities during this time were mostly in the field of political education for the young, telling them the truth about fascism.

In September 1944, as the first Allied units crossed the borders of Belgium and Holland, there were still hundreds of thousands of Wehrmacht soldiers in France and the tragedy of Arnhem was unfolding. But it did seem that the end of the war in Europe could not be far off. Having had parachute training, Anna volunteered to be dropped into France from an RAF special missions flight into the Reich, with all the risk that entailed. Dropped into a meadow near Thonon-les-Bains on the shores of Lake Geneva that had been used by SOE throughout the war, she made her way from there illegally to Bern, where the OSS wanted to equip her and three other ISK women to perform sabotage inside the Reich. While willing to risk their lives on courier missions, all four women refused on principle to carry out sabotage. After the war ended in May 1945 Anna returned to Frankfurt and political life, joining the Sozialdemokratische Partei Deutschlands (SPD) in local and then national politics as well as founding feminist groups.

Hilde Meisl[62] was 19 when Hitler came to power in 1933. Being Jewish and an outspoken social democrat living in Berlin – which was not a stronghold of Nazism – she was an obvious target for the Gestapo. Her childhood was marked by thyroid problems, which obliged her mother to take her several times into Switzerland for treatment. Able to travel to Britain in 1932 because she had an uncle there, who was a well-known composer, she studied at the London School of Economics and began contributing articles to ISK's magazine *Der Funke* on the economic problems of France, Britain and Spain, also writing for *Warte*. Using her cover name Hilda Monte, she also helped a number of comrades to leave Germany and begged her sister and others in Germany to agitate for the release from Dachau concentration camp of defence lawyer Hans Litt. The 26 January 1938 edition of the *Manchester Guardian* carried her article entitled *In Dachau Camp, the tragic case of Hans Litt*. This came too late to help the prisoner, who committed suicide a week later.

At the age of 24, Hilde gained British citizenship by a paper marriage to homosexual cartoonist John Olday and devoted herself to writing for socialist publications including *The Vanguard*, *Left News* and *Tribune*. Collaborating with ISK comrade Fritz Eberhard, she also boldly wrote *How to Conquer Hitler – A Plan of Economic and Moral Warfare on the Nazi Home Front*, which was a blueprint for economic warfare against the Nazis. Her book foreseeing a united Europe after the war, entitled *The Unity of Europe* was published by Victor Gollancz's Left Book Club. For unknown reasons, she left the ISK in 1939 to set up with the support of the British Labour Party an anti-Nazi German-language radio station using the call sign 'Der Sender der europäischen Revolution'. Broadcasting from a BBC facility, its editorial policy was to gain listenership by the BBC policy of never falsifying the news, in contrast to German radio, which put a pro-Hitler spin on everything. One transmission in December 1942 warned listeners that the liquidation of millions of Polish Jews was 'being done in your name, the name of the German people'.[63] In the build-up to the Normandy invasion General Eisenhower's Supreme Headquarters Allied

Expeditionary Force (SHAEF) was in desperate need of more intelligence about conditions in German-occupied territory. Hilde made two courier trips into Germany, dying when returning from the last. She was shot in the legs by a German frontier guard and, rather than be taken prisoner and tortured into giving away her contacts, bit into her cyanide capsule and was dead before the guard reached her.[64]

Lacking the tried and tested political motivation of the ISK members, other OSS German-speaking women spies were a mixed bag. Shortly after Hitler's final attack in the Ardennes, an OSS officer attached to the 7th US Army named Peter Viertel saw the advantages of using female agents, who needed fewer papers to travel within the Reich than did men, now that all fit – and many unfit – males had been conscripted. Based in Strasbourg, he picked three. Ada was an Italian circus artiste, stranded in the area, whose motivation was revenge for a gang rape by German soldiers that she had suffered. Maria was a buxom blonde Alsatian woman, whom Viertel found in a camp where collaborators were detained. Bilingual in French and German, she had worked in a Wehrmacht hospital during the occupation and been the mistress of a Gestapo officer. So far as Viertel knew, her reason for volunteering was simply to expunge her record of *collaboration horizontale* and avoid the humiliation of having her head shorn in public. The third woman, Emilie, was a pert brunette passed on to OSS by the Deuxième Bureau – French military intelligence. Apart from its recommendation, little was known about her.

In a secure mountain hideout requisitioned for training by OSS, the three women were taught the various skills necessary for their missions: parachuting, use of communications, recognition of military insignia and types of weaponry. Maria was the epitome of the woman agent against which many male controllers were prejudiced, causing problems by her flirtations and affairs with fellow agents and staff during training. Just before her departure from Lyons for the drop on 3 February 1945, she confessed to Viertel her true reason for volunteering: she was pregnant by her German officer and wanted OSS to reward her for a successful two-week mission by arranging an abortion on her return. He wanted to abort the mission, never mind the foetus, but she assured him her condition was not a problem as these were 'early days', so he let the mission proceed.

Maria dropped from the belly of a B-24, buried her jumpsuit and parachute, then started walking west through the chaos of the German collapse, using the identity of a Wehrmacht nurse. Meeting the first US troops, she identified herself, made a useful report of units and weapons encountered on her long walk, and was handed over to the OSS finance officer. He introduced her to an obstetric surgeon in Strasbourg with the alibi that she had shown incredible bravery behind the lines, but unfortunately had to undergo sex with a German officer to ensure she could return with valuable information. The surgeon discreetly performed the task for 'this loyal Frenchwoman'.

Emilie presented Viertel with a different surprise. On landing in Germany, she replaced the American frequency crystals for her transmitter with crystals locking it on frequencies used by the Deuxième Bureau in Paris – and sent all her reports to it, leaving OSS in the dark. As for Ada, she took off on five separate occasions, but each time was prevented from parachuting by weather conditions.[65]

One anti-Nazi agent, who did not spy for any of the Western Allies, was born Mildred Elizabeth Fish in Wisconsin, where she attended the state university. A bilingual literary translator, she met her future husband Arvid Harnack, a German lawyer and economist, while he was studying politics and economics in America. In late 1928, Arvid returned to Germany, where Mildred joined him the following year, aged 27. The couple eventually settling in Berlin, she completed her doctorate while working at the university there at the same time as Arvid received a second law degree.

Three years later, in 1932 amid the mounting pro-Nazi political pressure, she was dismissed from her university post and joined Arvid in a tour he organised of the Soviet Union for a group of friends who shared their belief that communism would solve the problems of unequal distribution of wealth in capitalist society, which they saw as the root cause of Nazism. After a brief stay back in Germany, Mildred made a short tour of American campuses to inform students of political trends in Europe and returned to Germany ostensibly as a lecturer in the foreign studies department of Berlin University but actually as a deep cover Soviet agent in what would become the Red Orchestra spy ring headed by Harro Schulze-Boysen. In 1937 both spouses joined the Nazi Party, as was required for all teachers in Germany.

The group's clandestine radio communications were detected and decrypted by monitors of the Oberkommando des Heeres or military high command, with the result that on 7 September 1942 Arvid and Mildred were both arrested. Exactly one week later Arvid wrote what he must have known would be his last letter to Mildred, of which this is an extract:

My dear, my beloved heart,
Despite all the severity I look back gladly on my life up to now. The bright outweighed the dark. And our marriage was for the greatest part the reason for this. Last night I let many of the wonderful moments of our marriage go

through my head, and the more I thought about them, the more memories came. It was as if I looked at a starry sky, in which the number of stars increase, the more meticulous [sic] one looks.

How often ... we [laid] our heads on each other's shoulders at night, when life had made us tired, either yours on mine or mine on yours; and then everything was fine. My greatest wish is that you are happy when you think of me. I am when I think of you.

Many, many kisses. I hug you tight.[66]

Five days after writing that letter, on December 19, Arvid Harnack was sentenced to death by the Reichskriegsgericht military tribunal and hanged at Plötzensee prison in Berlin–Charlottenburg three days later. Mildred was sentenced on the same day to six years' hard labour for espionage. Apparently on Hitler's personal instructions, she was retried for the same offence, with no further evidence being offered, and this time sentenced to death. She was beheaded, also in Plötzensee, on 16 February 1943.

A friend and colleague from their time at Wisconsin University named Clara Leiser wrote a commemorative poem entitled *To and from the Guillotine*, which includes the lines:

Oh Mildred, did your soft blonde hair get soiled?
Did your own bright blood spurt up into your face?
The executioner – had he the grace
To see what luminous beauty had been despoiled?
For never could his noose have been assigned
A fairer jewel – or his beheading block.
Reader, forgive this unaccustomed shock
To tender sensibilities of mind ... [67]

Mildred's body was released to Humboldt University professor Hermann Stieve to be dissected in the context of his programme of research into the effects of stress on the menstrual cycle. In this case, Mildred's stress was from spending a whole month in the condemned cell after her second trial. Her remains were later buried in Berlin–Zehlendorf cemetery.

6

The Human Submarines

Before the Second World War one-third of all German Jews lived in Berlin. The vast majority were assimilated; they might celebrate the high holidays by going to a synagogue, much as their nominally Catholic or Protestant neighbours went to church just at Christmas and Easter. Unlike the *shtetl* Jews of Poland with long side-curls speaking the medieval Rhineland dialect Yiddish, they spoke modern German, dressed, ate and lived their lives just like their Aryan neighbours. The men who had been of military age during the First World War had medals to prove the fulfilment of their patriotic duty to Kaiser Wilhelm II.

The Berliner Jews numbered 160,000 in 1933 when the Nazis came to power but, due to increasing anti-Semitic legislation – put on hold during the 1936 Olympic Games in order not to alarm foreign visitors – their numbers had been reduced by emigration of the more prudent and arrests of the less fortunate to 75,000 at the outbreak of war in 1939. Six years later, about 4,000 were still alive there, of which 1,400 had been hidden from the Gestapo by Gentile friends. The other 71,000 had been deported and killed by the state of which they were citizens, and for which they could have been working or loyally fighting when the Reich ran out of manpower in the last years of the war.

It was an accepted 'fact' for many years after the war that, until the Red Army liberated the extermination camps in Poland and other Central and Eastern European countries, nobody had known what was going on there. In fact, after a small number of heroic escapes from Auschwitz and other death camps,[68] accurate information about them reached the Western governments through the Polish underground and other sources as early as 1942. In addition, many Germans had learned about the mass executions on the Eastern Front, when tens of thousands of Polish, Russian and other Jews of both sexes and all ages were machine-gunned into ditches. They also knew that, in addition to the several hundred concentration camps in Germany and the occupied territories, there were other camps designated *Vernichtungslagern* – extermination camps, to which some 6 million Jews and other people designated as racially inferior by the Nazis were transported in trains that could have been used to move men and materiel for the war.

Civilians may not have known all the details of these death factories – indeed, the scale and methods of killing were too horrific to imagine, or even to credit if one were told in whispers about them – but they knew they were there and why they were there. In 1980 when the author and his wife visited the former concentration camp of Bergen-Belsen, where uncounted tens of thousands died in the last months of the Second World War, two miles down the road in the village of Belsen we were served coffee by two smiling, chubby ladies in their sixties. Most of the customers in the coffee shop were middle-aged ladies, all of whom must have been alive when the camp was producing an appalling stench of untreated excrement[69] and decomposing bodies. Also, prisoners sent to Bergen-Belsen were driven out of the cattle trucks at the railhead and marched the last 4km to the camp gates by armed guards with attack dogs. Regardless of whether they could do anything about it, can people living near the camps not have known what was going on behind the barbed wire and watchtowers?

By the time the tide of war turned against Germany as defeat at Stalingrad became inevitable towards the end of 1942, there were still some 33,000 Jews living in the capital of the Reich,[70] which ironically had never been a stronghold of the Nazis and had several militant communist districts. Many of these Jews were employed as slave labourers in major factories like that of the electrical giant Siemens, which had built a model township for its employees called Siemensstadt in western Berlin. The slave labourers did not, of course, live there but in designated *Judenhäuser* – cramped substandard apartments, to which they had been moved when evicted from their own homes, requisitioned for Party loyalists.

Two of the slave workers at Siemens were 19-year-old Erich Arndt and his older sister, Ruth. His girlfriend, Ellen Lewinsky, was a slave worker at the Schubert Flugzeug factory, which made parts for Focke-Wulf fighter aircraft. Working a twelve-hour night shift at Siemens with two hours' travel to and from work, they received half what Aryan workers living near the factories were paid for an eight-hour shift. Although working conditions were brutal, with physical punishment from overseers for the slightest shortcoming, the slave workers consoled themselves with the belief that their labour was too precious in the increasingly man-starved Reich for them to be sent to the camps. They had, however, failed to take into account the essential insanity of the *Endlösung der Judenfrage* – or Final Solution of the Jewish question – which had become state policy less than 10 miles to the south of the Siemens factory at the Wannsee conference during the previous February.

Among the slave workers, rumours were passed by *Mundfunk*[71] or word of mouth, by which it gradually became known that some Jews who did not turn up at work, despite severe penalties, had gone underground and were being sheltered by Gentile friends. It was an incredibly brave thing for these people to do since Hitler's propaganda minister, Josef Goebbels, had made it clear in November 1941 that everybody caught helping Jews would share their fate and be sent to concentration camps, or worse. On a number of occasions when Jews were being rounded up at random, Erich and Ruth had hidden for the night with a Lutheran friend, the widowed Martha Maske and a mid-40s couple of anti-Nazi pacifists, Max and Anni Gehre. Their daughter had been cured of the then lethal disease diphtheria by Erich and Ruth's father, Dr Arthur Arndt. It was one thing to ask such friends for a night's refuge now and again, but quite another to ask the same people to take the risks of long-term accommodation and sharing of their scant rations for months or years to come. However, the news from Stalingrad made these three young people think that the war must soon end in a total German defeat. There were also rumours that SS Obersturmbannführer Adolf Eichmann, the 'transportation manager' of the Final Solution, whose SS rank was equivalent to lieutenant colonel, was planning *Fabrikaktionen*. These were to be wholesale round-ups of Jewish slave labourers in the factories where they were obliged to report for work. Yet, when Anni Gehre went to Frau Maske to ask for her help in hiding the three young people long term, the widow's reply was a tearful refusal, softened by a promise of food from her rations from time to time, as the most she dared do.

However, another widowed friend of Anni Gehre named Frieda Lefèbre – known to her friends as 'Purzel' – had also been a patient of Erich's father Dr Arthur Arndt, and she immediately offered to look after his son and daughter in their hour of need. There were complications. Her one-bedroom apartment was small: to prevent neighbours hearing too much noise, they would have to wear no shoes and walk around in stockinged feet; also, Purzel's daughter Ilse had a boyfriend who was in the army but not, she thought, a Nazi. So, when he came to visit her while on leave, they would have to make no noise at all. It was the best that Anni could do.

Known as *Sylvesterabend*, New Year's Eve is a major festival in Germany. Erich and Ellen were invited on 31 December to a party, where they met a beautiful extravert former classmate of Ellen. Stella Kübler, née Goldschlag, was later infamous as a *Greiferin*, or catcher, meaning a Jewish woman who betrayed other Jews to the Gestapo in return for her own immunity. There were about twenty male and female *Greifer* in Berlin, of whom red-haired Stella was the most productive, fingering more than 300 victims, mostly colleagues or schoolmates. For each one arrested she received between 200 and 300 marks blood money.[72]

With Hitler insisting that the officers and men of General von Paulus' army at Stalingrad must die where they stood, with surrender or a strategic withdrawal forbidden, on 30 January 1943 Paulus and what remained of his Sixth Army were taken prisoner by Soviet forces. One of the fortunate men who were on leave from the Eastern Front at the time was the husband of Anni Harm, whom Anni Gehre had asked to shelter Ellen Lewinsky's mother, Charlotte. His experiences in the East had killed whatever belief he may once have had in Goebbels' claims about ultimate victory. Yet the draconian punishments for helping Jews made him think twice when his wife asked for his agreement to hiding Charlotte. He consented when she told him that Charlotte was 100 per cent Aryan in appearance, would cause no trouble and would pay 100 marks a month – which was more than enough to cover her food. It was a great relief for Ellen to learn that her mother had been accepted, since a further 3,000 Jews had been rounded up and deported to death camps in the first month of the year and the deportations were still continuing. This refuge did not last long, partly because Frau Harm had a bad heart, from which she died before the end of the war. Charlotte then spent some weeks sharing a prostitute's room, vacating it when it was in use for business.

The deportations continued, Goebbels noting in his diary on 27 February, when 7,000 had been deported that month, instead of his target of 11,000:

> 4,000 Jews are now wandering about Berlin without homes [and] are a public danger. I ordered the Police, the Wehrmacht and Party to round up these Jews as quickly as possible.[73]

Where were the missing 4,000 people? Some were being hidden by courageous and sympathetic Aryans, or for money; others were hiding in windowless store rooms, cellars and lofts with no running water or sanitation. Dr Arndt was hidden in the Gehres' pantry, where he would remain from January 1943 until the German surrender in May 1945, two and a half years later. Obtaining food was the greatest problem for the clandestine Jews. Emerging briefly to find food, the hidden Jews were referred to as *U-Boote* – submarines – because they could not risk appearing on the surface of everyday life.

Dr Arndt's son was not staying submerged because he had a job in a small metal-working factory belonging to Max and

Klara Köhler. Being of military age, Erich's morning and evening bicycle rides to and from work carried a strong risk of being stopped by civil or military police or the Gestapo and asked for identity papers, which he did not have. Anni Gehre's solution was to persuade the Köhlers to let Erich sleep on the factory floor, and she also procured two ration books for him and Ruth. With a great display of nerve, Anni also approached a known Nazi sympathiser and told her that Ruth and Ellen were undercover Gestapo agents, who needed a safe house. Eager to do her duty to the Führer, she agreed to let the two girls share a single bed in the pantry behind her shop. When it seemed prudent to end this extremely risky set-up, Ellen took a job as dressmaker in a brothel, where no one asked questions about her racial origin, and Ruth was found another job by Anni, doing housework for a rich lady living in the suburbs.

More complications for the *U-Boote* arose as 1944 brought daylight carpet bombing raids by the Americans in addition to the night-time raids by the RAF, demolishing thousands of homes in Berlin. Bombed out people were forcibly resettled in apartments where Jews had been hiding, obliging them to move in a matter of hours to new refuges. The loft above Köhler's metal works now became home to Erich, Ruth, their mother Lina and Ellen, plus eventually Ruth's boyfriend, Bruno. With nightly air raids, it was also the most dangerous part of a building in which to be, but they could not take the risk of going down to the shelter, or even a basement, in case they were asked for their papers. In the daytime, they had to be careful to make no noise that could be heard on the work floor below, where one young worker was an ardent Nazi. With the only sanitation being an open bucket, in order that the women could use it in working hours Erich had to pretend every so often to be checking noisily over his tool kit, kept in the loft. Inevitably, with everyone so long stressed out and malnourished – both women and men had lost half their body weight on daily rations that went as low as one slice of bread for each woman and two for a man – tempers frayed and small differences of opinion blew up into violent arguments.

Yet, thanks to Anni Gehre, the Köhlers and a few other courageous friends, they survived until the liberation of Berlin by Soviet forces in April and May 1945. That was an even more dangerous time for the women, with drunken soldiery intent of raping every German female in revenge for the excesses of German men on the Eastern Front. The temporary military governor of Berlin Lieutenant General Nikolai Bersarin was powerless to stop this, and many Soviet officers, while trying to prevent rape and robbery if personally appealed to by victims, thought that the conquered Germans deserved all they got. Yet Anni Gehre's *U-Boote* came through all this. The subsequent arrival of Western forces in July to take over the agreed British and American sectors of the city gradually imposed something like normal life.[74]

By May 1945 there were just 1,400 *U-Boote* who emerged from the shadows to register for food. Mostly, they 'surfaced' as lonely individuals, or couples, who had lost all their relatives. The group from the factory, saved by the courage of Anni Gehre, Max and Klara Köhler and their son Hans, was the largest single unit of survivors.[75] Erich married Ellen on 16 June and Bruno later married Ruth with Dr Arndt's permission, given reluctantly because he could not see how Bruno would support her. All the group emigrated to the USA and restarted their lives there, as did Max and Anni Gehre later. Perhaps the saddest fact of the liberation was the number who committed suicide when they realised that, although they were now safe, since all their relatives and friends had been murdered in the extermination camps there would never be a return to normal life.

Despite her enthusiastic collaboration in the Final Solution, Stella Goldschlag's parents were deported and killed, as was her husband and his family, in 1943. She continued working for the Gestapo and married a fellow *Greifer* named Rolf Isaakson in October 1944. Outed and arrested by the NKVD in May 1945, Stella was sentenced by a Soviet court to ten years in labour camps, although pregnant at the time by a lover named Heino Meissl, who refused to accept responsibility when her child was born in October. Forcibly removed from her mother, the girl was named Yvonne and given her father's name, Meissl. Stella served her time in Soviet zone labour camps, returning to the western sectors of Berlin at the end of her sentence. There, she was retried and sentenced again to ten years' imprisonment, but her imprisonment in the Soviet camps was counted as 'time served'. She married three more times. Using the name Yvonne Meissl, her daughter trained as a nurse before immigrating to Israel. Describing herself as 'a person who should never have been born', she had persistent dreams of shooting her mother. Eight years after her last husband died, aged 72 in 1994, Stella died by falling out of the window of her apartment in Berlin.[76] Did she jump, or had someone caught up with her and given her a push? We shall never know.

7

When the Men are Away …

Among the motives for resisting totalitarian power is the desire to protect a loved one, no matter what the cost. Charlotte Elizabeth Wust, known to friends and family as Lilly, was outwardly a typical 22-year-old Berlin housewife and mother of three sons when war was declared in 1939. With no interest in politics, she read her husband's copy of the Nazi *Volkischer Beobachter* each day and innocently repeated its coverage, assuming it was the truth. Her husband, Günther, was in civilian life a senior bank employee, who was called up soon after the beginning of the war and at first stationed near Berlin. He came home on leave one day a week – not always to see his wife, for he had had several affairs and was at the time besotted with a 19-year-old girlfriend. Lilly in turn had an affair during his absences that produced a fourth son. Although sex with men had never been a pleasure for her, she felt flattered when a man desired her.

One of the ways in which the Nazis encouraged women to fulfil their role as producers of the next generation of cannon fodder was to grant privileges for each child born: extra rations and domestic help were the most coveted. When Inge Wolf presented herself as a new home help for Lilly, sent by the labour exchange, she considered her future employer 'not very bright', but the two women got along all right, although Lilly was surprised when Inge was mildly affectionate. Without putting a name to it, she considered her home help 'different'.[77]

On 24 November 1942 it became public knowledge in Washington, London and Tel Aviv that extermination camps set up in Nazi-occupied Poland to wipe out European Jewry were already working. Although the news was broadcast into the Reich by the BBC's German service, few people were listening, that being an offence punishable by a hard regime concentration camp; repeating anything thus heard was a capital offence. Three days later, Inge took Lilly to a café to meet a younger friend of hers, introduced as Felice Shrader. This smartly dressed 17-year-old girl with varnished nails, wearing perfume and expensive silk stockings was unlike any woman Lilly had met before. Nazi propaganda decried cosmetics or any sexy dress for women. Felice smiled a lot at Lilly and looked her directly in the eyes, which was pleasantly disturbing. The first meeting led to many visits to Lilly's home, at which other women friends of Inge's came to enjoy the relatively generous rations available there. Lilly swiftly sensed that there were among them several couples: Inge and Felice were one, but Inge seemed equally close to Elenai, who also attracted another woman. Sometimes male friends were present – most men were away in the forces – and Elenai seemed to be having affairs with them, too.

On 30 January 1943, the tenth anniversary of the Nazis' coming to power was to be marked by a radio speech by Hermann Göring, who had boasted that the Ruhr in western Germany would never be bombed, let alone Berlin. Coming just after the terrible defeat at Stalingrad, it was a considerable embarrassment for the grossly overweight chief of the Luftwaffe that he had to postpone his speech for two hours due to the presence of RAF reconnaissance aircraft in the skies over Berlin. Although most Germans must already have realised by this point that Hitler's promised victory was becoming increasingly unlikely, two weeks later Propaganda Minister Josef Goebbels tried to erase the memory of Stalingrad by declaring all-out war on 'the internal enemy', i.e. the Jews, prematurely announcing a *Judenfrei* Berlin as a birthday gift for the Führer, who would be 54 on 23 April.

The Gestapo intensified its internal war, arresting hundreds of thousands of loyal Germans, who could have fought or worked for Germany as their parents had in the First World War. In the streets of German cities, convoys of military trucks disgorged battle-ready Waffen-SS soldiers with automatic weapons and Gestapo officers, who broke into houses and apartments to arrest Jews there and in the workplace. Pregnant woman and babies were thrown aboard the trucks. Anyone who resisted was savagely beaten up on the way to the collection centres – mostly former synagogues and official Jewish buildings, from which their next journey would end in a crematorium.

On 1 March the RAF bombed Berlin. By the time the last bomber turned for home after its bombing run, 65,000 people were homeless and 700 lay dead in the burning rubble, with several thousand injured. Goebbels racked up the rhetoric against the Jews, whose fault this was, according to Nazi logic – and Lilly unthinkingly went along with this, to the horror of Inge. Felice had absented herself from Berlin during all this, keeping in touch with Lilly by letters. She returned to find Inge looking after the four children because Lilly had been taken to hospital, suffering from a dental abscess which, in those days before antibiotics, could have led to a fatal septicaemia. Every day, Felice arrived at the hospital with a bouquet of roses – and Lilly came to realise that she had fallen in love with her bold and mischievous visitor.

By a decree dated 30 April 1943 German and Austrian Jews were stripped of all rights, their ration cards and even their nationality. Yet, about 5,000 were living illegally in Berlin alone, in addition to another 1,000 who were legal because they were protected by an Aryan spouse. The illegals known as U-boats existed on black market food and were sheltered by friends, neighbours and relatives who were technically Aryan. In all this turmoil, Felice confessed to Lilly that her real name was Schragenheim and she was Jewish – as were Elenai and a man who occasionally joined Inge's circle of women friends meeting in Lilly's apartment. Closer than that, Lilly's brother, Bob, was the result of an affair her mother had had with a Jew, although no one talked of that; it was bad enough that he was hunted by the Gestapo as a communist.

Gradually, Lilly learned Felice's family history. Her parents had been dentists during the Weimar Republic, when half of all the doctors, surgeons and dentists in Berlin were Jewish. After the Nazi takeover, her father was at first exempt from anti-Jewish legislation because he had fought in the 1914–18 war, and he died before the introduction of the Nuremburg racial laws in September 1935. In 1938 Felice's sister, Irene, managed to emigrate, thanks partly to Dr Schragenheim having invested funds for both daughters in Palestine. She left Germany just in time. On 1 January 1939 all Jews were required by law to add 'Israel' to their names if male and 'Sara' if female. So Felice became officially Felice Sara Rachel Schragenheim.

At the beginning of October 1942 she and Inge broke into the deserted Schragenheim family apartment, which had been sealed by the Gestapo, and 'stole' some family valuables, leaving a note on the kitchen table in which Felice declared she was going to commit suicide. She removed the yellow star from her coat and became a 'U-boat', living with Inge's parents. They pleaded with her never to go out in daylight as the hunt for Jews in Berlin was still ongoing, with Stella Goldschlag-Hubler, her husband and the other *Greifer* active in the streets and public places. For six months Felice lived mostly with Inge's parents, but the odds of her being 'outed' were growing shorter. She could have moved in with Elenai, but her 'half-Jewish' mother[78] was serving a ten-month sentence in the Moabit prison for an indiscreet remark someone had overheard and Elenai's family did not need any more problems. So Felice used the excuse that Lilly was still weak after her dental surgery to ask Inge if she minded her embarrassing lodger going to live with Lilly, to look after her.

By this time, Inge was relieved. For Felice to be hidden in the family home of a soldier's wife seemed the safest alternative and Felice's lack of food coupons would be compensated by Lilly's extra rations for her children, which Inge collected when she did Lilly's shopping. Also, she knew nothing of Felice's and Lilly's feelings for one another. The only problem was what to do during the increasing spate of Allied bombing raids, because Felice could hardly go down to the cellar of Inge's apartment block during a raid without pro-Nazi neighbours asking awkward questions.

So Felice moved in, happy to live with Lilly and the children, who adored her. During the day, she wandered from Inge's to Elenai's and other friends' homes, reasonably safe with a 'chaperone pass' for her to accompany children moving to the country to escape the bombing, which Lilly obtained for 2,000 marks through the man in Inge's circle. He was surviving by selling off, one by one, a collection of valuable rugs belonging to his father. Another method of earning some money that the women used was having a photographer take erotic or pornographic photo-graphs of them to sell to soldiers on leave.[79]

Although she did not mind Günther visiting the children or staying for a meal, Lilly filed for divorce because she wanted no excuse for him to demand his conjugal rights. Her parents and parents-in-law thought this was crazy, but she was influenced by the freedom that Inge and her friends flaunted: Inge, Nora and Elenai were a *ménage à trois*, but this did not seem to upset any one of them, nor scandalise the others. Although, when on leave, Günther spent the nights with his girlfriend, he decided to fight the divorce, at which point Lilly told him that the young-est child was not his. On one crucial Sunday afternoon, when she was in bed with Felice, Lilly's mother arrived and was let in by one of the children. Her initial shock soon wore off, as both parents recalled how all Lilly's adolescent passions had been for other girls, despite their best efforts to introduce her to suitable young men. The real shock came when Lilly told them that her lover, Felice, was Jewish, for each week that passed saw more of the 'U-boats' recognised and arrested, destination Auschwitz. By June 1943 the only Jewish institutions remaining in Berlin were the Jewish Hospital and the largest Jewish cemetery in Europe at Weissensee, north-east of the city centre.

On 12 October Lilly stood in court at the hearing of her divorce petition, citing Günther's repeated infidelity. When his lawyer introduced her refusal to have another child by him, the court decided in his favour, since in Hitler's Germany with the astronomical casualties on the Russian front, bearing four sons as Lilly had done was not considered a reason for a wife to refuse to bear another. So Günther was awarded the apartment, with the proviso that he could not turn Lilly and the children out into the street. When he reappeared in Berlin in April 1944, his girlfriend having moved to the country to escape the bombing,

Günther stayed in the apartment, seeming to find the company of Lilly and Felice – and Inge during the daytime – quite enjoyable. Their women friends were scandalised but, as Lilly said, Günther was supporting her and the children financially, so why not let him share the flat?

After his return to Romania at the end of his leave, he astonished the women by writing for Lilly's agreement to 'revive the marriage for the sake of the children' with him in paternal control.[80] Although regularly exchanging family news with him in a relatively friendly correspondence, Lilly left it to Felice to answer Günther's proposal. He in turn accepted that in 'his' household after the war, she would live with them in a larger apartment, as would Lola and the baby she was expecting. But the most important letters, kept by Lilly until 1992 when author Erica Fischer interviewed her at length to obtain the whole incredible story of these women in the war-devastated capital of the Reich, were the love letters and poems Lilly and Felice wrote each other whenever they were apart, Lilly being addressed as 'Aimée' and Felice as 'Jaguar'.

After the Allied invasion of Normandy in June 1944 and with the Soviet armies pressing in from the east, it seemed to Lilly, Felice and their women's circle that the war must soon end. This was also the professional opinion of most senior German officers, resulting in Stauffenberg's failed attempt on Hitler's life of 20 July, after which the Gestapo arrested *thousands* of people and sent them to concentration and death camps. Even Hitler's favourite soldier, Field Marshal Erwin Rommel, was given the choice of suicide or death for his whole family. He chose suicide. Since Goebbels twisted the facts 100 per cent to blame the Jews for the assassination attempt, that served as an excuse to step up the 'actions' against them in Berlin and other cities. It was probably this that impelled Felice to make a last will and testament leaving everything to 'Frau Elizabeth Wust, née Kappler, of Berlin-Schmargendorf, Friedrichshallerstrasse 23'.[81]

With the Nazi censorship distorting all war news, Felice and Elenai boldly took jobs at the *Nationale Zeitung* under assumed names. Arriving each day before the rest of the staff, they read all the incoming cables from Reuters and other international press agencies, updating their secret map of Europe torn from a schoolbook, which was pinned to the wall in Lilly's apartment, where Hitler's obligatory portrait had formerly hung before Inge and her friends opened Lilly's eyes to reality.

The fatal day – 21 August 1944 – was hot and sunny. As it was Lola's day off work, she agreed to look after the children so that Felice, who was also free, could cycle with Lilly to the bathing beach of Wannsee, in the south of Berlin where the Havel river widens into a lake. The joy of sharing a carefree few hours at the beach without thinking of air raids and the ever-present menace on the ground was preserved for decades to come in photographs taken with a self-timer on Felice's old Leica. One shows Lilly looking a little bit gauche in her bathing costume and Felice in a linen bathing suit looking bold and strong beside her. Another shows Felice kissing Lilly. Before they left the beach, Lilly also photographed Felice alone, looking masculine in a short-sleeved shirt and linen shorts. Neither woman imagining that there was so little time left them, they cycled happily back through the woodland, locked their bicycles in the cellar and ran upstairs to relieve Lola. She came to the door, her grey eyes wide with fright, mouthing the word, 'Gestapo'.

Two men standing behind her dragged all three women into the apartment and accused Felice point-blank: 'You are the Jewess Schragenheim.' Lilly was accused of sheltering a Jew – an offence for which the punishment was a concentration camp at least, but she was allowed to stay after the interrogation ended, because of the four children, while the Gestapo men prepared to take Felice away with them. No formal arrest was necessary, nor any warrant, because the Gestapo was above the law. With nothing to lose, taking advantage of a moment when both men were questioning Lilly, Felice made a run for it. Betrayed by the front door of the apartment slamming behind her, she was chased through the building by one of the Gestapo men. Hidden by a woman neighbour, she was betrayed by two male Nazi residents, who had seen where she was hiding. Dragged out, kicked and beaten, she was hauled back to the apartment, where the interrogation continued, the two Gestapo men attempting to frighten Felice and Lilly into giving names of others who had known what was going on and probing for details of how ID cards and ration books had been procured. Neither Lilly nor Felice gave any answers.

Two more Gestapo men arrived to take Felice away. One of the men lewdly told her to kiss Lilly on the lips before she left. By now both women feared they would never see each other again. Felice removed her ring and gave it to Lilly, planting a last, chaste, kiss on her forehead. After the four men left with their captive, Lilly was too distraught to do anything, but Lola went around the apartment, feeding all the documents she and Felice had brought there into the tiled stove and burning them. Neither of the two women slept that night, wondering hopelessly what they could do to help Felice. In the morning, preparing the children's breakfast, Lilly found Felice's last poem stuffed into a coffee cup. It read in part:

> Words exist, which when they're spoken,
> Cannot bear the light of day.
> Said aloud, something gets broken
> And can't be made right in any way.

So now you must bend down to me
And softly close your eyes.
I want to tell you silently,
My dearly beloved You.[82]

Lilly, who had never kept a diary, began one that day – some-times in the form of a letter to Felice, to have the feeling that she was in some way communicating with her. The first entry read:

Today it happened, the horrible thing I had blocked even the slightest thought of. They took my beloved away from me.

Dear God, protect the girl I love above all else. Give her back to me safe and sound. I screamed and cried, and the chil-dren with me, all except Albrecht [the youngest boy]. He just stood there and smiled, the chubby thing, because he doesn't understand. I came to my senses for the children's sake.

I didn't look out of the window. I simply didn't have the strength to, and I didn't want you to see my tears. Lola was so sweet. She saw you wave as they put you in that heavily guarded car and took you away. She was comforting, but what good is comfort?

She also wrote:

My God, six fearless men to trap one single girl. Six men![83]

Inge had an old schoolfriend named Berndorff, whose father was a *Sturmbannführer* working in Gestapo headquarters on the Prinz Albrecht Strasse. Imprudently, she and Lilly went there to ask him where Felice had been taken. As she described it in her diary:

As we went in, I remembered that [the Gestapo] had almost beaten my brother Bob to death in the basement of that same building. Inge was terribly afraid [there], but I had no fear at all.

When Sturmbannführer Berndorff said he did not know where Felice was, Lilly had the nerve to say, 'Unbelievable. You can't just misplace someone like that. I want to know where she is.'[84]

Her courage was rewarded that evening when the telephone rang and a man's voice said, 'Schulstrasse' before hanging up. That short phone call was an act of bravery by a Jewish orderly working in the former Jewish Hospital there, which was now the Berlin collection centre for Jews about to be deported to the East.

Next morning, Lilly went to the Schulstrasse with a present of fruit for Felice and was horrified to see the change in her usually bold and confident appearance. By flirting mildly with one of the guards to find out his duty roster, she managed, by small bribes of cigarettes, to continue visiting Felice when he was on duty, even taking the children with her sometimes – until the gross, bullying *Scharführer* in charge of the collection centre banned her from coming. On 5 September the helpful orderly at the Schulstrasse centre informed Lilly that Felice was going to be sent to Theresienstadt, a model concentration camp in what is now Terezin in Czech Republic. After a final half-hour meeting with Lilly on 7 September, Felice departed on transport 14890-I/116, the penultimate Jewish transport to Theresienstadt.[85]

On 7 October 450 Jewish prisoners working in the crematoria at Auschwitz attacked their SS Totenkopfverbände guards. Three guards were killed and all the prisoners were shot. Eleven days later, with the Allied armies closing in from east and west,

Hitler announced that all males between the ages of 13 and 60 capable of holding a weapon were to be called up in the Volkssturm as the Nazi regime's last line of defence. Since virtually all fit adult males were already in uniform, the 60,000 men conscripted in Berlin were unfit for service. In any case, half had only obsolete weapons and the other half no weapons at all. The decision to make this 'last ditch' stand would cause the deaths of another 1.5 million German men, for no purpose at all.

It was in this atmosphere of *Götterdämmerung*[86] that Lilly, in addition to sending food and clothing to Felice at Theresienstadt, obtained a travel pass made out in Lola's name to travel into the Sudetenland, to have her baby in her mother's home there. Arriving at Theresienstadt, she tricked her way into the commandant's office and demanded to see Felice, provoking a screaming fit, in which he accused her of lacking 'racial pride' for having anything to do with a Jewish woman. Obliged to return to Berlin frustrated, Lilly received five cards from Felice, acknowledging the receipt of parcels. Possibly because of Lilly's visit bringing her to the commandant's notice, on 9 or 10 October Felice was locked into a cattle car forming part of transport Ep-342, destination Auschwitz.

Nothing worked normally by now in the entire shrinking Reich, yet a letter from her dated 3 November arrived eleven days later at Lilly's parents' home, postmarked Trachenberg,[87] where Felice was in hospital, suffering from scarlet fever and lung problems, which were later diagnosed as tuberculosis. Even more strangely, an irregular correspondence ensued between Lilly in Berlin and Felice in the hospital, thanks to a helpful orderly. Felice's last proper letter was dated 12 November, by which time it was unlikely that she would end up at Auschwitz, as Himmler was already preparing the destruction of the gas chambers and crematoria there in an attempt to erase all the evidence before the first Soviet troops arrived. Felice wrote three days later in wobbly handwriting on a scrap of paper:

> My Beloved,
> The nurse just came in and said we're being taken away. Pray for me and keep your fingers crossed!
> Always, your F-------

It seems that Felice was transferred to the slave labour camp at Gross-Rosen, which was the third largest of all the camps for women.

On 8 December 1944 Lilly was ordered to report to Gestapo Section IV D1 in the Französicherstrasse, which investigated 'U-boats' who had been caught and the Aryan Germans who had helped or sheltered them. Five men and a woman took part in her interrogation, during which she said that she had not known Felice was Jewish until she was arrested on 21 August. Refusing to change that alibi, she was informed that she belonged in a concentration camp herself, but would be allowed to return home 'for the sake of the four children'.

On 5 January 1945 Lilly received two non-committal letters from Felice, forwarded by her parents and dated 18 and 26 December, but she had no address to which to reply. Central Berlin was being bombed flat. The city's gasworks no longer existed. The electricity supply was unpredictable. The main railway stations were shattered, as was much of the S-Bahn and U-Bahn transport systems. The telephone did not work.

She had met three other Jewish women who had survived the war thus far in a summer house without running water or sanitation, washing themselves and their clothes in restaurant toilets and drying them on the chairs where they sat. When Lilly took them in, pretending they were relatives from out of town, her

Nazi neighbours had given up commenting on her, to them, bizarre behaviour. In early April 1945, with the end of the war only weeks away, rations were cut yet again, making it nearly impossible to feed four adults and the children. Much of the time they lived in the cellar, while outside *die goldene Fasanen* – 'golden pheasants' was the Berliner's sarcastic nickname for the brown-uniformed Party hacks – fled the city in their big cars with full petrol tanks, terrified of being caught by the approaching Soviet forces.

It was the women of Berlin who paid the price for Hitler's obstinacy after he committed suicide on 30 April 1945 and the guns fell silent a week later. Understandably, none of them wanted to talk about it afterwards, but nearly all, from infants to grandmothers, were raped by Soviet soldiers, some victims dying in the act. Others caught gonorrhoea or syphilis from their violators, but few became pregnant since malnutrition during the battle for Berlin had stopped their ovulation weeks or months before. Lilly, the children and her three 'lodgers' were given places in a cellar with 100 other women and children. Every few minutes, a woman was taken away and raped. The only German words most of the Russians knew were, *'Frau, komm.'* When Lilly heard these words and felt a rifle muzzle rammed into her chest, another soldier pushed her back into her seat, calling her *matka* – Mummy – because her children were with her, but some women were raped in front of their children.

All over Berlin, house ruins were plastered with notes asking for news of people who had lived there, and giving the address of a relative or friend. Lilly posted details of Felice wherever she could and, whenever she met groups of concentration camp prisoners, understandably on the rampage, stealing property and food, she asked whether any had been at Gross-Rosen, but none could give her any word about Felice. On 3 August, the poem she wrote in her diary included the lines:

> With hope, my days I justify,
> I hate my night dreams fervently.
> It doesn't make sense, I don't know why,
> This waiting. Have you left me?
>
> But deep within I know the reply
> And that is why I take it calmly.
> It does make sense. I do know why.
> If alive, you would never leave me![88]

As 21 August – the anniversary of Felice's arrest – approached, Lilly grew increasingly depressed. When her illicit lodger, Lucie, took an overdose of sleeping pills, getting her to a hospital and forcing staff to admit her to wards already overflowing was a full night's work. Lucie died, partly from malnutrition during the battle for Berlin. The only other mourners at Lucie's burial were the other two lodgers, but Lilly felt thousands were there, unseen. One paradoxical problem for the 'U-boats' who now emerged from hiding was that, unlike the survivors of the camps, they did not qualify for the new identity cards marked *Opfer des Faschismus* – victim of fascism – which entitled the bearers to go to the head of the ubiquitous food queues, and gave priority on the waiting list for accommodation.[89]

Lilly's hunt for news of Felice was reinvigorated on 18 August, when she received a brief letter from a Dr Grünberger:

> Fräulein Schragenheim took the same path as my daughter, and therefore probably was in Bergen-Belsen. Further details in person 12–1pm, 6–7pm.

Lilly hurried to see him and learned from the good doctor, who had himself just returned from Auschwitz, that the Allgemeine-SS had closed Gross-Rosen at the end of January and sent the women west to Bergen-Belsen. Lilly went to see another woman who had responded to her notices asking for news from camp returnees. She had been in Theresienstadt and recounted how Felice had been a tower of strength there, adding that she was always together with 'a woman who wore pants'. On 21 August, Lilly confided to her diary the burning jealousy that sentence aroused in her. Who was the mysterious woman? Had Felice gone abroad with her?

When Aryan visitors came and were introduced to Jewish friends, Lilly watched them shaking hands – something they would never have done in what was already called *die Hitlerzeit*. Dr Grünberger came with a tin of liverwurst and some other food, but had no more news. On 5 June 1946, almost two years after Felice's arrest, a letter arrived from Dr Grünberger's daughter, including the lines, 'I never met your friend anywhere along the way. Unfortunately, she probably shared the fate of millions of concentration camp inmates'.[90] That was a euphemism for dying due to malnutrition, exacerbated by sickness, such as Felice's tuberculosis, contracted in the camps. There were at the time between 11.5 million and 13 million Germans heading, mostly on foot, westwards from as far away as Romania and Hungary; 2.2 million were expelled from Czechoslovakia alone; an estimated 600,000 were murdered in revenge killings on the way.

The simile of a needle in a haystack is nothing compared to Lilly's hunt for news of Felice in all this confusion and tragedy. On 14 February 1948 – St Valentine's Day – Felice was officially declared dead by a court in Berlin–Charlottenburg.

8

SOE SOS

One German-occupied country about which a great deal was
known before the Normandy invasion of June 1944 was France
– thanks to the several thousand agents sent in by the British
SIS, Section F of SOE and the Free French Bureau Central de
Renseignements et d'Action (BCRA). Yet when the Wehrmacht
occupied the country in May 1940, the mood of the population was one of stunned acceptance, apart from a few isolated
anti-German gestures and the execution of those who had made
them. Most French people were too busy tracing relatives –
even children – who had been lost in the mad rush away from
the north-east of the country, organised by local and regional
authorities in sheer panic when the Wehrmacht and Waffen-SS
spearheads ignored the supposedly impregnable Maginot Line
and drove, cycled or marched around it, following more or less
the same route as in 1914.

With several million French civilians trying to return home
through a country in chaos, seeking papers entitling them to
food or a roof over their heads or simply getting money when

all the banks were closed, organised in-country resistance was slow in getting off the ground. In addition, for the first twenty months of the war, the Parti Communiste Français (PCF), which was later an important element in the armed Resistance, was actively pro-German in line with the Nazi–Soviet Pact of 1939 – a fact that it would try to cover up after the war by labelling itself 'the party of the martyrs'.

When Winston Churchill decided to 'set [German-occupied] Europe ablaze' in July 1940, one of the organisations created to do that was Special Operations Executive (SOE), whose Section F was tasked with espionage and sabotage in France. Its most famous boss was Old Etonian Maurice Buckmaster, a former Ford motor company manager in Paris, who took over in September 1941. In charge of welfare and 'prepping' female agents for their missions was the cool and competent Intelligence Officer, Vera Atkins, who hid her exotic Romanian–Jewish origins under very English speech and manners. The predominantly male British intelligence community was strongly prejudiced against women, who were thought liable to change allegiance in the field for emotional reasons, to refuse to kill when necessary and to be physically vulnerable when caught. Yet, particularly after the introduction in autumn 1942 of forced labour service[91] in Germany for French males between the ages of 18 and 50, women were far less likely to be stopped and searched or have their papers checked than men. They were therefore recruited especially as couriers and for the dangerous job of operating clandestine transmitters and moving their bulky sets from one safe house to another. Also in their favour was the traditional German male's belief that women would not volunteer for dangerous military work and, of course, the susceptibility of most men to a disarming smile or mild flirtation by a pretty girl. The age of female agents ranged from 19 to 52. The older ones had in their favour that young Germans in uniform saw them as grand-mothers, even less likely to be dangerous.

The SOE agents' training course for both sexes was so tough that a failure rate of twelve from a course of fifteen recruits was not unusual. It included fieldcraft such as detecting and losing surveillance, and the use not only of British weapons but also of American and enemy small arms, which had to be stripped down and reassembled in darkness. Target shooting was rendered more difficult by being scheduled at the end of an exhausting mock battle course and training included practice parachute drops at Ringway airport near Manchester,[92] from which the older train-ees were excused as they were inserted by fast motor boat on the coast of Brittany or by Mediterranean *feluccas* on the southern coast of France.

Considering that memoirs of agents began to be published soon after the end of hostilities in Europe, it is surprising that no two authorities agree a figure for exactly how many were sent, how many were caught or killed at the time of capture, or how many died under torture and in prisons, concentration and death camps afterwards. Part of the confusion is due to the reluctance of successive British governments to admit the scale of losses. The post-war destruction of 87 per cent of the per-sonnel files – partly deliberate, partly accidental – is another reason why figures are hard to determine.[93] The best guess is that around 1,600 agents were despatched, many on Lysander flights from RAF Tempsford airfield. British Intelligence (SIS), Colonel Buckmaster's Section F in SOE and the Gaullist BCRA each had its own agenda and networks, yet elementary security was often neglected by two or more agencies having to share the same RAF flights to infiltrate and exfiltrate their agents. Of the between fifty-two and sixty SOE women agents, seventeen were caught and twelve died in captivity. Every one of them deserves a book about herself. What follows is an account of several very different women.

As a public school man, Buckmaster had a penchant for girls who had been to 'good schools', which he considered built character. This was due to the public school ethos that protected long-term traitors including Philby, Burgess and Maclean. Elizabeth Devereaux-Rochester,[94] born in December 1917, certainly fulfilled Buckmaster's educational–social background requirements, being educated at Roedean School, having lived with her British mother in Paris before the war and attended Swiss finishing schools. With the US staying neutral until 11 December 1941 and Elizabeth having American nationality through her divorced father, she chose to do jobs such as driving ambulances for the French Red Cross after the German invasion, occasionally begging petrol from Wehrmacht tankers. After that date, Elizabeth went underground, surviving by her own wits as she escorted Allied escapers and others across the French–Swiss frontier. When the Swiss closed the frontier, she took her charges across the Pyrenees to Spain. It was by that route that she made her own way to London via Spain. There, she was recruited by SOE as a fluent French-speaker, despite her tall build and looks described by several people as unmistakably English. If she did not relish the physical side of the training course, she was able to cope with it and did find the explosives instruction fascinating. She particularly enjoyed blowing things up after she returned to France, including steel bridges and several locomotives parked for the night in Annecy station.

In October 1943 Major Richard Heslop of SOE and Captain Jean Rosenthal of the BCRA, who was a high-class Parisian jeweller and furrier in civilian life, reported back to Buckmaster that Resistance leaders on the remote Glières plateau of eastern France could assemble a force of 2,350 male and female

maquisards there as a self-contained army needing only to be supplied with arms and ammunition by air across the Mediterranean
from Allied-occupied North Africa. This, it was thought, would
enable them to hold off any attack on this wild upland area near
the Italian frontier, whence they would emerge at the right
moment to harass the Germans in the rear during the planned
Allied invasion of southern France.

After fewer than forty-eight hours in London, Heslop and
Rosenthal were back in south-eastern France commanding
the Marksman mission, with Elizabeth as their courier. Apart
from participating in a number of sabotage operations because
she enjoyed working with explosives, she was regarded as too
undisciplined for clandestine work. In her own words, she was
'a spoiled brat', unaccustomed to doing anything except what
she wanted. Ordered back to Britain in the spring of 1944, she
refused to comply. On 20 March 1944, it is unclear what she
was doing in Paris, which was not part of her sector, when she
was arrested by two Gestapo men in plainclothes and a lout-
ish *milicien* armed with a sub-machine gun. Because she had a
false identity card, she was taken to Gestapo HQ in the rue des
Saussaies, where torture was routine, but talked her way out of
more than a short roughing up by persuading her interrogator
that she was just a crazy American girl who had been on the run
for months all over France, supporting herself by selling off her
personal jewellery, piece by piece. Her motive, she said, was that
she had a terror of being behind barbed wire and did not want to
be locked up with all the other American civilians, including her
mother, in a concentration camp at Vittel.

Next followed a spell in solitary confinement in the Gestapo
wing of Fresnes prison, with women in neighbouring cells being
regularly dragged off for torture. Just after the Normandy invasion in June 1944, Elizabeth was interviewed by a Wehrmacht

legal officer, who believed that she was a harmless eccentric American and said she would be sent to Vittel after finishing the last twelve days of a three-month sentence for having a false ID card. After this relatively luxurious way of waiting for liberation in September 1945, she stayed in Europe until 1974, doing various jobs in advertising, trying to make a living as a writer and falling in love and out again. Returning to America, where she had spent little time before, she wrote an account of her experiences.[95] After inheriting a comfortable legacy, she fell ill and was diagnosed with multiple sclerosis. This, she said, made her glad she had never married because it would have been a terrible affliction to foist on one's partner. Although she is believed to have died in St Mâlo between 1981 and 1983, sources differ as to exactly when.

Another female agent of F Section, who did not go through the training course, was born Countess Krystina Skarbek to an impoverished Polish aristocrat and his rich Jewish wife, but chose the *nom de guerre* Christine Granville when she started working for SOE. Thought to have been the inspiration for Ian Fleming's first Bond girl, she avoided the usual long training course by virtue of having already performed brilliant undercover work in German-occupied Poland and Hungary for Section D of SIS – the predecessor of SOE. This petite and pretty 29-year-old was described by Vera Atkins as 'a very brave woman, but a loner and a law unto herself. She had tremendous guts.'[96]

Parachuting on 7 July 1944 to the Maquis groups assembling on the Vercors plateau in eastern France – shortly to be the scene of appalling tortures, murders and massacres of *maquisards* and civilians of all ages and both sexes by Central Asian Waffen-SS troops – Christine did everything a male agent could have done and also, on her own initiative, hiked over the mountains into Italy to persuade Polish conscripts in German uniform to desert and join partisan bands.[97] Her most amazing exploit was the very courageous rescue of Francis Cammaerts, head of the Jockey network, whose lover she had become. After escaping from the encircled plateau, he was arrested with two other Allied officers at a roadblock near the town of Digne, where a sharp-eyed Gestapo man noticed that the SOE office in Algiers had, in providing their forged ID papers, committed three appalling errors. One document was out of date. Another had not been date-stamped. Worst of all, the three men were carrying a large amount of cash. Their alibi that they had only met while hitch-hiking that morning – was blown when a body search revealed that all the banknotes they carried had numbers in the same series. Within an hour they were all thrown into a cell in the Gestapo wing of Digne prison.

They were still there on 15 August, when 94,000 men of the US 7th Army and the Free French 1st Army landed on the beaches between Toulon and Cannes in Operation Dragoon – the invasion of southern France. The breakout from the beach-heads and subsequent progress up the Rhône valley was so fast that the Gestapo in Digne panicked and prepared their escape, their normal practice including the execution of all prisoners and hostages before departure. The lives of Cammaerts and his two companions hung on a thread. When the news reached Christine, liaising with anti-German Italian partisans, her first plan was to organise an armed attack on the prison in Digne. This proved impossible to set up in time, so she took what she later called a calculated risk. Had the three prisoners been just rank-and-file members of the Jockey network, her duty was to stay clear and not get involved, but only Cammaerts knew how to contact and activate the many watertight cells, into which he had prudently divided Jockey. It was thus her duty to risk her life to save his.

After a 40-mile bicycle ride across mountainous country, she arrived at the prison and chatted up an elderly gendarme under the pretence of being Cammaerts' wife, saying that she wanted to leave a parcel of food and clothes for him. The gendarme introduced her to Albert Schenk, a bilingual Gestapo liaison officer from Alsace. Christine had learned while working undercover in Poland that, when you have to bluff, you bluff big. So she told Schenk that she was General Bernard Montgomery's niece, in daily radio contact with the Operation Dragoon forces advancing up the Rhône valley! To her request that he release the prisoners in order to save his own neck, Schenk replied that he did not have the necessary authority and introduced her to Max Waem, a more senior Gestapo colleague from Belgium.

To back up her story when meeting Waem that afternoon, Christine took the additional risk of showing him some of the crystals used to lock her SOE transmitter on fixed frequencies for transmissions. That they were old ones that had been damaged was irrelevant because, in doing so, she had given a *Sicherheitsdienst* officer proof that she was an Allied spy. She also told Waem that the local Resistance planned to assassinate him shortly, unless the Americans arrived first, in which case he would either be lynched in the post-liberation frenzy or hanged by the Americans as a war criminal for having ordered the arrest and execution of what she called 'the three most important prisoners in France'.

The only chance of Schenk and Waem staying alive, she said, was for them to help get 'her' three prisoners out of the prison alive and well, in return for which she would hand over enough money for the two of them to make good their escape. Probably at no other time would her incredible story have been believed, but in the confusion generated by the speed of the Dragoon forces' advance, Waem and Schenk were rightly worried about their fate, if they left their departure too late.

Either of the men she was dealing with could have had her arrested and shot. Indeed, Waem repeatedly threatened her with a loaded pistol but, as the negotiations dragged on, Christine knew she had judged her adversaries correctly. After three hours' haggling, impressed by her apparent total calm – she said afterwards that she was too busy to be frightened – Waem named his price for liberating the prisoners. He wanted a hand-written note confirming that he and Schenk had saved their lives and 2 million francs in cash as getaway money.

Christine hurriedly left town and made her way to where she had hidden her transmitter, to radio news of the deal to Algiers. In what must have been one of the swiftest operations mounted in the entire war, the cash was dropped that night in the hills close to Digne. Returning to the prison the following day, she handed the money over and waited for Waem to deliver. Nobody knows what bluff she used at that stage to stop him simply pocketing the money and shooting her with the three men.

When footsteps were heard approaching the condemned cell, Cammaerts woke up: exhausted by the months of clandestine life, he could fall asleep anywhere. He and the others had just been served the best meal since their arrest. Suspecting this was 'the condemned men's last meal', they saw Waem standing in the doorway, wearing a Wehrmacht uniform jacket over civil-ian clothes. He motioned them outside with his revolver. As Cammaerts walked out, Waem said, 'What a wonderful wife you have!'

Waem marched his prisoners out of the main gate and then turned right, instead of left towards the football pitch, used as an execution ground by the Germans. A few hundred yards from the prison, he hustled them into the rear seat of a waiting car and got in beside the driver. His uniform jacket guaranteeing them safe passage past the German checkpoint at the edge of town, Waem ordered the driver to halt at the first bend, where the slim figure of Christine was waiting. Waem got out and buried his uniform jacket as the first step in his personal getaway. With the car heading for the mountains, Cammaerts and his companions realised that Christine had saved their lives by risking her own.[98]

One always wonders how incredibly brave agents like Christine Granville settled down to peacetime living after all the adrenaline they had burned up. The answer is often tragic, for many committed suicide. Stranded in Cairo with one month's salary when SOE terminated her contract in 1945, she applied for British nationality in the belief that London would welcome with open arms a woman holding the MBE, the George Medal and the Croix de Guerre. Yet some ignorant bureaucrat in London turned down her application because she could not prove the requisite five years' previous residence in Britain. Eventually reaching London as a stateless refugee after borrowing the money for her fare, she worked as a switchboard operator and sold dresses in Harrods department store before signing on as a stewardess aboard the SS *Rauhine*.

Vera Atkins once said of Christine, 'She was no plaster saint. She was a vital, healthy, beautiful animal with a great appetite for love and laughter. She lived for action and adventure.'[99] In a sense, that also caused her death, when a schizophrenic senior steward aboard *Rauhine* became obsessed with her. To escape him, she jumped ship but her unwanted suitor followed her ashore. After persistently stalking her, on the evening of 15 July 1952 he accosted Christine and stabbed her through the heart. For this crime he was hanged two weeks after his trial that September.

The sanitised dramatisations of SOE and other female agents[100] on the ground in occupied France tell only part of the story. They could not function without support from ordinary French people who provided raw intelligence and safe accommodation, despite knowing the risks they ran. They were the people listening to all those mysterious personal messages broadcast by the BBC French service at 1 p.m. as a standby and at 6 p.m. as confirmation, subject to weather conditions, availability of the aircraft and the possibility that it would be intercepted and shot down en route. One of these *messages personnels* was '*Jacqueline a une robe rouge. Je répète. Jacqueline a une robe rouge*'. Broadcast on 21 August 1943, this was picked up by 17-year-old Cathérine Bouchou in the hamlet of St-Antoine-de-Queyret, a few kilometres from the author's home in south-west France. It meant that an RAF aircraft, from Tempsford or Tangmere airfield, was due to drop that night by parachute a cargo of arms, ammunition and, in this case, an agent.[101]

Her father being the mayor's part-time secretary, Cathérine helped him make false papers with genuine ID cards and the Mairie's rubber stamps. Her mother and younger sister knew nothing of this and the mayor turned a blind eye. Jacqueline's red dress was to be 'Annette,' an SOE radio operator arriving to replace an arrested predecessor working for SOE officer George Starr, who was staying in the Bouchou house. Her real name was Yvonne Cormeau, widow of a Belgian RAF officer killed during the London blitz when a bomb destroyed their house while he was home on leave. Mother of two young children, Yvonne joined the Women's Auxiliary Air Force (WAAF) and volunteered to work for F Section as a way of avenging her husband's death.

Cathérine still recalls the drop taking place behind the family home at 1 a.m. on 22 August because it signalled the end of her family life. In the light of the full moon, the small reception group organised by family friend Rodolphe Faytout saw the aircraft flying in so low that they thought it was going to hit the house. Anxious not to drop Yvonne in the surrounding woodland, the pilot overcorrected, landing her in the Bouchous' vineyard, where she lost a shoe and tore her skirt on the stakes before recovering the transmitter and a suitcase of money dropped with her. Beneath each of nine other parachutes blossoming in the moonlight swung a man-size container. In desperate haste, the group of friends hid their contents temporarily in the Bouchous' barn and then made their way home. But the Germans had also heard the RAF aircraft flying in low, so Faytout's original intention to disperse and hide the weapons next day was frustrated by a Heinkel He 46 spotter plane repeatedly flying low and slow over the area.

Although locating a transmitter requires just two direction-finding aerials, whose bearings converge on the point of transmission, to speed up the detection process, the Germans were using three *camions gonométriques* together, disguised as local baker's or tradesmen's vans. Yet Cathérine Bouchou clearly recalls that Starr kept Yvonne transmitting his backlog of urgent messages from her family home for five days. However big the backlog of messages, this seems an appalling lack of security. Yet, with a combination of nerve, caution and luck, Yvonne went on to make a record 400 transmissions over thirteen months without being caught. She did not meet Cathérine again until they met on the set of a *This is Your Life* television programme devoted to Yvonne Cormeau's life on 8 November 1989.

Faytout's group received several other drops, unaware that SS-Officer Helmut Demetrio, based in the nearby town of Castillon, had them in his sights. Slender build, spectacles and habitual slight smile did nothing to soften Demetrio's face,

marred by duelling scars on upper lip and chin. With his interpreter Heinrich – called 'Cosh' because of the way he punctuated
questions during interrogation – Demetrio had already tortured
many local people.

The last and fatal drop took place on 20 October near the
village of Pujols, after which the parachuted ammunition and
weapons were hidden in a woodshed for dispersal when fog
grounded the spotter plane. But Faytout was arrested next day,
swiftly followed by several others in the group, making it plain
that he had talked. The farmer who had hidden the arms was
arrested while his wife, Lucienne, was out shopping. Four days
afterwards, a black Citroën drove up to his farm. Faytout got
out and indicated the shed where the arms had first been hidden.
French-speaking SS men jumped down from the truck behind
the Citroën and started hunting for them, but they had already
been buried elsewhere. When Demetrio and 'Cosh' came into
the farm kitchen, the latter's first words to Lucienne were, 'Your
husband has spilled the beans. He said you would tell us where
the arms now are.'

She knew that was a lie because, if he had cracked, they would
already know. Seated on the kitchen table with a loaded pistol
pointed at her, but trusting her husband not to have involved
her, even under torture, she was alternately threatened and
beaten for four or five hours. Knowing that one of the arrested
men had hanged himself in his cell after an eye was torn out of
its socket during interrogation by these two men, she became so
traumatised that her throat dried up completely and she could
neither speak, nor move. Faytout was called in to break the
deadlock, but could only stare at the floor in silence until told to
'piss off back to the car' by Heinrich the Cosh.

With a mine detector, the buried arms were soon located. By
dusk, everything was loaded on the truck, which headed back to

Castillon. Some time after the Germans' departure, Lucienne's paralysis wore off and her voice returned. Realising that she had forgotten all about her daughter, who should have been home from school long since, she ran to a nearby house, hoping she was there. Refusing to open the door, the neighbours warned her to go away, in case she was being watched. Telephones being few and far between, she spent the night anguished for her husband and child, only learning next morning that other neighbours had heard about the raid on the farm and taken her daughter home with them.

One by one all the others were picked up, including Cathérine Bouchou's father. There were not many cars on the road in that rural area, so she clearly remembers the black Gestapo Citroën coming to take him away. A few days later, her mother heard the distinctive *gazogène* engine returning and told her two daughters to hide in the woods. Concealed there, they saw her taken away too, leaving the old grandmother alone in the house. That day marked the end of family life: Cathérine's father had been working hard to buy their rented house, but with both parents gone and no income, the sisters and their grandmother had to spend all their savings on rent.

On arrival at the Gestapo's Fort du Hâ prison in Bordeaux, all the prisoners were facially unrecognisable after beatings from 'Cosh.' From there, they were shipped, starving, to the death camps at Neue Brem, Buchenwald, Nauegamme, Mauthausen and finally Dora. During one transfer in cattle trucks, Cathérine's father died in another man's arms, worn out with beatings, overwork and starvation. At Dora, two of the men toiled for months in the vast underground factory assembling Hitler's V-weapons, allowed outside only to witness the hanging of fellow prisoners. On the death march westwards as the Red Army approached, 2,400 prisoners from Dora were locked inside a barn beside a

Wehrmacht half-track park that was bombed by Allied aircraft, but these two survived. Yet when they returned to France after the end of the war, their families, visiting them in hospital, could not recognise them. Lucienne's husband, a strong peasant farmer weighing 102kg when arrested, was reduced to a skeletal 43kg. Cathérine Bouchou's mother returned from concentration camp, prematurely aged and with broken health, unable even to smile for the ritual photograph at her daughter's wedding.[102]

The financial cost and the suffering among the thousands of French men and women punished for espionage and sabotage operations planned safely in London can never be calculated. When the author asked Cathérine Bouchou's husband why Faytout had not been killed in revenge after the Liberation, he replied, 'We wanted to forget all that.' Pierre Mignon, one of the men from Faytout's group who did survive, wrote a comprehensive account of what happened. It begins:

> Having no literary pretensions, I never intended to publish my notes. Yet now, when so many people want to forget it all happened, we must go on record.[103]

Francis Cammaerts' system of watertight cells was the only safe way to organise a large network. In 1942 Buckmaster decided to set up a totally new network in northern and western France under Francis Anthony Suttill, a 33-year-old lawyer qualified in both Britain and France. He may have been a good lawyer but lacked the paranoia necessary for clandestine work. Someone who knew him summed up Suttill as 'more suited to be an officer in a gung-ho cavalry regiment than for clandestine warfare'.[104] He christened the new network Prosper, after a fifth century theologian named Prosper of Aquitaine. On 24 September 1942 First Aid Nursing Yeomanry (FANY) Lieutenant Andrée Borrel, who had previously spent months with the Resistance, helping to get downed Allied airmen out of France,[105] was parachuted by the SOE into France in preparation for Suttill's arrival in the early hours of 2 October. Once on the ground, he immediately set about recruiting agents with very poor security until several *thousand* people were involved directly or indirectly, many of them knowing the identities of far too many other members of the network. Suttill was also linguistically unsuited, having an appalling accent when speaking French, so it was Andrée who took the brunt of all this work and the repeated exposure that came with it.

Why were the elementary principles of security ignored? At Norfolk House in St James's Square in London was the office of Chief of Staff to the (yet to be appointed) Supreme Allied Commander (COSSAC). This was also the umbrella beneath which several shadowy sub-organisations lurked – in particular, the London Controlling Section run by Colonel John Bevan. Bevan's predecessor, Colonel Oliver Stanley, had resigned rather than deliberately misinform Resistance agents regarding the Dieppe raid with a view to letting them be caught and reveal under torture their false information in an effort to convince Hitler that the disastrous raid on Dieppe was a prelude to a full-scale invasion. Bevan, in civilian life a stockbroker, was made of sterner stuff. Unfortunately for history, he removed all his secret files on leaving office and left instructions for them to be destroyed after his death, which was done.

It is against that background of cynical deceit that the Prosper network must be assessed. At first, Prosper seemed to be working out brilliantly. During April and May the network received drops of 1,006 Stens, 1,877 incendiary devices and 4,489 grenades; in June it took delivery of another 190 man-sized containers of materiel on thirty-three landing grounds spread

over twelve *départements*. Prosper already had two radio operators. When Suttil requested another, SOE sent out Noor Inayat,
an Anglo–Indian who had impeccable French, having grown
up in Paris and written children's stories for Radio Paris while
studying child psychology at the Sorbonne. A clandestine agent
should be able to pass unnoticed even on an empty street. Yet,
Noor Inayat was so stunningly beautiful that men stared wherever she went.

Two other women on her training course wrote to Vera
Atkins that she should not be sent to France because her Sufi religion forbade her to tell an untruth. Her instructors also assessed
her as too gentle and lacking in deceit. Another wrote: 'Came
here without the foggiest idea what she was being trained for.'
As one French agent said after meeting Noor in Britain during
training, he was convinced after talking with her that she had
no idea of the work ahead of her – and that it was *intended* she be
caught, tortured and killed after revealing false information.[106]
Her final report included, 'Not over-burdened with brains …
it is very doubtful whether she is really suited to the work in
the field.' Buckmaster wrote on this report: 'Nonsense … makes
me cross.'[107] A convinced advocate of Gandhian non-violence,
Noor's motive in volunteering for the SOE was the naïve hope
that if some Indians gave significant help to the British war
effort London would be more likely to grant independence after
the war. She was, in short, unsuitable in every way for a clandestine career.

Flown in with three other agents to a field north of Angers
on the night of 16 June 1943, she did not transmit the customary
confirmation of arrival. She also muddled up her passwords when
meeting contacts, behaved in obviously English ways and even
handed a map to another agent in the open street. Her security
codes were left lying around and were picked up by outsiders.

She ignored warnings not to meet people who might remember her from before the war and even told them that she was a British agent. That *not overburdened with brains* seems an understatement. On 20 June another operator informed SOE that Noor's transceiver had been damaged on arrival, and requested that a replacement be flown out. On 24 June a communication from Suttill stated that Noor had narrowly avoided arrest when visiting a blown safe house. By the time that message arrived in London, Suttill and Andrée Borrel had been in Gestapo cells for twenty-four hours. A flash message was received from an agent in another network that Suttill and his male chief radio operator had disappeared and were feared under arrest. Hundreds of members of Prosper were rounded up, with some of them confessing under torture that they had been preparing for an Allied invasion planned for autumn 1943, causing Oberkommando der Wehrmacht (OKW) to keep in northern France many divisions that could have been deployed elsewhere.[108]

SOE panicked and ordered many of those still at liberty to get out of France as swiftly as possible, but in July Noor informed London that she was the only one of Suttill's core members still free. One can imagine the loneliness and fear she must have felt, stranded in occupied France, knowing that some of the arrested people must have given her description under torture to the Gestapo. A double, or treble, agent named Déricourt tried to persuade her to return to Britain on a Lysander flight he was organising, but she refused, suspecting he would hand her over to the Germans after bringing her to the landing field. Ordered by London to stay in Paris and make contact with agents from a third network, Noor betrayed increasing stress in her transmissions and her schedules were repeatedly missed.

Handwritten notes from Noor requesting new radio crystals arrived with Lysander return flights in August and September

– proof that she was still working, but with an alarming lack of security in failure to encode her requests properly, in case they fell into enemy hands.[109] On 13 October she was betrayed and arrested. Although she apparently did not talk under interrogation, the Gestapo discovered her notebooks in the room where she had been living, containing all the messages she had transmitted to SOE, which should have been destroyed immediately after sending. From these, they learned enough to send many false messages to London. Sonya Olschanezky, a locally recruited SOE agent, did send a warning to Buckmaster that Noor had been arrested and to disregard any further transmissions from her set, but he ignored this because he did not know who Olschanezky was. How, after this warning, the SOE monitors failed to realise that the continuing transmissions lacked security checks – which meant they had been sent under enemy control – and did not detect the different 'fist' of the new operator, is a mystery. This negligence resulted in a number of agents sent to France being immediately captured by the Germans on landing.

On 25 November 1943, Noor and two male SOE agents escaped from their Gestapo cells over the rooftops of their prison, but were recaptured almost immediately because their absence was noticed when an air raid required a roll-call of all prisoners. Refusing to give her word that she would not try again to escape, Noor was transported to Pforzheim prison in Germany two days later and shackled to the wall in solitary confinement for twenty-four hours a day during most of the following ten months. On 11 September 1944, after the breakouts from the Normandy beachheads made it obvious that Germany would lose the war, Noor and agents Yolande Beekman, Madeleine Damerment and Elaine Plowman were transported to Dachau concentration camp. Thereafter, the only concrete record of Noor's existence is a sad little plaque at Dachau, recording the deaths of these four women on 13 September 1944 after a near-lethal beating meted out for his personal pleasure by the sadistic Allgemeine-SS officer Friedrich Wilhelm Ruppert, subsequently executed for this and other crimes.

Their deaths came more than two months after the killing of agents Andrée Borrel, Diana Rowden, Vera Leigh and Sonya Olschanezky at Natzwiller[110] concentration camp in Alsace, as recorded on an equally saddening plaque that was affixed to the camp crematorium there and is now in the memorial museum. As *Nacht und Nebel* ('Night and Fog' – a 1941 directive targeting political activists and resistance members) prisoners destined to vanish without trace, so that families, friends and comrades would never know where, when or how they died, the SOE women agents ceased administratively to exist. Vera Atkins, on her own initiative after the cessation of hostilities, travelled extensively through formerly German-occupied territory in an endeavour to trace the 'lost agents' and give their families some closure.

SOE agent John Stonehouse miraculously survived four different concentration camps, his captors never realising he was Jewish. One of the camps was Natzwiller in Alsace, then incorporated into the Reich, where being gay without being Jewish was enough to provoke the most brutal treatment. Created as an SS enterprise titled Deutsche Erd- und Steinwerke for the mining of a rare pink granite used in Nazi monuments, Natzwiller was not designated a *Vernichtungslager* death camp, but as a Lagerstufe III, meaning the hardest regime in the concentration camp system. Together with its subordinate camp in neighbouring Schirmeck, more than 40 per cent of its eventual 52,000 slave workers died in the quarry from overwork, ill-treatment, malnutrition, exposure in the minus 30°C winter weather, random killings and 'medical experiments' including deliberate burning with mustard gas and injection with lethal diseases. In addition, from time to time the camp inmates observed groups of *Nacht und Nebel* prisoners assembled in front of the administration building, who were driven with whips and blows into a sand quarry and there shot by firing squad, their bodies incinerated in the small camp crematorium.

In August 1943, while the famous Parisian boys' choir Les Petits Chanteurs à la Croix de Bois were singing in Berlin, the insanity of the Final Solution saw eighty-six female detainees transported 1,200km *westwards* from Auschwitz through Poland and Germany to Alsace. One would think that, with Hitler desperately trying to stem the reverses all along the Eastern Front after the disastrous tank battle of Kursk and the Allies already on Italian soil, every available railway waggon would be pressed into service for the armed forces, but Dr Josef Hirt, director of the Institute of Racial Anthropology at Strasbourg University wanted freshly killed Jewish bodies undamaged by bullet wounds or ill treatment for his experiments. These unfortunates were thus to be gassed at nearby Natzwiller.

The camp is now a memorial to those who died there. In the museum is a letter dated 8 December 1943 to then camp commandant Josef Kramer, later to command Bergen-Belsen. It reads:

Re Christmas Bonus. For faithful service, head office chief SS Obergruppenführer/General Pohl has authorised payment of a Christmas bonus to you. Please find enclosed cheque for 500 Reichsmarks.

A receipt for the money was requested. The 'faithful service' in question was Kramer's gassing in the improvised gas chamber of the eighty-six Jewish women so that their skulls could be boiled clean and sent to the 'anthropological' collection of Dr Hirt in Strasburg, generously subsidised to prove the insane Nazi racial theories. The women were made to strip before going into the gas chamber, one woman resisting so furiously that she had to be shot outside.

On the afternoon of 6 July 1944 when the four SOE women agents arrived in this obscene universe, carrying little suitcases containing their few belongings, Stonehouse was in a labour detail working near the wire and saw them walk down the *Lagerstrasse* – the central track between the huts. Natzwiller being a camp for male prisoners – all veterans of the Resistance in different countries – he was surprised, not only to see four women, but also that they were quite smartly dressed, walking confidently and not in the shuffle of long-term camp prisoners. A Dutch Resistance officer in Natzwiller later told Vera Atkins that all the prisoners were intrigued by what he called 'these first class women' and speculated they had been brought in to set up a brothel for the SS. A graphic artist with excellent visual recall, Stonehouse described clearly to Vera one of the women as being 'of middle height, rather stocky build, with shortish fair hair tied with a coloured ribbon, aged about 28. She was wearing a grey fingertip-length flannel swagger coat with a grey skirt that I thought looked very English'.[111] Vera recognised this description of Diana Rowden. She could not identify another woman described by Stonehouse because she had never met locally recruited agent Sonya Olschanezky.

By the time the four women were escorted down the flight of steps leading to the holding cells, everyone in the camp except them knew that they had been brought to Natzwiller to be murdered. Before that moment, there had already been an argument between the camp staff about the method to be used. They could have been hanged in public during roll-call, which was the usual way prisoners were executed, but executioner Peter Straub said that hanging these women would cause *ein grosses Theater* – a lot of trouble. It was then decided to tell each woman she must have an inoculation against typhus, and inject her with a fatal dose of phenol. Natzwiller being a concentration camp and not an extermination camp, no one knew whether they had enough phenol in stock. A junior medical orderly was told to check in the pharmacy and found 80cc of phenol, which he was ordered to bring to the crematorium block with a 10cc syringe and one or two large-gauge needles, plus some ampoules of Evipan, a powerful barbiturate. A Belgian doctor prisoner, working in the camp hospital next to the cell block, managed to establish vocal contact with one of the women, which would have been punished by hanging, if he had been overheard. She told him her name was Denise. This was the cover name of Andrée Borrel.

Normally, Natzwiller prisoners were allowed to stay outside the huts until 8.30 p.m.. But that evening they were ordered to be inside by 8 p.m. and to close the shutters because anyone looking out would be shot by the sentries. By then, the unusual flurry of SS activity and the smoke coming from the furnace chimney made it obvious that the women were shortly to be killed and their bodies burned.

A recidivist common law prisoner named Berg later testified that he had been given the job as stoker of the camp crematorium, where bodies were burned three times a week. When two English and two French women were brought to the camp in July 1944, he was ordered to pre-heat the furnace to maximum temperature by 9.30 p.m. and then go to his own cell in the crematorium block and stay there with two other prisoners. The women were being held in separate cramped holding cells in the nearby detention block. A Belgian prisoner, watching through a knot-hole in the shutter, saw two SS men fetch the first woman from the cells and return at fifteen minute intervals for the others.

Inside the crematorium block, the women were told to undress, which they refused to do unless a female doctor was present. They were given the injections anyway, in the upper arm and, when drowsy, three were undressed, although one woman was too rigid to undress completely. In Berg's cell, the three prisoners who shared it heard the sound of four heavy burdens being dragged along the corridor with loud groaning noises. His statement continued:

> The fourth [woman] resisted in the corridor. I heard her say 'Pourquoi?' and one of the camp doctors said, 'Pour typhus.' We then heard the noise of a struggle and muffled cries of the woman. I assumed that somebody held a hand over her mouth. I heard this woman being dragged away too. She was groaning louder than the others. From the noise of the crematorium oven doors which I heard, I can definitely state that in each case the groaning women were placed immediately in the [preheated] crematorium oven.[112]

Another SS man at Natzwiller said that Straub told him next day, 'When the last woman was halfway in the oven – she had been put in feet first – she came to her senses and struggled [presumably roused by the searing pain as her skin came in contact with the hot oven]. As there were sufficient men there, they were able to push her into the oven, but not before she had resisted and scratched Straub's face.' Straub also told him, 'I was in Auschwitz for a long time. In my time about 4 million people have gone up the chimney, but I have never experienced anything like this before. I am finished.'

Several prisoners in neighbouring huts, watching the flames flare from the chimney each time the furnace door was opened, heard repeated screaming – from which it seems that all the women may have regained consciousness, due to the agonising pain of being burned alive. When all the SS had gone away – to a farewell drinks party for the chief doctor who had been posted elsewhere – Berg and the other two prisoners in the crematorium block came out of their cell and found four charred bodies in the oven. From photographs, Berg positively identified SOE agent Vera Leigh and thought Sonya Olschanezky was possibly Noor Inayat, whom she did slightly resemble.[113]

When Vera Atkins tracked down and interviewed Straub three months after the end of the war in Europe, his face still bore the scars from the nails of the courageous woman who fought all those SS men pushing her into the crematorium oven, alive and conscious.

9

Heroine or Liar?

On 5 September 1941 an exhibition under the title *Le Juif et la France* opened in German-occupied Paris. Allegedly scientific, it was the first big manifestation of the Vichy government's anti-Semitism supporting Nazi racial theories. After it closed to go on provincial tour four months later Paul Sézille, the director of Vichy's Institute for Jewish Questions, wrote to his colleagues at the Commissariat Général des Questions Juives boasting that paid attendances had totalled 500,000, which because of free and reduced price admissions meant a total attendance of close to one million. This was eyewash. The less racially prejudiced German ambassador in Paris, Otto Abetz, recorded that a total of 250,623 visitors was closer to the truth.

Sometimes propaganda achieves the reverse of what its promoters hope. Among the visitors to the exhibition in France's second city Lyon was Lucie Aubrac, a 28-year-old history teacher who had helped her husband Raymond to escape from a German POW camp, after which he had changed their surname from Samuel firstly to Valmont and then Aubrac, to gain an apparently Aryan identity. Both PCF members, the couple were active in a Resistance network called Libération-Sud, publishing an anti-German news-sheet entitled *Libération*. Lucie was so horrified by the blatant anti-Semitism of the exhibition that she decided to put her infant son in a children's home, which left Raymond and herself free for the dangerous activity of rescuing captured comrades from Vichy and German prisons. Inevitably, one member of the gang was captured in a prison raid and tortured into giving away the identities of some thirty others, including Raymond. Before they could be handed over to the Gestapo, Lucie hurried to the office of the Vichy Procurateur de le République. The tide of war was turning against Germany, so she threatened this state prosecutor with dire punishment by the Allies post-war unless he released Raymond, which he did.[114]

But the Gestapo was on Raymond's track, and heading the Gestapo in Lyon was *SS-Hauptsturmführer* Klaus Barbie. Working out of an office in the luxurious Hôtel Terminus adjacent to Lyon's main railway station, he was a psychopath who enjoyed personally whipping prisoners, pulling out fingernails and toenails, pistol-whipping faces, burning his naked victim's sensitive body parts with heated pokers and applying electric shock to their sexual organs during torture sessions in the Ecole de Santé Militaire. When bored, he interrupted interrogations at which he fondled a French prostitute further to disturb his victims, in order to play the piano. His prisoners frequently saw their predecessors at Barbie's interrogations returned to the vermin-ridden, unventilated holding cells of Lyon's Montluc prison bleeding, unconscious, with broken limbs and eyes literally gouged out. To demonstrate his contempt for the *Untermenschen* he was terrorising, Barbie strolled through the city centre streets without a bodyguard each evening to dine in one of Lyon's many gourmet restaurants. This was the man intent on arresting Raymond Aubrac.

General Charles de Gaulle – the leader of the Free French forces – had sent into France a political representative in the person of Jean Moulin, a former prefect of Chartres endowed with considerable diplomatic skills, who managed to set up an umbrella organisation to co-ordinate the activities of the main Resistance movements, often at odds for political and personal reasons. This was called 'les Mouvements Unis de la Résistance' (MUR). The plurality of the title betrays the fact that none of the movement leaders would accept orders from any other one. That they came together at all was due to Moulin handing out large sums of money from the Gaullist headquarters in London and threatening to withhold this and airdropped arms supplies when someone was being unco-operative.

Diplomat, Moulin undoubtedly was but, as a clandestine agent, he committed a fatal error. Although well aware that he was being hunted all over France by the Gestapo and its French collaborators, Moulin called a meeting on 21 June 1943 of the heads of eight major Resistance movements in Caluire, a suburb of Lyon. With every one of the attendees likely to be under surveillance and thus liable to lead his German or Vichy French shadowers to the meeting, it is hard to find a sane reason for such a major error, which may have been due to Moulin feeling a disarming sense of triumph at getting this group of powerful men to set aside some of their differences in the common cause.

The venue for the meeting in the afternoon of 21 June was in the house of dental surgeon Dr Dugoujon, chosen because Moulin thought they could enter and leave unnoticed among the comings and goings of Dugoujon's patients. Representing Libération-Sud was Raymond Aubrac. A missing right-wing movement leader was ex-army officer Henri Frenay of the

Combat group, who was in London for a briefing by the Gaullist BCRA. He was represented by his deputy, who brought along a man named René Hardy as his assistant.

The dentist's house was already staked out by the Gestapo before they arrived and the meeting had no sooner begun than German and French agents burst in and handcuffed everyone, including genuine patients awaiting treatment. As they were all being herded into closed vans, Hardy made a run for it. Despite several Gestapo men turning automatic weapons in his direction, he escaped with only a slight leg wound – a remarkable achievement for a man running with his wrists cuffed behind the back, and who was not pursued very far, despite the importance of the arrests.

The local French police noted the incident routinely, between reports of ID cards stolen from a town hall and an increase in thefts of vegetables from private gardens. In the torture chambers at the Ecole de Santé Militaire, Barbie ignored Moulin's alias, calling him by his Resistance code name, Max. What happened in the following thirty hours is best left to the imagination. On the evening of 23 June the 'trusty' prison barber in Montluc prison was ordered to shave an unconscious man, who had obviously been tortured nearly to death, and whose flesh was cold to his touch. Moulin mumbled something in English and asked for water. The guard rinsed out a shaving mug and the barber held it to Moulin's mouth, but he could only swallow a few drops before losing consciousness again.

Driven to Paris, he was locked up in a suburban villa used by the Gestapo as an interrogation centre. De Gaulle's military representative in occupied France, General Charles Delestraint – who had been captured after using his real identity when signing in for the night at a Paris hotel! – was brought there from

Fresnes prison two weeks later to be shown Moulin lying on a stretcher. Noting that his skin had turned yellow and his respiration was hardly noticeable, the dignified Delestraint, who could speak German, replied coldly to the Gestapo questions with, 'How do you expect me to identify a man in that condition?' Officially, Jean Moulin died in a train taking him to Germany on 8 July 1943, aged 44. General Delestraint was transferred to the concentration camp at Natzwiller in Alsace and from there in September to Dachau, where he was shot and cremated on the morning of 19 April 1945, aged 64.

In one successful operation the Gestapo had neutralised the two men who might have united all the different Resistance movements. Barbie's masterstroke of 21 June was rewarded by a personal citation from Himmler on 18 September 1943 and the award of the Iron Cross first class with swords on 9 November 1943.

Two days after the arrests in Dr Dugoujon's waiting room, Lucie Aubrac arrived at the Ecole de Santé Militaire. Expensively dressed, she said her name was Ghislaine de Barbantine and she wished to speak to Barbie. Most French people avoided the sadistic Gestapo officer and his colleagues like the plague, so Barbie was intrigued and agreed to see her. He was smartly dressed, she afterwards recalled, in a light summer suit and pink shirt, and had an attractive woman with him, as usual for these sessions. When he asked what she wanted, Lucie cried hysterically that she came from a respectable conservative family and was ashamed to be carrying a child by 'Claude Ermulin' – which was Raymond's alias – especially since she now realised that he was a terrorist. She begged Barbie to allow her to tell 'Ermulin' just what she thought of him and to force him to marry her before he was executed, which French law permitted for a prisoner under sentence of death.

This first request was rejected, but she returned on 21 October visibly pregnant and succeeded in meeting Barbie again by dint of bribes to French prison staff working for the Gestapo. As she had astutely deduced, the idea of a wronged woman tongue-lashing a tortured detainee whose child she was carrying so appealed to Barbie's perverted sense of humour that he ordered 'Ermulin' to be brought to the Ecole de Santé. Apparently unmoved by his pitiful state after four months in Montluc Prison, Lucie raved at 'Ermulin' that whatever was happening served him right as far as she was concerned, but she needed the father's name on her child's birth certificate and expected him to 'do the decent thing' and marry her. 'Ermulin' was hardly in a condition to marry anyone. The whole point of the danger-ous pantomime was to have him brought to the medical school for the confrontation. As the police van was returning him and Barbie's other victims of the day to Montluc prison after interro-gation, two cars closed in on it and automatic fire from silenced weapons killed the men in the driver's cab and mowed down the guards who jumped out, except one who escaped. The prisoners were released, but some reports said Raymond was wounded in the attack. By risking her own life and that of her unborn child, Lucie Aubrac had saved that of her husband.[115]

She had also put herself in the line of fire, with the Gestapo and their French collaborators intent on tracking down her and Raymond – and their son, now 3 years old, whom they collected from the children's home an hour before the Gestapo arrived. In a remote hideout in central France, they lay low and waited for a flight from RAF Tempsford to bring them all safely to London. Given Lucie's condition, they had to wait for favourable condi-tions for a comfortable landing and take-off but the weather was against them. Meanwhile, Raymond's parents were arrested, but could not divulge the runaways' whereabouts, even had they been tortured. With thousands of Germans and *miliciens* searching all over France for Lucie and Raymond and the meteorological conditions continuing unfavourable for a clandestine landing, they were moved to the Jura region of eastern France.

At 3 a.m. on 9 February 1944 a Hudson piloted by Flight Lieutenant Johnnie Affleck – one of Tempsford's courageous special missions officers who serviced the drops and landings in France – touched down in a field near Bletterans, south-west of Besançon. The Aubrac family and four other passengers were quickly embarked, but their added weight drove the Hudson's port wheel into the muddy ground. The team of *résistants* who had held torches to mark the landing strip urgently rushed from farm to farm through a snowstorm to get help until nearly 200 adults were heaving on ropes and pushing to free the aircraft, only to find that the tailwheel had become trapped in the mud. While some of them dug ramps for the wheels, others harnessed a team of horses or oxen to the undercarriage and pulled the Hudson free – at which point the pilot gunned the engine and cautiously took off, to everyone's great relief. For once, there was a happy ending: after the mud-splattered Hudson landed at Tempsford at 6.40 a.m., Lucie was rushed to hospital in London to give birth to a daughter, who was baptised Cathérine Mitraillette – the second name meaning a sub-machine gun, as used by the Resistance. For this hair-raising mission, Affleck was rightly awarded the Distinguished Flying Cross.[116]

After the liberation, René Hardy was twice charged with betraying the MUR meeting to the Gestapo – before a civil court in 1947 and a military tribunal in 1950. He escaped conviction on both occasions for lack of proof, but the trials left a big question mark in public opinion. In post-war France the PCF was very important, as was the legend of the Resistance saving

French honour, and Lucie Aubrac, widely regarded as a great heroine, wrote several books about the Resistance.

That would have been the end of the story except that, in 1972, a French television journalist named Ladislas de Hoyos 'outed' Barbie, living as a German refugee in Bolivia under the name Klaus Altmann. Although there are gaps in his story after the German surrender, he was known to have been recruited by the US Counter Intelligence Corps (CIC) in 1947 as a useful source in its struggle against Soviet infiltration of the western zones of Germany. When the French authorities discovered that this man whom they had already sentenced to death *in absentia* was being protected by their American allies, they requested he be delivered to them. CIC refused. In 1965 Barbie was employed by the West German intelligence agency Bundesnachrichtendienst in Pullach, Bavaria, and submitted a number of reports, although where he was living is unknown because his salary was paid into a bank in San Francisco. At some point in this tangled tale CIC arranged with a ratline organised by pro-Nazi Croatian Catholic priests for this embarrassing asset to be smuggled to Bolivia. There he was involved in the arms trade, which earned him the rank of lieutenant general in the secret police and the protection of high-ranking military and political friends.

After a *coup d'état* these friends could no longer protect him and, following a very shady deal between the governments in La Paz and Paris, Barbie was eventually extradited from Bolivia to France on 5 February 1983. When first detained in Montluc prison, his undiminished hatred of the French was manifested in repeated threats to 'tell the truth' about some scandals of the Resistance, one of which, he said, was that Raymond Aubrac was a double agent, working for the Gestapo.

Barbie's trial for crimes against humanity – the only charge still possible under the French statute of limitations – opened on 11 May 1987 in Lyon. With financial backing from François Genoud, a Swiss banker involved in the 'Nazi diaspora' at the end of the Second World War, the senior of three defending lawyers was *Maître* Jacques Vergès, a francophobic French–Thai–Algerian lawyer who professed to be both a communist and a Muslim, was a personal friend of the insane Cambodian dictator Pol Pot and had gained notoriety by defending extremely unpopular clients such as the assassin Ilich Ramírez Sánchez, nicknamed 'the Jackal'. Given the wealth of indisputable evidence against this client, all Vergès' courtroom skills could not prevent Barbie being found guilty and sentenced to life imprisonment. In October a second trial opened, which Vergès was determined would discredit the Resistance by proving Barbie's allegation that Lucie Aubrac was a liar and that her husband was the traitor who had betrayed Moulin, having agreed to act as a Gestapo informer when released in March 1943. According to Vergès' account, Barbie had personally planned the seemingly miraculous rescue from the prison van in return for this collaboration.

On 25 September 1991, when Barbie died in prison of leukemia and prostate cancer at the age of 78, the matter was officially closed. However, in April 1997 the Lyonnais journalist Gérard Chauvy published *Aubrac, Lyon 1943* repeating Vergès' accusations against Lucie and Raymond Aubrac, who sued for slander and demanded the withdrawal of Chauvy's book. They assembled a number of eyewitnesses to the events of 1943, including the man who organised the raid on the prison van, all of whom testified that Chauvy had never bothered to interview them to obtain the true facts. The tribunal imposed fines of 60,000 francs on him and 100,000 francs on the publisher, Albin Michel. Their appeal being rejected, the fines were raised to a global sum of 400,000 francs.

Lucie Aubrac naturally did everything to refute Barbie's story, but some people in France do believe his version of the events in 1943, rather than credit her with the courageous rescue of her husband. Which is the truth? It is hard to credit the account of a pathological sadistic torturer and murderer like Barbie, as manipulated by the francophobe lawyer Vergès, but was he telling the truth or, with nothing to lose, simply attempting to besmirch the record of a real French heroine who had out-smarted him?

10

Rape as a Tool of War

Just ten years after the ravages it had suffered in the Second
World War, in 1954 North Africa was the setting for another war
which from time to time spilled over into Morocco to the west
and Tunisia to the east, but was mainly fought in Algeria, then
legally a part of France. During seven years and five months,
the French Army and Air Force, the Foreign Legion, French
colonial troops and *harkis* – Algerian troops in French uniform
– used all the currently available hardware – fixed-wing aircraft
and helicopters, mortars, artillery, electrified border fences –
against the Armée de Libération Nationale (ALN), whose small
mobile groups of fighters armed with rifles, grenades and light
machine guns emerged from remote mountainous areas to ter-
rorise the countryside. In the cities, urban guerillas armed with
knives, automatic pistols and home-made bombs targeted not
only Europeans but also anyone who collaborated with the
French administration. As far as the government in Paris was
concerned, Algeria was part of France, not a colony, and the
armed forces were putting down a rebellion there fomented by

the Comintern and supported by the Parti Communiste Français (PCF). Algeria was divided into three *départements* centred on the cities of Oran in the west, Algiers in the centre and Constantine in the east – in exactly the same way as mainland France has been divided into *départements* since the Revolution, when the *ancien régime* duchies and counties were abolished.

All civil wars are fought with bitterness, which in this case was exacerbated by race and religion. More than 1 million Algerians were of European origin; their families had lived there for several generations – some ever since the country was created from a scattering of hereditary tribal lands in 1830. But the majority of the population was Arabic- or Berber-speaking, nominally Muslim, and for the most part deprived of education and political rights. The territory was fertile ground for a war of independence, triggered by the Soviet-supported Viet Minh's victory in 1954 over French occupation forces in Vietnam, which showed the world that the day of European empires was over. Paradoxically, both Washington and Moscow wanted to destroy the British, French, Belgian and Portuguese empires, the US administrations intending to open the whole world to American Big Business and Stalin's regime determined to subject the entire planet to Soviet hegemony.

There had been anti-French riots in Sétif and Guelma in May 1945, but in 1954 it was evident from the first day of hostilities that the war just starting was going to be a very dirty one, with a concerted programme of assassinations of Europeans and Muslim civil servants followed by brutal retaliation from the French authorities. From the very start, rape of European women and defilement of their corpses was practised by the guerilla fighters of the ALN, which was the military wing of the political Front de Libération Nationale (FLN), and who were known as *fellagha* or *les fells*. French soldiers also raped Muslim women when deployed into the countryside, away from the oversight of senior officers. Benoist Rey was a young conscript serving in the French zone of Germany in 1959 when he was posted to Algeria. He kept a secret diary of the atrocities he witnessed and published it as a book after his demobilisation[117] entitled *Les Egorgeurs* – the cut-throats – having witnessed at least 100 prisoners killed by his comrades slitting their throats during his service as a medic in Algeria. Under the censorship of the time, the first edition was seized immediately after publication; it remained subject to censorship until reissued in 2012.[118] He wrote:

> In my unit, rapes happened all the time. Before we raided a village, the officer said, 'Rape them if you want, but be discreet.' It was regarded as a perk for the lads. The way guys thought of it was, it was only women and Arab women at that. From the hundred men of my unit, twenty or so took advantage of their opportunities on every raid. Apart from two or three, the other guys kept their mouths shut for fear of being accused of supporting the FLN if they had spoken out. On one operation, a girl of fifteen was raped by seven soldiers and another of thirteen by three other men.[119]

The 1.5 million professional soldiers and conscripts shipped across the Mediterranean said little about their deeds in Algeria when returning home. More than 30,000 never came home and many others returned crippled or mentally disturbed. Nearly everyone in France knew a man killed or wounded during the long conflict. Afterwards, it took four decades before the truth began leaking out in responsible journals such as *Le Monde* of torture by both sides, summary killing of prisoners and rape of women used as a routine instrument of war. No written orders for rape have ever been found. Men serving in Algeria said that some units did not rape; it all depended on the commanding officer or senior NCO present. If he sanctioned it, it happened; if not, it did not.

With most of the men of military age absent from the *bled* and *mechtas* – remote villages and isolated farms – fighting with *les fells* in the mountains, one routine was *le viol à quatre* where two soldiers stood guard at the two ends of the village, a third rounded up the women and children at gunpoint, to keep them out of the way, and a fourth raped one or more selected young women. When he had finished, they swapped roles until each soldier who wanted to had sated his lust. Usually, men with wives or fiancées back home did not take part, but kept their mouths shut about what they had seen. As in the former Yugoslavia, the victims of these rapes could not pretend it had not happened because too many neighbours knew the truth. So they were for the most part rejected by their husbands when the men returned at the end of the war. As one Muslim ex-*fell* said in the television programme *Envoyé Spécial – Les viols d'Algérie*,[120] the rape of his wife by French soldiers was an insult to his masculine dignity, so he could have nothing further to do with her. She was then an outcast, a non-person, effectively dead already as far as he and the family were concerned.

Mohamed Garne considers himself 'French by crime'. Born in 1960 after his pretty 16-year-old mother, Keïra, was gang-raped by guards in the concentration camp at Teniet-el-Haad in western Algeria the previous year and later severely beaten about the belly by their comrades in unsuccessful efforts to abort the fœtus so she could not give birth to a tell-tale pale-skinned baby, he was brought up by nuns in an orphanage and in foster homes. Unable to trace her for twenty-eight years, he eventually found his mother living like a wild animal in a cave among the graves of a large cemetery overlooking Algiers – fit only to live with the truly dead, in her own words. After using his money to build her a small house in the cemetery, he came forward to demand reparation on her behalf. On 22 November 2001, the Court of Appeal in Paris granted her the status of 'civilian victim of war' and a pension.[121]

Posted in 1961 to the infamous Villa Sesini interrogation centre in Algiers,[122] conscript Henri Pouillot recorded being present at 100 or so rapes during the ten months he served there, although he did not participate himself because he was engaged to a girl in France. Like Benoît Rey, he too later wrote a book, entitled *La Villa Sesini:*[123]

> I suppose nine out of ten of the women there were raped, depending on their age and looks. When there was a 'ratissage' in Algiers, it was usual to capture one or two young ones just to serve the lads. They stayed in the villa one, two or three days, sometimes longer. The fifteen men stationed in the Villa Sesini had total control over them. Nothing was forbidden. The rapes were just another form of torture made possible by women's bodies. Sometimes it was to make them talk and other times just for pleasure when they were taken to the guys' bedrooms.

A former reservist sent to Algeria confided to the author that *of course* he had taken part in torture of male prisoners:

> We had to make them talk, so they were taken to the MT section and trussed hand and foot on a metal work bench, scorching hot from the sun. The electrodes were clipped on their sensitive parts, they were hosed down to make a better

contact with the wet metal and the current from a *gégène* field
generator turned on.[124]

Former sergeant Jean Vuillez served in the Constantine region
starting in October 1960. The prisoners he saw tortured for
information were nearly all female because, in his sector, all
the men were away fighting or locked up behind the electrified
fences of the concentration camp at El Milia. He wrote:

> You cannot imagine how those women were treated. Three
> of the NCOs 'interrogated' them regularly in their barrack
> rooms. In March 1961 I saw four women locked up in a cellar
> for a week, tortured each day with salt water to drink and
> beaten on the breasts. The naked corpses of three of those
> women were eventually dumped beside the road to Collo.

Historian Claire Mauss-Copeaux believes that the nationwide
rapes during and after the battle of Algiers in 1957 began with
the practice of soldiers having to feel the genitals of *burka*-clad
women during street searches of the casbah, to check the real sex
of a person dressed like this. When a woman's identity papers
revealed that she was the wife of a man known to be with the
ALN, Army nurses and secretaries made a quasi-gynaecological
examination: if her pubic hair was shaven, it meant she was
receiving visits from him; if not, they had not recently been
in touch. Feminist lawyer Gisèle Halimi wrote that nine times
out of ten, the women she interviewed had been raped in many
different ways, but their shame was so all-pervading that they
begged her not to reveal these crimes that made them, in their
own minds, human trash. It is unknown how many suicides
this provoked. Jacques Duquesne included in his book *Pour com-
prendre l'Algérie* a photograph showing a naked young Algerian

woman held up by two grinning, uniformed, French soldiers like a hunting trophy. The picture is reminiscent of the GIs' trophy photos of captured Viet Cong women and the naked, humiliated detainees in Abu Ghraib prison in Iraq being taunted by male and female US soldiers.

On 26 November 2001 a much-decorated retired French general was on trial in Paris, not for having ordered the torture of suspects during the 'battle of Algiers' in 1957, which he admitted, but for publishing a book about it.[125] On 25 January 2002 General Paul Aussarès was fined 7,500 euros. When interviewed by an *Envoyé Spécial* reporter, who asked whether arrested women had been tortured, as well as men, he replied politely, 'Of course, madame.' When she asked, 'Were they raped?' his emphatic reply was, *'Jamais!'* Never.[126]

Where is all this leading? Despite General Aussarès' denial, the evidence is overwhelming that many women were both tortured and raped during the Algerian war. What then was the fate of PCF members who actively supported the FLN? A number of male party members acted as *porteurs de valises*, travelling to Algeria with suitcases of money collected, voluntarily and by force, from Algerians working in metropolitan France. Some funds were also given freely by PCF sympathisers and cash subsidies originated in eastern bloc embassies in Paris. This practice soon came to the knowledge of General Aussarès and his fellow intelligence officers with the result that any men caught doing this were treated as traitors and tortured to death, their corpses afterward being dumped in the Mediterranean, so that they disappeared without trace, like the prisoners designated *Nacht und Nebel* in Nazi Europe. Former PCF member Hélène Lenoir[127] recounted to the author how the worst and most prolonged tortures were reserved for men such as her lover, a party member who had completed his compulsory military service and volunteered to train FLN recruits in the *bled*, participating with them in attacks on European civilian and military targets. After being caught, he disappeared.[128] Journalist and PCF member Henri Alleg was arrested by paras on 12 June 1957 and tortured for a complete month with beatings, electric shocks and waterboarding. He was also threatened that his wife would be similarly maltreated, like a famous actor's wife, Madame Touri, tortured in front of her husband to make him talk.[129] In the paras' torture centre, Alleg frequently heard women screaming in a separate wing of the prison while undergoing torture.

The family of Louisette Ighilahriz, a 21-year-old using the *nom de guerre* Lila, were all active in the struggle for independence. She acted as a liaison agent for the FLN, carrying small weapons to be used in urban attacks and messages reporting movement of army units. Possibly, she was a member of the *réseau bombes* of young women commanded by Yacef Saadi, which included Samia Lakhdari, Zohra Drif, Djamila Bouhiridet and Hassiba Ben Bouali – the four of them shown in a photograph to be seen on French Wikipedia holding automatic weapons and hand grenades.[130] Louisette, her mother and sister were all tortured – in her case by men commanded by a para captain named Gradiani in a villa she identified for the camera in a 2002 French television current affairs programme[131] as the HQ of the 10th Para Division, in an endeavour to make her name all her pro-FLN contacts. Interviewed to camera, she found it difficult, half a century later, to find words for what happened there. Her ordeal began with being punched and slapped by several soldiers calling her 'whore' and 'slut'. Cigarette burns all over her body and electrical torture were followed by *le viol partouze*, in which several torturers raped her for their own pleasure, all the time hitting and screaming abuse at her.[132]

In 1954 Annick Castel Pailler was the 20-year-old wife of a PCF schoolteacher who had volunteered to run a school in a small town 200km south of Constantine in the Aurès Mountains. Although she was not actively enagaged with the FLN, after he was arrested soldiers came for her, too. She was driven to the hospital of Birtraria, which had been taken over as an interrogation centre, where a young recruit warned her that he had overheard some of the guards talk of coming to rape her in the night. She says that only one did rape her and that, when she screamed for help, he warned her to shut up unless she wanted him to bring all his comrades, to use her one after another. The next morning, the young conscript was near tears for what had happened and gave her a present of a baguette loaf and some butter. To no avail, she pleaded to her rapist that she was married and had a little daughter, but it seems she had to endure his nightly visits for three awful weeks.[133] Unusually – as raped women so often prefer to keep quiet, rather than talk about their suffering – Annick had the courage in 1958 to accuse her rapist. The court handed him a suspended sentence of two years' imprisonment.

When the PCF in Paris decided it was too dangerous for male party members to continue transporting money to Algeria, and it was thought that French *women* would not be suspected, female comrades were asked to volunteer. A number did so, some carrying the money in their luggage and others having it stitched into their undergarments. When they fell into the hands of the paras in Algiers or Oran, they automatically suffered torture and rape, as General Aussarès must have known. Although many disappeared, including Hélène Lenoir's fiancé, one was released after several weeks in hospital to frighten off her comrades by telling how she had been raped with a broken bottle.

The most famous case concerned a 22-year-old Algerian woman from a comfortable middle class family. Djamila Boupacha[134] was an FLN militant using the *nom de guerre* Khelida living in a middle class suburb of Algiers, who placed a bomb in the Brasserie des Facultés bar on 27 September 1959. The bomb was defused before exploding. With no witnesses to accuse her, she was not arrested until 10 February 1960, when fifty gendarmes, *harkis* and police burst into her family villa outside Algiers, beating up everyone inside. Together with her father, sister, brother and brother-in-law, she was arrested on the grounds of confessions obtained by torture, and taken to El-Biar where a para captain supervised a severe kicking that broke several ribs. After five days of beatings, she was transferred to the prison of Hussein-Dey, where a team of three harkis, two soldiers and three plainclothes police officers tortured her. For exactly how long this continued, is unknown because no record was kept of her detention, but it lasted more than a month.

Electrodes were attached to her ear lobes, lips, nipples and labia or inserted into the vagina and anus with the current turned on at increasing power. Lit cigarettes were applied to sensitive body areas. Tied to a bar, which produced excruciating cramps, she was suspended, head down, over a bath of filthy water and lowered into it until she nearly drowned, time after time. Reduced to a soaking, haggard wreck of the person who had been arrested, she was then raped or sodomised with a bottle.[135] After a month of this, she was to be tried in Algiers for the crime of planting the bomb, but became a *cause célèbre* for left-wing sympathisers who feared she would be murdered in her cell to prevent any further publicity. In May 1960, Parisian lawyer Gisèle Halimi volunteered to act for her and travelled to Algiers. She was allowed to interview her client, but was arrested and expelled back to France on the same day.

She invoked the support of Simone de Beauvoir, who wrote an article in *Le Monde* about Djamila, after which a committee of intellectuals and female *résistantes* who had suffered torture and deportation during the German occupation succeeded in having the trial moved from Algiers to Caen in Normandy, thanks to the intervention of Simone Veil, then a magistrate.

On 21 July Djamila was transferred to the prison of Fresnes, outside Paris. Her trial began in Caen at the end of June 1961. Questioned in court by Halimi, Djamila named several of her torturers, but was condemned to death for her terrorist activities on 28 June. Fortunately the Evian agreement of 18 March 1962, which ended the war in Algeria and amnestied all crimes committed during it, saw her liberated on 21 April 1962. After briefly seeking refuge with Halimi, Djamila was taken back to Algeria, now an independent one-party state, and used as a symbol of the FLN/ALN struggle for freedom, her bourgeois origins being 'corrected' by the socialist government to 'working class'. In 1974 the minister responsible for benefits to former freedom fighters admitted that, of a total of 10,949 female FLN activists, 2,000 worked like Djamila in the towns and cities, of whom 948 were killed.[136] However, within a few months of Djamila's return, the idea that women had shared the fighting and the suffering, and were thus partly responsible for the country gaining independence became politically unacceptable in Muslim–socialist Algeria and a political veil was drawn over Djamila and all the other female fighters, living or dead.

11

The Whore of the Republic

Sometimes current sleaze reveals even worse things in the past of the protagonists. In April 1999 an article in the French daily *Libération* commented on Christine Deviers-Joncour, ex-mistress of disgraced Foreign Minister Roland Dumas, giving her friend, Lucienne Goldfarb, 1 million francs in cash in November 1997 to look after her mother and children because Deviers-Joncour expected to be sent to prison for her involvement in the gigantic petroleum bribes scandal that rocked the French government and caused Dumas' fall from power.[137]

Contacted by *Libération* for a comment, Goldfarb confined her answer to, 'Let them prosecute me. I'll know what to say.' Tough talk from a woman of 74 with friends in several police and intelligence services, who would not want her in court and talking. As to how Deviers-Joncour and Goldfarb first met, we have to go back half a century.

Ever since the French Revolution, republican France had been a *pays d'accueil*, initially welcoming refugees from the monarchist states of Europe and continuing that policy until by 1940 tens of thousands of refugees at risk from Nazi racial and political policies had been given asylum there, many of them in Paris. One network of young male and female immigrants who fought the occupation under the communist Francs-Tireurs et Partisans organisation was the Main d'Oeuvre Immigrée network (FTP–MOI), commanded by an Armenian refugee named Missak Manouchian. It included two women: Anna Richter and the Romanian Olga, or Golda, Bančic. The method of the group was for the men carrying out attacks on German and French Vichy targets to travel to the scene without the revolvers and grenades to be used, in case they were stopped and body-searched. These were brought for them by the two women. After the attack, because the group had very few weapons, these were hidden and recovered by the women, who brought them back to base while the men cycled off with no evidence to connect them with the deed should they be stopped. Since the area in which the attack took place was immediately cordoned off by German security troops, there was a colossal risk of the women being caught with the evidence on them. They did this in at least 100 operations.

Being both an active communist and Jewish, Olga had been arrested and maltreated several times in her native Romania. After arriving in France, she was active in support of communist groups fighting in the Spanish Civil War, married a Jewish writer and gave birth to a daughter. After the German invasion, she entrusted the 1-year-old girl to an uninvolved French family living in the country, to save her from any reprisals, and went underground, using the *nom de guerre* Pierrette. A former comrade afterwards recalled how she was always especially tense on Friday operations because Saturday was her day to go and visit the daughter in the country.

Olga was arrested by the anti-terrorist police Brigade Spéciale No. 2 on 6 November 1943, together with sixty-seven other members of Manouchian's group. Of these twenty-three were locked up in Fresnes prison and tortured while awaiting their trial on 15 February 1944 and subsequent execution by firing squad on 21 February at the Mont Valérien fortress. After enduring prolonged torture, Olga was transported to Karlsruhe on 19 February and transferred to Stuttgart on 3 May, to be beheaded by guillotine there one week later on her 32nd birthday. Shortly before her execution she managed to throw out of the window of her cell a letter addressed to the Red Cross. Whether picked up by a French forced worker or some other well-wisher, it eventually reached its destination, with the note:

Dear Madame, Please be kind enough to forward my letter to my little daughter Dolores Jacob after the war. This is the last wish of a mother who has only twelve hours to live.

The letter, in rather stilted language with many spelling and grammatical mistakes, was written in French because her daughter had never learned Romanian:

My dear little daughter, my dear little love,

Your mother is writing her last letter, my dear little girl. Tomorrow, at six o'clock on 10 May, I shall be no more. My love, do not cry, as I do not cry either. I die with a quiet conscience and the conviction that you will have a happier future than your mother. I still have your picture in front of me. I believe that you will see your father again and hope that he will have a better fate. Tell him that I have always thought of him and of you.

I love you with all my heart. Both of you are so dear to me. Your father is, from now on, also a mother to you. He loves

you very much. My dear child, I end this letter in the hope
that you will be happy all your life with your father.

   With all my love, goodbye,

   Your mother.

On 4 July 2013 the municipality of Paris erected a plaque on
the wall of No. 114 rue du Château in the XIVth *arrondissement*,
where Olga had lived, commemorating her Resistance activities
and death in Stuttgart, ending '*Morte Pour la France et la Liberté*'.

   As to who betrayed all those people, after the liberation of
Paris on 25 August 1944 survivors of FTP–MOI pointed the
finger at a plump, red-haired 20-year-old girl named Lucienne
Goldfarb, who came from a very Jewish area in the eleventh
arrondissement of Paris. Two years before, it had seemed quite reasonable when Lucienne asked an old school friend to introduce
her to someone in touch with the Resistance 'so I can avenge my
family'. Her father had been deported to a German death camp
in 1941 and her mother and brother were currently held in the
French concentration camp at Drancy, en route to the same fate
in Germany. So her request seemed genuine.

   Her first contact passed her with a favourable recommendation to a superior, and eventually she was cleared by Henri
Krasucki, head of the youth groups. Very soon afterwards, the
arrests began. Krasucki managed to get a warning from his cell
after seeing Lucienne chatting to police in the courtyard of
a police station where he was being held. One of the arrested
women was told that she had been betrayed by an attractive
young redhead and a woman identified as Lucienne was seen
being driven in a car with two German officers.

   After the liberation, Krasucki formally placed charges against
two of the Brigades Spéciales officers who had tortured him and
also against Lucienne. Many people who had lost relatives and

friends were angry when nothing was done about the latter, for lack of witnesses. Even a police officer who had warned people about her at the time refused to 'stir the muddy waters of the past'. However, in 1950 Simon Rajman, brother of a *résistant* named Marcel Rajman, who was arrested and executed after betrayal by Lucienne, recognised her working as a streetwalker in the Boulevard Sebastopol. To escape him and a friend who accosted her, she jumped on to the platform of a passing bus. There was a struggle before she was pulled off the bus. After a police patrol car answered bystanders' calls for assistance, all three were driven to the local *commissariat*. To everyone's surprise, Lucienne was completely calm, ordering the *commissaire* to call a telephone number in the Préfecture de Police. He did so, listened to the line, and said, 'OK, I'll let her go.'

Simon Rajman was furious. The only thing in his possession to remind him of his brother was a note to Marcel's nephew, written in the condemned cell shortly before he was shot as a member of the Manouchian group who had assassinated *SS-Standartenführer* Julius Ritter, the deputy organiser of Fritz Sauckel's compulsory labour conscription in France. It read, 'Be happy and make Mummy happy as I should have wanted to do, had I lived'.[138] In a longer letter written to his wife at the same time, Marcel Rajman's commander, Missak Manouchian, wrote:

> I should have so liked to have a child by you, as you always wanted. So please get married after the war and have a child in my memory. I have no hatred for the German people or anyone else – except for whoever betrayed us and those who sold us. Everyone will have his due reward or punishment.[139]

Well, some did: traitor David Davidowicz was very slowly strangled to death by surviving members of the Manouchian gang, as the German security forces called it. Seeing the black-and-red posters announcing their executions, Simone de Beauvoir wrote, 'I looked for a long time [at the young faces in the photographs] under the arches of the Metro, thinking with sadness that they would soon be forgotten.'[140] As they mostly were.

Lucienne Goldfarb was not prosecuted after the liberation. On the contrary, she was protected by the Paris vice squad 'for services rendered'. In March 1946 a hardened ex-prostitute named Marthe Betenfeld succeeded in having all the licensed brothels in France closed down. The result was that all the sex workers took to the streets, some of them opening *hôtels de passe*, where the other girls could take their clients for a 'short time'. In 1958 Lucienne Goldfarb opened her own *hôtel de passe* under the working name of Katia le Rouquine, or red-haired Katie. Prospering in this business, she later opened a highly lucrative brothel known as '10-bis' on rue Débarcadère in the seventeenth *arrondissement* under the protection of the vice squad in return for her activities as informer for them and La Direction de la Surveillance du Territoire (DST) – the French equivalent of MI5.

In 1975 an official investigation into this cosy arrangement irritated Lucienne, who thought she was above the law, causing her to write a book about her scandalous life, but omitting any mention of her activities during the occupation. The publicity this created brought its author to the notice of relatives of those she had betrayed. Aged 79, Parisienne Madeleine Meyer had lost several relatives through wartime denunciations by Goldfarb, and called the publisher, demanding that the book be withdrawn from sale. She also called the very expensive lawyer who acted for Katia la Rouquine, a man called Roland Dumas, who had been active in the Resistance and lost his own father, executed by the Germans. She asked him whether he knew of his client's

traitorous activities during the occupation. When he claimed
not to, she filled him in and the book was suppressed. Dumas
proposed a meeting between Meyer and Katia in his office – an
idea that was angrily rejected, Madeleine Meyer refusing to be
heard on an equal footing with an informer who had betrayed so
many people.

And that is how the brothel madame Katia la Rouquine met
the eventual mistress of France's future Foreign Minister. As to
what the voluptuous and vivacious Madame Deviers-Joncour
had received for her clandestine intermediary roles during her
relationship with Dumas, it was reported in 2006 that the French
fisc considered that she still owed 11 million euros in unpaid tax!
This was after she was sent to prison for eighteen months and
ordered to pay a fine of 1.5 million francs, so giving the cash to
Lucienne Goldfarb was a way of keeping the taxman's hands out
of her purse. Unabashed, Deviers-Joncour, who was dubbed *la
putain de le République* – the whore of the Republic – by a judge,
went on to publish several books, one of them using that insult
as its title. So the two women had much in common.

Three very different women: Andrée Borrel (left), Diana Rowden (below, left) and Vera Leigh (below, right). SOE agents caught in France, they were burned alive with a fourth woman agent in the crematorium of Natzwiller concentration camp.

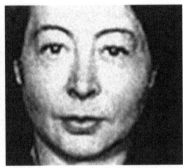

In the English Civil War so many women were heroines that King Charles I forbade them to dress as men and fight. Poet, playwright and spy Aphra Behn (above, left) was the most famous. Wardour Castle was commanded by 61-year-old Lady Blanche Arundell (above, centre) while parliamentarian besiegers demolished the castle around her. Lady Banks (above, right) held Corfe Castle for the king during a three-year siege.

Charles II disguised as the servant of Jane Lane riding the same horse as her halfway across England (above). Betrayed, she had to walk all the way across England disguised as a peasant girl to take ship for safety in France. Lady Anne Halkett (right) disguised James, teenage Duke of York, as a girl to rescue him from Parliament's hands. She thought he looked 'very pretty'.

Known as 'la belle rebelle', Belle Boyd spied for the Confederacy during the American Civil War, riding her horse between the lines at breakneck speed.

Quaker-educated anti-slavery activist Elizabeth van Lew spied for the Union and was treated as a traitor by her neighbours in Richmond, Virginia, after the war.

Canadian Emma Edmonds (above) avenged her fiancé's death by disguising herself as a black male slave to spy for the Union.

Rose O'Neal Greenhow was allowed to keep her 8-year-old daughter with her (left) in Washington's Old Capitol prison when caught spying for the Confederacy.

Margarete Zelle (left) with her boring husband, Dutch Army officer Ralphe McLeod and (above) in a sexy pose as the pretended Indian princess and temple dancer Mata Hari. Her tragedy was that she lived her fantasies, and was shot as the spy she never was in real life.

Two real heroines of the First World War: Although French, Louise de Bettignies (above left) spied for Britain. Belgian girl Gabrielle Petit (statue, above right) swallowed her messages when arrested, aged 21, but was shot by the Germans anyway.

Raised as a girl with both masculine and feminine names, the transgendered Chevalier Charles Geneviève d'Eon captivated Tsarina Elizabeth the Great and won a treaty for France. D'Eon's last years were spent in England, reduced to earning a pittance by giving exhibition fencing matches (above right).

French diplomat Bernard Boursicot fell in love with Chinese actor Shi Pei Pu in Beijing, aged 20, and believed that Shi had borne him a son. Twenty years later (above), they were on trial for espionage, Shi looking a shadow of his formerly glamorous self.

The handsome young couple to the right are Frieda Truhar and her first husband and fellow agent Pat Devine. She carried Moscow's secret funds to the Chinese Reds sewn into her corselette.

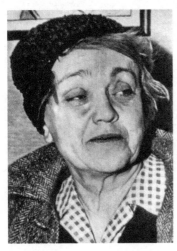

Agnes Smedley in middle age (above left) does not look like a glamorous spy who seduced men in the 1930s to serve in Stalin's war against the democracies. But take a look at her in her prime (above right).

Edith Tudor-Hart was a Viennese photographer who also had a good eye for traitors. Her best catch for the Comintern was Kim Philby.

Women against Hitler? Aenne Kappius (below) was a German vegetarian, like the Fuhrer, but her passionate socialism made her a traitor to the Nazi fatherland.

Hannah Szenes, seen here relaxing on her *kibbutz* before her mission in Hungary (right) suffered torture and execution there, rather than lure RAF aircraft over German ack-ack sites.

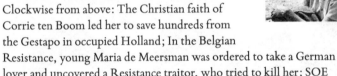

Clockwise from above: The Christian faith of
Corrie ten Boom led her to save hundreds from
the Gestapo in occupied Holland; In the Belgian
Resistance, young Maria de Meersman was ordered to take a German
lover and uncovered a Resistance traitor, who tried to kill her; SOE
agent Kristina Skarbeck fought the Nazis under cover in Poland,
Hungary, Italy and France.

In the Cold War, US-born Ethel
Rosenberg (mugshot above) went
to the electric chair for stealing
nuclear secrets, but was innocent.

Ursula Kuscinski married British
communist Len Beurton. Using
a pram and nappies on the line to
conceal their espionage roles, she
transmitted thousands of secrets
to Moscow, but escaped in time.

British Cold War spy Ethel Gee (left) spied for her lover, Harry Houghton. He did it for money. Both went to jail for nine years. The Royal Navy secrets they stole were transmitted to Moscow by Leontina Cohen (below on 1998 Russian stamp) posing as Helen Kroger, a rare book dealer living in Ruislip.

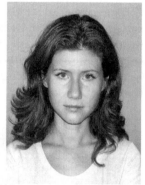

A gallery of modern Russian spies. Caught in a grainy FBI surveillance shot (above left), Anna Chapman (back to camera) swaps identical bags in a bookshop. But even in her mugshot (above right) she managed to look pretty and innocent. Expelled with her in 2010 (below, left to right) were fellow SVR spies Cynthia Murphy, Patricia Mills, Tracey Foley and Vicky Pelaez.

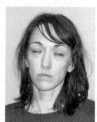
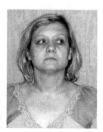

12

Sayonara, SIS

CIA websites do not customarily celebrate agents' birthdays, but on 3 March 2015 one of them carried the headline *'Spy Girl' Betty McIntosh Turns 100 Years Old*. This tough old lady who had served with CIA and its predecessor, the Office of Strategic Services (OSS), in the Second World War was invited back to Langley. There CIA Director John Brennan shared a 100th birthday cake with her and said:

> CIA is honored to count Betty McIntosh as one of its alum-
> nae, and we are very fortunate to have her at the Agency
> today. Her many achievements and storied (sic) life are an
> inspiration to all women and particularly so to those of CIA
> … It is fitting that Women's History Month begins each year
> on 1 March, the birthday of Betty McIntosh.

Elizabeth Peet McIntosh was one of the comparatively few women agents sent overseas by the predominantly male OSS during that war. Although born in Washington DC, on

1 March 1915, she grew up in Honolulu, Hawaii, where she became fluent in Japanese. Both her parents were journalists, so it seemed natural that, after graduating from the University of Washington School of Journalism, she moved back to Hawaii, writing for local papers and the *San Francisco Chronicle*. When Japanese forces attacked Pearl Harbor on 7 December 1941, she covered the event first-hand, which earned her a job with the Scripps Howard News Service, based in Washington D.C..

In 1943, Betty was sent to write a story about a man named Atherton Richards, who had been the head of a firm in Honolulu working on the mechanisation of sugar cane harvesting, and who was then one of the top men in 'Wild Bill' Donovan's OSS. Years later, she recalled, 'He was a friend of my father's. It was very difficult to get a meeting with him, but I finally managed to. After our interview, he said, "Wouldn't you like to get into something more interesting than the work you're doing?"'

Betty was covering the White House, particularly stories on Eleanor Roosevelt, the president's wife, which was an important assignment, but she said she would be interested if it meant going overseas. Richards said, 'I can promise you that.' There was no mention of undercover work, just that 'something more interesting'. She described her first visit to the OSS as 'very strange'. When she reported for duty, nobody told her what those duties would be. She was fingerprinted and told not to speak about anything to anyone, although, as she said, she did not know anything, about which to speak.

She was assigned to the Far East section of OSS Morale Operations (MO), whose purpose was to mix genuine information and disinformation, targeting Japanese troops in south-east Asia and the Pacific. Like her, most of the others working there were newsprint and radio reporters and other media folk, who were instructed in how to prepare black propaganda. The group included several Chinese artists and captured Japanese soldiers who were artists in civilian life and prepared to work for the Allies rather than stay in a POW camp.

As in most other irregular outfits, she recalled that they did not take well to military discipline:

> I remember the artists and writers lounging around in the office, and when an officer entered the room they would just say, 'Hi, fella', or just 'Hi'. They wouldn't say 'Colonel', 'Sir' or anything like that. And they never learned to salute. Their uniforms were awfully sloppy too.

After completing basic training, she was posted to India in the summer of 1943 and wrote false news reports, radio messages, and other propaganda designed to spread disinformation that would undermine the morale of Japanese troops fighting in Burma. The most successful operation came the following year when the enemy advance into north-east India was halted at Imphal. In her words, 'The Japanese government told their soldiers that if they surrendered they would lose their birthright and would not be able to go back to Japan. So consequently very few Japanese surrendered. They cost us a great deal because they fought to the very end and many of our people, too, were killed. So the idea was to try to get them to give up without feeling that they had lost their identity.'

Betty and her team forged a Japanese Imperial order permitting troops to surrender under certain conditions. This was a believable scenario because there had recently been a leadership change in the Japanese government, which led to a window of uncertainty. A Burmese OSS agent was tasked with assassinating a Japanese courier en route through the jungle and inserting the forged order into his knapsack. The agent then reported to the

Japanese on the whereabouts of their dead courier. Predictably, and according to plan, the Japanese retrieved the body with its mailbag and concluded that the forged order was authentic.

Betty's next major assignment was to fly 'over the hump' of the Himalayas to Kunming in China, behind enemy lines. Being a newspaper journalist, she had never worked in radio, but her new challenge was to create scripts to be broadcast by a black radio station to Japanese troops fighting in China and to the home islands of Japan. Somebody dreamed up a make believe fortune-teller, whose broadcasts allegedly reading the stars attracted a large listenership.

She recalled going in to the studio very late in the war, and one of her supervisors saying, 'We've got to get something on the program that will just shake the Chinese and the Japanese.'

She replied, 'Let's predict a big earthquake in Japan.

He objected, 'They're always having earthquakes.'

So she said, 'Then let's have a tsunami to go with it.'

That was also turned down, so, instead of being too precise, the fortune-teller announced, 'Something terrible is going to happen to Japan. We have checked the stars and there is something we can't even mention because it is so dreadful and it is going to eradicate one whole area of Japan.'

Shortly afterwards, the first atomic bomb was dropped on Hiroshima and Betty was asked by the OSS boss in China, Colonel Richard Heppner, how she could have known in advance. Her answer was, 'We just made it up, because that's the sort of thing we did.'

In 1929 Secretary of State Henry Simson shut down the State Department's cryptography department, saying famously, 'Gentlemen don't read each other's mail.' There was something of the same attitude in Washington after the end of the war in the Pacific. On 20 September 1945 President

Truman signed Executive Order 9621, under which the OSS was wound up, but three months later he created the Central Intelligence Group (CIG), which was the direct precursor to the CIA. The National Security Act of 1947 established the CIA as the United States' first permanent peacetime intelligence agency. Meanwhile, Betty was flown back to the US and demobilised, taking a job in New York with *Glamour* magazine, which she found 'underwhelming' after her wartime activities. Then an opening occurred with the Voice of America radio propaganda organisation, doing the work she had enjoyed with the OSS.

She married Colonel Heppner in May 1946 and moved with him back to Washington, working on assignments for the Joint Chiefs of Staff, the State Department and the infant United Nations Organisation, which regularly brought her into contact with General Donovan. She also wrote a humorous account of her time overseas with the OSS entitled *Undercover Girl*, published in 1947, and later two children's books. But after Heppner's death she felt at a loss and old OSS friends persuaded her to ask CIA Director Allen Dulles for a job. She was taken on immediately, but found the atmosphere far more rigid than it had been in the OSS. One thing that was the same was the predominantly male hierarchy: female officers who had proved their courage and competence during the war were treated like secretaries.

As to her duties in Langley, six decades later she still would not talk about them, except to say they were similar to what she had done in the OSS. While serving in Asia, she met fighter pilot Fred McIntosh and married him in May of 1962, continuing to work for the CIA until she retired in 1973 after forty years of service in the field of intelligence. In 1998, at the age of 83, she published *Sisterhood of Spies: The Women of the OSS* – a tribute to all the women who have served in the still male-dominated CIA. Who better to do that?

Born in November 1910, Amy Elizabeth Thorpe came from a respectable Minnesota family. Her mother was the daughter of a state senator and her father an officer in the US Marine Corps, but there was a spark of devilry in their daughter. Enjoying the high life of Washington while still in her teens, she practised her German, French and Spanish on lovers chosen from the foreign diplomatic corps, especially older, senior men seduced by what William Stephenson – Churchill's spy chief in the USA – described as 'her bright auburn hair, large green eyes… and a slender yet voluptuous figure'.[141] In 1936 her parents heaved a sigh of relief when she apparently settled down with Arthur Pack, the sober Second Secretary at the British Embassy in Washington, and departed with him to Warsaw, when he was posted to the embassy there. Marriage, especially staying quietly at home during his frequent travels, soon lost its charms for her and she sought excitement in the company of other men in the embassy cocktail circuit of pre-war Warsaw. Of this period, she later remarked, 'I discovered how easy it was to make highly-trained, professionally close-mouthed patriots give away secrets in bed. The greatest joy is a man and a woman together. Making love allows a discharge of all those private innermost thoughts that have accumulated. In this sudden flood, everything is released.'[142]

Canadian-born millionaire William Stephenson met her in 1937 and made a mental note of her name and rather special qualities, giving her the cover name 'Cynthia' when she commenced working for him at British Security Co-ordination (BSC), a cover for MI6 during the Second World War. Although in his book, written after the war, he alleged that Cynthia obtained key information regarding the Enigma encoding machines used by the Axis forces by seducing an Italian admiral, since the admiral's family later sued for defamation and won their case this was probably a smokescreen for the brilliant work of the code-breakers at Bletchley Park. However, when he needed an agent to penetrate the Washington embassy of Vichy France in May 1941, knowing that many of the embassy staff had been in post before the French surrender and thus had no love for Marshal Pétain and his collaborationist regime, he gave the job to the girl with green eyes. Installing herself at 3327 O Street in fashionable Georgetown, Cynthia posed as a freelance reporter and applied for an interview with Vichy ambassador Gaston Henry-Haye. Her request was channelled through the 49-year-old press attaché Charles Brousse, who told her at their first meeting that he was a former naval air pilot with the rank of captain who had served on the Anglo–French Air Intelligence Board prior to the German invasion of France. He said he had many English friends, although he had not forgiven British Prime Minister Winston Churchill for ordering the Royal Navy attack on the helpless, decommissioned French fleet at Mers el-Kebir on 2 July 1940 – but then, neither could many RN officers who had been involved.[143]

Cynthia's interview with the ambassador went well. He was still furious after a meeting with Secretary of State Cordell Hull, at which he had had to listen to Hull's criticism of Vichy's collaborationist policies, but Cynthia's personality, sophistication, fluent French and genuine love for France – plus a little flirting – calmed him down and enchanted him, to the point of him escorting her gallantly to the embassy gates on her way out. On the following day she received his invitation to an embassy party and a bouquet of red roses from Brousse. A handsome womaniser married to his third wife, he set out to seduce the charming American reporter, eighteen years his junior, who spoke French so well. Their first lunch date ended in her bedroom at the house on O Street.

Cynthia soon discovered that Brousse, unlike his boss, was not an apologist for Vichy's policies and he soon realised that he was not the seducer, but the seduced – not that it mattered because he swiftly fell in love with her. Although she was theoretically on 'home ground', J. Edgar Hoover's FBI was as territorially possessive as a robin in winter and Cynthia had to avoid their surveillance of her foreign diplomat target. The method she chose was to move into the Wardman Park Hotel, where Brousse and his wife were living. There, he could easily slip along the corridors to her room without being seen by Hoover's watchers in the lobby. Quite early in their relationship she revealed her true colours to Brousse, who began helping by passing over small items of confidential material.[144]

In July of 1941, for reasons unknown, Ambassador Henry-Haye terminated Captain Brousse's employment as press attaché, but retained him as an aide paid from secret funds at a lower level. Cynthia to the rescue! At her suggestion, Captain Brousse began accepting regular payments for daily reports of happenings inside the embassy and copies of cables between Washington and Vichy. For some months Cynthia was away from Washington on other work, but was called back by Stephenson in March 1942, three months after America's entry into the war. Although she did not know it at the time, the Combined Chiefs of Staff were already planning what became Operation Torch – the invasion of French North Africa – and urgently needed to be able to read encoded French naval radio traffic. She called Brousse, who met her in her room at the Ritz-Carlton hotel – some spies lived well in those days – and was stunned to learn that she was planning to steal the codes from the French embassy safe. It was, he said, impossible because only the two cipher clerks could open the safe in which they were kept, in a part of the embassy patrolled at night by an armed guard. Neither of the cipher clerks could be bribed, he said, and when Cynthia suggested seduction, he laughed: the senior man was too old to remember what that was and the younger one was 'not interested in women'.

Cynthia nevertheless paid a visit to the senior man out of office hours, but found him to be a man of honour: he admitted disapproving some of his government's policies but his personal code of loyalty would not let him betray its trust in him. Shortly afterwards, he was retired and returned to France, being replaced by a young nobleman, whose wife was about to give birth to their second child and who was short of funds on a junior diplomat's salary. Cynthia sounded him out before taking to BSC in New York that week's crop of diplomatic cables handed over by Brousse, with the result that he arrived at her hotel when his wife was out of town. Aware that FBI watchers might be lurking nearby, she whisked him up to her room but, before this eager visitor got too excited, Brousse rang from the lobby, saying he was on his way up. It was a scene from a French farce: Cynthia ushering the young count along a corridor away from the lift, hoping Brousse would not catch sight of him. But Brousse did, and was furious with her. Using sex to vent his anger, she calmly told him that it was all his fault: if he had got the codes when she asked, none of this need have happened.

After a number of twists and turn in the plot – Cynthia was never at a loss for new ideas – she told Brousse he must pretend to take the night security man into his confidence by telling him he needed to use the embassy for late night meetings with a girlfriend, so that, if his wife called to check up on him, he could tell her he was working late. Once the guard was accustomed to her coming to the embassy for romantic assignations, Cynthia thought she could find a way to open the safe and copy the codes. Fortunately, Stephenson was a close friend of 'Wild Bill' Donovan, the director of OSS, who was let into the secret and supplied a Canadian safe-cracker, recently released from prison in return for doing clandestine jobs and keeping his mouth shut. Called simply 'the Cracker', he was placed on standby while the alibi was prepared. Each evening Cynthia arrived, smiled at the security man who had been suitably bribed and spent a couple of hours making love with Brousse on the ambassador's sofa.

Before leaving the building, Brousse shared a drink or two with the guard. One night, he was given a glass of champagne containing a tasteless knockout drug, permitting Brousse to let the Cracker into the embassy, where he set to work, grumbling that the safe was an old model and its combination not easy to crack. Eventually he succeeded when it was too late to copy the codes. It was, in fact, dangerously close to dawn when they left the embassy with the guard thinking he had taken a glass or two too many. Having the Cracker write down the combination for her, Cynthia was confident she could open the safe herself. That evening, when the guard made his rounds while she was on her knees at the safe, Brousse said she was in the bathroom and the man left. Try as she did, the safe would not open. Brousse becoming worried that his sexual technique was suffering with all the intrusions and stress, it was decided to sneak the Cracker into the building again through a courtyard window on the following night. He reported that two FBI men had chatted with the guard while he was waiting in the shadows, making Cynthia wonder how that looked on her file in Mr Hoover's office. It was soon apparent that her problem had been the lock's need of lubrication; it was simply too stiff for her to manipulate. After the Cracker opened it without too much trouble, with the help of another BSC man coming through the same window the code books were copied using a camera in five hectic hours, during which the sound of the guard's return forced Cynthia to do a rapid strip and let his torch light up her naked body lying on top of Brousse. After a muttered apology, he left them alone for the rest of the night.

With the Cracker and photographer leaving through the courtyard window and Cynthia by a side door, Brousse made a joke to the guard about insatiable women to account for his exhaustion, and the embassy woke up to a new day. A few hours later, the film was being flown across the Atlantic, destination Bletchley Park, where not only could the French naval codes be read, but having them would enable the code-breakers to use those messages, once deciphered, as a key to break the same messages in German Enigma code.[145]

In a newspaper interview after the war, Cynthia was asked whether a woman from her respectable family background was not ashamed of the many occasions she used sex for espionage. Completely unembarrassed, she replied, 'Wars are not won by respectable methods.' She was last heard of living in a castle in France with Charles Brousse, an apparently happy and faithful couple. She died of throat cancer in December 1963, with Brousse dying ten years later when a fault in his electric blanket set the castle on fire. Their years of married bliss were due to Stephenson blocking all Cynthia's attempts after the codebook operation to be parachuted as an SOE agent into occupied Europe, where he considered such a beautiful woman would be too noticeable to survive for long.

13

Two Daughters of Israel

People with little knowledge of Middle Eastern history may think that the present conflict in Israel is a modern phenomenon. Yet the countries of the eastern Mediterranean littoral have been the scene of bloodshed for millennia because they are the only land route from Africa to Europe. Long after prehistoric mankind travelled this way from Africa to spread north, west and east – killing off competing species on the way – in Biblical times Gaza was where Samson demolished the temple of the Philistines' god, Dagon, after being blinded and having some vital part of his anatomy cut off when caught dallying with Delilah. In historical times, with blood and fire, Gaza City fell to the Egyptians, the Philistines, the Hebrews under King David, the Assyrians, the Babylonians and the Persians. It was a prosperous trading centre that rated a mention in the Tel el-Amarna tablets thirteen centuries BCE because of its strategic position on the Via Maris, the ancient coastal route linking Egypt with Palestine and lands beyond.

Visiting the remains of Biblical Jericho today, with its walls 9 metres thick in places, one has to reflect why that was necessary.

Although the Old Testament is not regarded as historically reliable, it was during Joshua's ruthless conquest of Canaan that Rahab the harlot sheltered two Hebrew spies in her house in or on those walls during Joshua's conquest of Canaan *c.* 1,400 BCE. When soldiers came hunting for them, by virtue of her profession she was able to claim that she had treated them like any other clients, and had no idea where they went afterwards. After thus talking her way out of a sticky situation, she helped the two Hebrews escape the city and return with the intelligence they had gathered to Joshua's forces encamped on the other side of the River Jordan ... and the walls came tumbling down. We do not know whether she chose to do this because she was a Hebrew slave, forced into sex work by Canaanite captors, but the Book of Joshua records that Rahab received her reward. Told by the spies to hang a red cloth outside her window, she saved the people in her house from massacre when the city fell and the rest of its inhabitants were put to the sword.

Angered by the stubborn resistance of the Gazans in 332 BCE, Alexander the Great sold into slavery those who had not starved to death during his five-month siege of their city. Between 1096 and 1291 the several major crusades continued the bloodshed. For the Ottoman Empire (1299–1923), Syria, Lebanon and Palestine were the vital land link between the empire's capital at Constantinople and the province of Egypt, resulting in Allied–Turkish hostilities there during the First World War. After the withdrawal of the Turks and the installation of the British Mandate, hostilities between Muslim Palestinians and their Yiddish- and Hebrew-speaking neighbours became an undeclared war, with recurrent rapes, murders and massacres. In 1948–49 British occupation forces arrested, shot and hanged Jewish independence fighters, who retaliated with bomb outrages and hanging of British servicemen. Far from being a land of milk and honey, this has more often been a zone of blood and fire.

During the First World War, the first wave of Jewish return-ees to Palestine also had to combat endemic malaria, drought and swarms of locusts. A Jewish agronomist named Aaron Aaronson in the settlement of Zihron Ya'akov – just south of the port of Haifa – decided with a group of trusted friends, including his 20-something sister, Sarah, and brother, Alex, to form a spy ring in mid-1915. The aim was to reveal the plans of the Turkish occu-pation forces in the area to the British expeditionary force under General Allenby, which was based in Egypt. They reasoned that the British might, in gratitude, liberate them, whereas the Turks never would. The code name they chose was Nili, an acronym of their password *Netzah Yisrael lo yeshaker* – meaning, the eternal one of Israel will not lie.[146]

Sarah Arensohn's formal education ended at age 12, but she was highly intelligent, speaking Hebrew, Yiddish, Turkish, French, Arabic and English. Employed as Aaron's assistant in the agricultural research station of Atlit on the coast below Zikhron Ya'akov, she often accompanied him on his travels around the province of Palestine, which the Turks accepted as necessitated by his work combating the scourge of the locust. Sarah was an accomplished horse-rider and a good shot. When dressing as a man on her travels and speaking gendered languages, she had to be careful to speak of herself as male. When her brother, Aaron, was away, she was in charge of co-ordinating the activities of up to forty Nili spies and running the research station at Atlit.

Already in the early years of the twentieth century, some young Israeli Jewish women were starting to reject the tradi-tional sequence of dutiful daughters becoming obedient wives and ultra-supportive mothers of their sons. Sarah took as lover a founder member of Nili named Avshalom Feinberg, but family pressure ended her affair with him and obliged her to 'make a good match' with Chaim Abraham, a rich merchant who took her to Istanbul in 1914. Aged 24 and seeing no reason to stay with a man who did not please her, Sarah returned home a few months later. That overland journey through Anatolia was to change her life – and indirectly cause her death – because on it she witnessed first-hand the Turkish genocide that killed off more than a million Armenian men, women and children living in what had been western Armenia, but was now politically Eastern Turkey. It was news of this holocaust that made the Jews in Palestine fear they would be the next category of *gavour* or infidel to be eliminated by their Muslim Turkish overlords.

Sarah took advantage of the Turkish disdain for women to travel to Egypt carrying secret despatches. It was a dangerous journey that cost Feinberg's life, robbed and murdered by Bedouin in the Sinai desert while carrying reports to General Allenby's forces advancing towards Beersheva and Jerusalem. In between her trips, to get the collected intelligence of Turkish fortifications and troop movements, desert routes and water sources as fast as possible to the British, Sarah flashed frequent updates in Morse code to a Royal Navy frigate moored off the coast. When German submarines in the eastern Mediterranean made this too risky, messages were also transmitted by carrier pigeon. In September 1917, one of the birds from Zihron Ya'akov landed on the house of the Turkish governor in nearby Kessariya, where it was caught and its coded message deciphered, leading the Turks to surround and search Zikhron Ya'akov.

One by one, the members of the Nili network were identified, arrested and routinely tortured. One was smuggled by friends from village to village until it was decided that he must die in case the Turks caught up with him and tortured him into giving away the whole network. An assassination squad tracked him down, but only managed to wound him. Trying to get to safety in Egypt, he was caught by Bedouins and handed over to the Turks. Following his interrogation under torture in Damascus, he and another man were eventually hanged there in public on 16 December 1917.

Knowing that she too would shortly be arrested, Sarah worked fast to protect her agents, but some of the arrested Nili members talked after brutal Turkish interrogations. So, on 1 October, she too was arrested. Despite three or four days of torture,[147] she gave nothing away. Told that she was to be transferred to a Turkish prison inland at Nazareth, where worse treatment awaited her, she requested to be allowed to return home, to change her blood-stained dress and pack some belongings.

Going into the bathroom, Sarah wrote a hurried suicide note, expressing her fear that further torture would make her betray her comrades, and took a pistol hidden behind a loose tile, to shoot herself in the mouth. This was on Friday 5 October. Unfortunately, she held the pistol horizontal, not pointing upwards at the brain. Although the bullet severed the spinal cord, she survived in great pain until 9 October. Jewish Orthodox religion refusing burial to a suicide, there was no place in the cemetery for her body until the rabbi gave way to popular feeling that she was a martyr and the burial was allowed, with a small fence placed around the grave to obey the letter of the law and separate it from the other graves.[148]

The ultimate betrayal, of course, was the letter signed by British Foreign Secretary James Balfour on 2 November 1917, which became known as 'the Balfour Declaration'. It appeared to represent a firm British intention to reward Sarah, her Nili comrades and other Jews in and out of uniform for their support in the First World War by promising a 'national home' for the

Jews in Palestine after the Turks were driven out. This was on a par with Lawrence of Arabia's unfulfilled promises to Prince Feisal during the Arab Revolt against the Turks. It would take another three decades after Sarah Aronsohn's death before a bloody war of independence drove the British Army out of the land that is now the state of Israel.

Sometimes a historian stumbles by chance over a little-known piece of history. While exploring the archaeology of Herod the Great's city of Caesarea Maritima – modern Kessariya – the author was staying in a guest house on the neighbouring *kibbutz* of Sdot Yam. Poking through the excavation relics in the museum there led me to find the Hannah Szenes Study Centre, dedicated to keeping alive the story of a very brave young woman. On 17 July 1921 a daughter was born to a Jewish journalist-playwright called Béla Szenes in the Hungarian capital Budapest. In assimilated families such as hers, Zionism was thought of as an idea for poor Jews and inappropriate for prosperous middle class families living in the tolerant ambiance of what had been the Austro–Hungarian Empire. Why exchange that for the constant struggle of life in a primitive semi-desert country? When her father died, Hannah was only 6 and recently enrolled in a Protestant school for girls that also accepted some Catholic and Jewish pupils. The parents of most Jewish pupils had to pay three times the fees for Protestants, but after Hannah was assessed as a gifted pupil the family only had to pay twice the Protestant rate. Not a lot is known about her childhood, but at the age of 13 she began a diary. The entry for 18 June 1936 reads:

> When I began writing a diary, I was determined not to blabber about boys, as do other girls, but my diary is becoming like that of any other girl.[149]

About the same time, anti-Semitic legislation under Hungarian regent Admiral Miklós Horthy was becoming increasingly menacing, causing her to join Maccabea, a Zionist student organisation. By the time of her graduation in 1939, for a combination of realpolitik and commercial interests, Hungary had been nudged further and further into the Nazi camp. On 17 July 1939, her entry read:

> Today is my birthday, and I am eighteen. One idea occupies me continually. There is but one place on earth in which we are not refugees, not immigrants, but where we are returning home – Eretz Israel.[150]

When Hannah made the decision to immigrate to Palestine, she was hoping to make a living there as a writer like her father, but this was not relatively civilised Central Europe. Arriving in the Promised Land, she quickly realised there were many priorities more important than her personal ambitions, and instead enrolled at the Girls' Agricultural College in Nahalal, a village between Haifa and Nazareth.

In 1941 German pressure on Horthy to rid Hungary of all its Jews resulted in the expulsion of 20,000 refugees without Hungarian citizenship to Ukraine, where all the Jews among them were massacred by SS troops under *Obergruppenführer* Friedrich Jeckeln in what may have been the first mass killing of the Holocaust. Learning of this, Horthy halted the deportations, instead conscripting many Jews and political prisoners to serve with the Hungarian Army on the Russian front in forced labour battalions tasked with clearing minefields, where they had at least the chance of survival. At about the same time, Hannah joined the *kibbutz* or collective farm named Sdot Yam – meaning 'flowers of the sea' – adjoining Herod's still impressive seaside palace of Caesaria Maritima. Life there was tough, with Hannah and the other volunteers sleeping in tents pitched on the poor soil, which they hoped to turn into productive farmland. However, she was healthy and athletic, taking in her stride the heavy labour, dressed in the only clothes available – men's shirts and shorts or trousers from the communal clothes store. If some evenings she looked at her sore and work-scarred hands with wonder, she felt, as all the *kibbutzniks* did then, that this was the price for building a homeland for their people,

Before the end of 1942 the leaders of the Jewish community in Palestine were aware that the pogroms of Eastern Europe, which had killed so many Jews, were nothing compared to Hitler's death factories killing thousands of their relatives each day. Although they begged to be allowed to send Israeli rescue teams to Europe, neither the Western Allies nor the Soviet government were prepared to do anything about it. In January 1943 the Red Army annihilated Hitler's 2nd Hungarian Army on the River Don – a defeat ascribed with Nazi 'logic' to the negative attitude of the country's Jewish minority. So he ordered that all the Jews in Hungary be sent to Auschwitz, but Horthy temporised, giving up only 10,000 of them, who were drafted into penal battalions.

Hannah joined Haganah, the embryo paramilitary organisation that later became the Israel Defense Forces. Palestine then being administered by Britain under the League of Nations Mandate, the London government refused to let the Jews of Palestine serve in the armed forces, rightly fearing that they would use any military training after the end of the war against Germany to fight the British army of occupation. Certainly, Hannah did not support the British occupation of Palestine, but it seemed that the only way she could help her people under threat in Hungary was to join the British armed forces when this policy was changed towards the end of 1943 and any operation that promised to hinder German ability to repulse the planned invasion of Normandy was given the go-ahead. Parachuting several hundred spies and saboteurs with local knowledge and perfect mastery of the languages of their intended areas of operation into German-occupied territory was one of these ideas.

Hannah was one of 240 young men and women shortlisted by Haganah for service with the British. In Egypt, they were given training in parachuting, sabotage and use of weapons and radio by SOE. They were also very fit, accustomed to living rough and were highly motivated to combat the German war effort. What the Haganah men and women intended was to use SOE's claim on RAF aircraft to get into Hungary and there organise resistance of their people to the disaster they could see approaching. In January 1944 twenty-four men and two women, one of whom was Hannah Szenes, completed training in Cairo. She left behind in Sdot Yam the diary she had kept, as well as poems, letters and a play she had written. Her last entry in the diary, dated 11 January 1944, read:

> This week I am to leave for Egypt, enlisted, a soldier. I want to believe that I have done, and am going to do, the right thing. For the rest, only time will tell.[151]

Given the rank of Aircraftwoman 2nd Class in the Women's Auxiliary Air Force, Hannah was dropped on 14 March 1944 with two male comrades into a partisan-held region of northern Yugoslavia to make their own way across the Hungarian border. They lived for several weeks with Tito's communist partisans, who were suspicious of all foreigners. The food was poor and the camp was frequently moved when German and Četnik hunter-killer squads closed in. Toughened up by *kibbutz* life, Hannah could take all this in her stride.

Inside Hungary, events were moving fast. With Soviet forces steadily pushing back the German and other Axis forces facing them and rapidly approaching eastern Hungary, the government feared that they would rapidly occupy the country and therefore began to explore contacts with the Western Allies in the hope of negotiating some surrender deal. Learning of this, Hitler summoned Horthy to a meeting and required him to supply more troops and to deport all Hungarian Jews immediately to Auschwitz. It was a trick. While Horthy's train was deliberately delayed en route back to Budapest on 19 March 1944, German forces occupied Hungary in an operation dubbed *Fall Margarethe*.[152] A new pro-Nazi government was forced on Horthy that was prepared to hand over all the Jews in the country for extermination. When Hannah's two comrades learned this, they thought they had arrived too late, but Hannah argued that there could be no going back. If it was too late to save all the Hungarian Jews, at least they could smuggle some of them out.

On 15 April the entire gamut of Nazi anti-Semitic laws were enacted in Budapest by ministerial decree rather than act of Parliament, because Horthy had refused to sign them into law.[153] Hungarian *csendőrség* or gendarmerie units thereafter assisted SS troops to drive the country's Jews into ghettoes, from where Hitler's deportation supremo Adolf Eichmann began on 29 April shipping 12,000 a day to Auschwitz – a process that continued for three months. Five days before this, two Slovakian detainees named Vrba and Wetzler managed against horrific odds to escape from Auschwitz-Birkenau and, after ten days, reached Slovakia to give eyewitness accounts of the daily mass gassings in the camp. At the beginning of May, the Vrba–Wetzler Report, as it became known, was translated into Hungarian and reached Budapest. Just before the end of the month, two other Jews who had escaped from Auschwitz confirmed to the Jewish Council in Bratislava that the extermination of the Hungarian Jews was in full swing.

Hannah and a comrade named Palgui crossed the frontier clandestinely on 13 May, and were swiftly arrested by the *csendőrség* frontier guards, who discovered the hiding place of Hannah's SOE transmitter, of a model well known to the Gestapo and Abwehr. This negated any possibility of using her cover story. She was taken to a prison, stripped, tied to a chair and whipped and clubbed for three days. When meeting her in prison later, Palgui testified to this:

> They had whipped the palms of her hands and the soles of her feet. They had tied her up, forcing her to remain immobile for hours. They had beaten her so violently that her body was completely covered with bruises.[154]

The beatings also knocked out several of her teeth. The aim of this savagery was to force her to divulge the security codes that would have enabled an English-speaking Hungarian or German operator to use Hannah's transmitter to lure RAF bombing missions over anti-aircraft batteries. Transferred to a second prison in Budapest, Hannah continually underwent interrogations, but refused to give more than her name and rank, even when her mother was also arrested. Palgui's account continues:

> The Germans knew what they were doing. They threatened to torture her mother and to execute Mrs Szenes before Hannah's very eyes, if she continued refusing to divulge the codes. But she did not yield. Only those who knew how much she loved her mother could begin to imagine her suffering. For my part, I was shaken by her account and could

not hide my bewilderment. How could she remain outwardly so calm and so steadfast? Where did she find the courage to sacrifice her mother, whom she so loved, rather than reveal a secret, upon which, it is true, the lives of many depended? Who knows? Perhaps her determination indirectly contributed to saving her mother? Had Hannah yielded, the Germans would surely have executed her, sending Mrs Szenes to the gas chambers in Auschwitz.

Fellow prisoners who had known the family before the war or had heard about them, did what they could to help. For example, they managed to arrange that Hannah and her mother be placed in adjacent cells so that they could see each other. Once or twice a week, the prisoners were allowed to take a walk in twos in the miniscule courtyard of the prison under the surveillance of guards who dealt severely with the slightest conversation. In my cell, I could hear the footsteps of Hannah and her mother and, from the window of my cell I could see the two of them walking side by side, holding hands. [155]

By October 1944, with the Red Army advancing in the east and the Allied forces closing in in the west, it was obvious to any professional soldier that Germany could not win the war. On 15 October Regent Horthy signed an armistice, but fighting continued. On 28 October, Hannah appeared before a military court, where she accused her judges of collaborating with the Nazis. Legally, as a Hungarian-born citizen in the service of an enemy power, she was being justifiably tried for treason. Palgui's account continues:

After a week's delay [possibly because her judges had been drafted to the front] on 7 November the military prosecutor, Captain Simon, came to [Hannah's] cell and announced that she had been condemned to death. He then asked, 'Do you wish to petition for a reprieve?' Instead, Hannah asked to appeal the decision, and to see her defending lawyer. Capt Simon said that was not possible, and told her, 'You must prepare to die. You may write farewell letters. But hurry. You will be executed in one hour.'

She requested a pen and some paper and wrote two letters, one to her mother and one to us, her comrades in the pioneer movement. Only Captain Simon knows what she wrote, because the letters never reached their addressees. At ten o'clock, he returned to the condemned cell and ordered her to follow him. Two soldiers escorted her to the courtyard. A wooden box filled with sand with a stake driven into it stood near the grey brick wall at the side of the small prison chapel. They tied her hands behind her back and tied her to the stake. Capt Simon offered her a blindfold, which she refused. At that moment three shots were fired.

Half an hour later, a car came to take the body, which was buried in the Jewish cemetery in Budapest, in the section for martyrs alongside countless anonymous victims of the Nazis. We do not know who buried her there. The Jewish Burial Society had been disbanded and Jews were not authorized to leave their homes. Perhaps an unknown admirer wanted to render her this final honour.[156]

As she was being buried, a letter to her mother was found in her clothes, as well as Hannah's last poem:

One … two … three … Eight feet long,
two strides across, the rest is dark.
Life is a fleeting question mark.
One … two … three … Maybe another week

or the next month may still find me here,
but death, I feel is very near.
I could have been twenty-three next July.
I gambled on what mattered most.
The dice were cast. I lost.

Many of her other poems and writings were posthumously published, and some of the poetry was set to music, sung by Israeli and other artistes. In the small museum of Kibbutz Sdot Yam the Hannah Szenes Study Centre has a repository of writing by and about her, as well as audio-visual material. In 1950 her remains were reinterred in the military cemetery on Mount Herzl in Jerusalem. At the end of the Cold War, a Hungarian military court officially exonerated her, but this was little consolation for her relatives in Israel when the news reached them on 5 November 1993.

14

The Pearl in the Lebanese Oyster

Born in 1920, just one year before Hannah Szenes, Dvorah was the fourth of twelve children born to small-time Jerusalem businessman, Tuvia Meir.[157] She spent part of her childhood in Argentina, where her father and his brother owned a clothing company until declining business forced their return to Palestine, then occupied by British troops under the League of Nations mandate. Thereafter, the family lived in a Jewish neighbourhood of Jerusalem with little money. To alleviate their financial straits, Dvorah's father arranged her marriage at the age of 16 to a prosperous businessman from Beirut named Yitzhak Dror. Balding and more than twice as old as her, he was the antithesis of Dvorah's adolescent fantasies about boys of her own age. On the contrary, she realised that she had effectively been sold to him when she learned that the marriage contract waived any dowry and instead gave her father a favourable loan to restart his failing business.

Dror took her back with him to Lebanon, where their marriage was celebrated on 2 November 1936. The Lebanese capital

Beirut then had a population of 105,000 inhabitants, of which only 5,000 were Jewish. The others included both Shiite and Sunni Muslims, Armenians, Maronite, Greek Orthodox and Greek Catholic Christians and Druzes, each community living in its own quarter and having a proportionate share of political power. The city was also the seat of the French administration of Syria and Lebanon under the League of Nations mandate, so French was everyone's second language. With her husband rising early for morning prayers in the synagogue and then spending a long working day in his shop, returning late for supper and bed, there were few pleasures for Dvorah, confined to the home in deference to Middle Eastern custom and constantly reminded of her junior status there by her mother- and sister-in-law, whose house it was. After her second child – a son – was born, Yitzhak bought a separate apartment for his new family, while she 'did her duty' as his wife, bearing seven children for him in all. The boredom and frustration of her married life can be sensed in her reply to a younger sister's letter in 1944, asking her about married life:

> You asked whether a marriage can wither and die. I really don't know. My marriage never really blossomed ... He goes to work and I have babies.[158]

She was by then a citizen of Lebanon, which became a founder member of the Arab League created in October 1944, yet was still occupied by French Mandate forces that eventually left on 7 April 1946. For prosperous middle-class people such as Dvorah and Yitzhak, life there was as good as it gets. When President Bishara al-Khuri declared his country 'the Switzerland of the Middle East', who could disagree? One could ski on Mount Lebanon in the morning and surf in the Med on the same afternoon; the banks welcomed money from all over the world and guarded client confidentiality as closely as the gnomes in Zurich. Although each community had its own concept of what an independent Lebanon should be like, so long as they were all prospering, who cared? Everything changed when the United Nations voted Resolution No 181(11) on 29 November 1947, approving the establishment of a Jewish state in Palestine after the end of the Mandate in May the following year. Riots erupted in Beirut but, although some Jewish shops were looted, government guards around the Jewish quarter of Wadi abu-Jamil deterred any violence to homes there.

With thousands of Jews in Iraq and Syria desperate to escape increasingly anti-Semitic regimes, Dvorah set up an escape route through Lebanon, arranging for as many as 500 people at a time to be hidden in Wadi abu-Jamil until they could be conducted by paid smugglers across the southern Lebanese frontier to Misgav 'Am, the northernmost Jewish settlement in Palestine. Yitzhak did not want to get personally involved, but financed her work with the refugees. After accidentally overhearing some loose talk about Arab League plans to drive the Jews out of Palestine, Dvorah put the information in a letter to one of her brothers in Jerusalem, sent via her people-smugglers. Her brother passed it to the Haganah – the Jewish underground army preparing for a war of independence.

This brought her to the attention of the embryo Jewish intelligence organisation that would become the Mossad.[159] Asked to spy for Israel on a permanent basis, for the following fourteen years Dvorah used her connections with the top layers of Lebanese society to gather intelligence about Arab intentions and military capabilities. Using the code name Pearl, she sent regular digests of this intelligence to the Haganah in invisible ink it had supplied on otherwise innocuous family correspondence.

The Arab leaders of neighbouring states had assumed that the comparatively few Jews in Palestine could easily be wiped out by the Arab Liberation Army led by Fawzi al-Kaukj, but the tide of what would turn into the War of Israeli Independence went the other way and plans were laid for all the regular armies of the Arab League to invade simultaneously on 15 May 1948, when the British troops left, and 'finish off the Jews'.

As the fighting spread in the new state of Israel, 140,000 Palestinian Arab refugees flooded over the frontier into Lebanon. In this chaos, Dvorah had to slow down her people-smuggling in the other direction, but she continued sending intelligence, although her husband grew increasingly worried because some spies had been publicly hanged in Damascus. Far from giving up, Dvorah identified strongly with the desperate struggle going on south of the border and accompanied one party of refugees, to meet her Haganah controller in Tel Aviv at the end of the year. He predicted that that the Arab armies would withdraw, which turned out to be correct. In February 1949 Egyptian and Israeli delegates met under the auspices of the United Nations on the Greek island of Rhodes and signed a ceasefire. Lebanon was the next country to make peace, followed by Jordan. Left alone, the hardline Syrian government was the last to accept the status quo.

Peace of a kind had come to Israel, but not to Dvorah, who was informally arrested and taken to the Sûreté Générale offices where the charming 35-year-old Major Georges Anton interrogated her very politely, but made it clear that he had evidence of her clandestine activities for Israel. He warned her not to attempt to leave Beirut because she would be required to answer more questions and was facing a trial in a military court after two of her associates had confessed. At their subsequent meetings, she found her feelings in turmoil, falling in love for the first time in her life. Major Anton could have her sent to prison, yet was considerate enough to have her driven home in his own car after each interview and even admitted that he had wanted to meet her face-to-face since first seeing her at a parents' meeting in the school their children attended.

Despite all the pregnancies, Dvorah was an attractive woman in her prime, well dressed, expensively perfumed and elegant. More importantly, she was yearning for love and Georges Anton was a far more romantic suitor than Yitzhak had ever been. Using the alibi of the frequent unexplained absences from home necessitated by her clandestine work for the refugees, Dvorah began an affair with Georges that started with dinners in expensive restaurants out of town, in the course of which she learned that he belonged to the Maronite Christian minority, which genuinely wanted at least one non-Muslim country in the Middle East. This explained why he was feeding her strategic information in the belief that she would pass it on to the Mossad.

Ultimately, to her amazement, late in 1951 he agreed to meet her controllers – not in Israel but in neutral Turkey. When Tel Aviv approved the idea, Georges and Dvorah travelled on the same plane to Istanbul, able for the first time to spend a whole night together in their hotel. After continuing on to Rome, to her disappointment Georges was whisked away to be separately briefed by the Mossad officers. This compartmentalisation, although normal in intelligence for security reasons, as she realised, drove a wedge between them when they met after returning to Beirut because she was aware for the first time that he was keeping secrets from her.

On 20 July 1951 Jordan's King Abdullah was assassinated outside the al-Aqsa mosque in Jerusalem – not by a Jew but by a Palestinian Arab in revenge for the way Abdullah had wisely accepted the existence of the Israeli state. That winter was one of appalling weather, with travel so difficult in the Middle

East that few refugees made it to Beirut, but those who did warned Dvorah to be prepared for a flood of Jewish refugees when spring came, in response to the increasing anti-Semitism in neighbouring Arab countries. Realising that her small network of smugglers would be inadequate, she joined forces with abu-Saïd, a big-time Christian casino owner who smuggled everything from hashish to gold and prostitutes by air, ship and even the traditional camel trains, throughout the Arab world. At first she feared this powerful and ruthless man wanted to become her lover, but afterwards she said he wanted her as his confidante with no hint of impropriety in their relationship.

Through him she was able to buy genuine passports from a contact in the Interior Ministry for the new flood of refugees, but because abu-Saïd had no influence in the Muslim underworld she also had to make a deal with his opposite number there, a Shiite gang boss named Darwish Baidon, who was able to move larger numbers of people – until a group was betrayed and arrested on a beach near Beirut while being ferried out in small boats to a ship lying offshore. This landed Dvorah in court on 12 June 1952 – the summer when a coup by Egyptian Army officers deposed their corrupt King Farouk and sparked political unrest throughout the Arab world.

There were tensions between her and Yitzhak, who accused her, with good reason, of neglecting her family responsibilities in favour of her clandestine work, which included setting up, with Israeli money, the small and exclusive Rambo bar/nightclub on the fashionable al-Hamra street, where important men could be entertained by attractive hostesses in the hope that alcohol and sex would loosen their tongues for the benefit of the Mossad. Yitzhak's attitude changed when Dvorah became pregnant again. When the postponed trial of those accused after the incident on the beach saw her back in court in October and condemned to

forty days' imprisonment, she was visibly pregnant. Her punishment was deferred until after the birth in December. Three
weeks later, accompanied by her infant son, she was driven to a
comfortable impromptu 'prison' in the village of Judeida in the
mountains north-east of Beirut – a favour that had been arranged
by one of her contacts. It was more like an informal house arrest,
with Yitzhak paying for her keep and large bouquets of orchids
and other presents arriving from abu-Saïd. The greatest pain for
Dvorah was not to hear from Georges, who had been promoted
within Lebanese intelligence and had to be very careful not to
draw attention to their relationship. At their first meeting after
her release from Judeida, he explained that Syrian intelligence
was now watching him very closely and monitoring his phones.
The good news was that his new rank entitled him to an apartment at the luxurious officers' club in Beirut, where they could
meet on the pretence that he was continuing her interrogation. It
was a strange love nest for two Israeli spies.

A change had come over Dvorah during her enforced rest at
Judeida, which had given her the time to reassess her life. She was
33 years old and the mother of seven children, but her work and
her relationship with Georges had given her a sense of empow-
erment. No longer did she feel that she was just an obedient wife
and mother, who must ask her husband for permission even for
such minutiae as which dress to wear for an evening out. On the
contrary, she was an important individual taking enormous risks
of her own choosing and changing many people's lives for the
better. Yitzhak was frightened that her activities might harm his
business and the family, so she arranged for her two oldest sons
to travel to Jerusalem and stay there. Later, their oldest sister
joined them. What perturbed Dvorah was Georges' warning
that Syrian intelligence was convinced she had paid traitors in
Damascus to facilitate the departure of her refugees, and might

arrange to kidnap or kill her in revenge. That she was also being watched by the Egyptian Mukhabarat secret service was obvious when two agents from Cairo tried to intimidate her and made an attempt to kill her after she brushed them off.

With contacts in the Lebanese Cabinet and the general staff, Dvorah was inevitably above the radar horizon of several Arab intelligence services. Georges' warning about her enemies in Syria was proven timely when abu-Mustafa, their hit-man in Beirut, known as The Tiger, arrived at her apartment at 2 a.m. one night with two of his armed gang members to kidnap her and three other Jews at gunpoint and drive them to prison in Damascus. Dvorah had already met him and knew his mother, but he had only known her under her Arabic name, Um-Ibrahim – mother of Ibrahim. Perplexed to find that his mother's friend was also the wanted Israeli spy Dvorah Dror, abu-Mustafa was in a quandary until she arranged a fake passenger list for the previous day's flight to Istanbul – 'proving' that the targets he was supposed to kidnap had already fled after being forewarned by someone in Damascus. She then left on the very next flight.

In February 1958 Egypt and Syria formed the United Arab Republic, which looked like the same enemy both north and south of Israel. With increasing unrest in all the Levant, Beirut became the listening post for outsiders like the Soviets, the CIA and Britain's MI6, intent on learning what was happening, especially in Syria and Egypt, and spreading their own disinformation – all of this like a froth on top of the bubbling sectarian turmoil of Lebanese politics. Throughout that spring, outbursts of violence grew into street battles throughout Beirut. On 15 July US Marines landed in Lebanon and RAF aircraft flew British paras to Amman and Zarka in Jordan. The unrest in the streets of Beirut calmed down temporarily and Dvorah resumed her people-smuggling, developing new routes via Athens and

Cyprus. But the stress was telling on her: she had lost her appetite and developed a nervous twitch in one eyelid. The pressures on Georges after the forced resignation of President Camille Chamoun, and his own obligation to work with the Syrians, who were grabbing more and more power in Lebanon, contributed to the final breakdown of their relationship.

On her next clandestine visit to Tel Aviv, Dvorah paid a visit to her daughter, Chanah, in Jerusalem. Now engaged to be married, she lectured her mother: 'Do you really think I don't know what you have been doing all these years? How else does a Jewish woman from Beirut manage to visit Tel Aviv every few months? Haven't you done enough? Please don't return to Beirut. Stay here with us. Daddy will bring the other children and we'll all be together again. And I'll be able to sleep at night without worrying about you!'[160] If that was an emotional appeal from her adult daughter, the advice of Dvorah's Mossad controller – a cold, unlikeable man named Shimshoni – was identical. She was too exposed, he said unemotionally. The attempted assassination and failed kidnapping proved that she should 'come in from the cold' and not return to Beirut.

But Dvorah did go back, because it seemed to her that Israel was under threat from all sides and needed every piece of intelligence she could glean from her sources. At least, that is what she later said, although her relationship with Georges may have played a part. Back in Beirut, he had no good news for her, having lost his privileges, among them the apartment where they used to meet. He had, however, placed watchers on her house in the Wadi abu-Jamil in the hope this would guarantee her safety as long as she stayed within the Jewish quarter. His department was being sidelined by Muslims in the Interior Ministry, which he read as a warning to leave Lebanon with his family while he still could – or risk assassination by a Syrian hit squad. Dvorah was distraught. Although their past intimacy was lost, she depended on him for wise and helpful advice. When, one week later abu-Saïd casually mentioned that Colonel Anton had moved to South America, she felt as though the bottom had fallen out of her world.

Her alibi for leaving Lebanon so often – although never direct to Israel, which would have been unwise – was a letter from her gynaecologist referring her to a specialist in Rome for tests. The next trip was for the wedding of Chanah and her husband but, on the return leg, an error by a Turkish immigration officer meant that her Lebanese passport had to be flown to Israel to be 'doctored' by Shimshoni. Instead of being returned in the promised two weeks, it was delayed by him for two and a half months in the hope that this would give Dvorah time to reconsider her position and stay away from Beirut for good.

Meantime, after a 28-year-old Lebanese counter-espionage officer named Milad el-Korah had convinced one of Dvorah's agents in Beirut that he could supply false passports for her smuggling activities, el-Korah travelled to Rome to persuade her that she risked nothing in rejoining Yitzhak and the children in the Wadi. It was a trap. On 22 February 1961 she returned to Beirut with him and reactivated her network. All seemed as before until the night of 9 August, when a midnight raid of security men burst into her home, with el-Korah in handcuffs. Later, she learned that this was a piece of play-acting: he had been an *agent provocateur* all along. With the four young children screaming and crying, and Yitzhak distraught, every room was searched roughly, leaving the floors covered in clothes and books and papers. Dvorah was arrested and driven to a military police prison in southern Beirut. The shock of her arrest provoking a heavy period, she was relieved when some medication and feminine hygiene materials were procured for her in the morning.

Left alone with no interrogation for two days, she began to think that all her important contacts were actively working for her.

It was an illusion. On 12 August her interrogation by four military intelligence officers began. She was prepared to confess to the people-smuggling, but they were not interested in this. Soon, leaks to mass circulation newspapers in the Arab world resulted in front-page stories about the 2,000 top secret documents she was supposed to have passed to Israel and the 20 million Lebanese pounds she had allegedly spent in bribes. She was also presented as a whore and brothel madam – this last because of her connection with the nightclub on al-Hamra street. After six weeks, Yitzhak was allowed to visit her, and she learned that all her important friends had abandoned her, to save being implicated in her alleged crimes, which would be treasonous if proven because she held Lebanese citizenship.

Her stubborn refusal to admit the espionage charges and confess resulted in more and more brutal methods being used. Bruised all over her body, Dvorah also suffered a dislocated jaw and several teeth knocked out by blows to the face. Underlying the habitual use of violence in Lebanese interrogations was also the anger of the four men mistreating her, due to the fact that she – a woman – had succeeded in outwitting some of the most important and influential men in Lebanon. Their ultimate threat was that, if she continued to refuse a full confession, she would be transported to the al-Maza prison in Damascus, where even more terrifying tortures would await her.[161] When her interrogation was ended after several miserable months in solitary confinement, she was sent to a women's prison, sharing a communal cell with prostitutes, murderers, drug addicts and dealers awaiting trial. In the way of prison inmates, who pick on the most vulnerable person, they all ganged up on 'the Israeli spy'. It was a different kind of hell, in which the sadistic wardress was even crueller than her charges. On the outside, Yitzhak was prepared to spend all the family's savings on lawyers' fees, but it was hard to find one who was prepared to take on such an open-and-shut case. Surprisingly, the first friend to alleviate Dvorah's conditions was the gang boss abu-Mustafa, who called on the family, told them that Dvorah was entitled to receive kosher food and 'persuaded' the wardress's drunkard lover to make her behave correctly – to this prisoner at least.

Conditions improved, especially after Dvorah began receiving food parcels she could share. Yet the months dragged by, during which the prosecution's main witness against her dropped dead in his prison cell from causes unknown, but his 319 pages of confession, detailing names, places and dates, was already in evidence. Fifteen months after her arrest, the trial of Dvorah Dror and three of her associates commenced and the several judges – who were never all in court at the same time – were inundated with sworn testimony that the woman in the dock had repeatedly betrayed her adopted country. Dvorah, however, clung to the belief that she would be found guilty only of smuggling the refugees, for which the penalty was three years in prison. As the day of sentencing approached, her 17-year-old son Tuvia whispered on his last visit that everyone who mattered in the legal system had been suitably bribed and the important friends she could have implicated in any confession of espionage must surely show gratitude that their names had never been mentioned. So, with the time she had already served and the customary remission of one third of the sentence, she hoped she would soon be free.

On the morning of the verdict she dressed in her court clothes, brought from the Wadi abu-Jamil by Miriam, her eldest daughter still in Beirut: a black suit over a white blouse. With no make-up allowed, the choice seemed appropriate for a respect-able mother of seven children, aged 43. After her final plea, the judges retired for thirty minutes – which stretched into two hours. When she was taken back into the courtroom, it was to hear the clerk of the court read out the verdict:

> All charges against [Dvorah Dror] have been proved beyond any shadow of doubt. The court is convinced that she has worked in the services of an enemy state and has greatly harmed the Republic of Lebanon, the country that granted her citizenship. Using financial and other forms of temptation, she deceived and corrupted the morals of many people ... and has smuggled valuable state documents out of the country. The court accepts, because of the great sums of money placed at her disposal, that it was the accused's intention to overthrow the Lebanese government. Therefore the Lebanese Military Court unanimously sentences the accused to be hanged.[162]

There was uproar in court, with newspaper reporters fighting to be first out and telephone the story to their editors. In deep shock, Dvorah was taken down to the cells and brought back into court an hour later, to hear the clerk announce that the sentence had been commuted to twenty years' hard labour on the grounds that she was the mother of seven children. When she was recalled again, she hoped that some other extenuating circumstance had been taken into consideration. Yet, it was to hear that Yitzhak had been sentenced as her accomplice to ten years' imprisonment, reduced on account of his age to two years. This leaving the four children in Beirut without either parent, relatives planned to divide them up: one here, two there. The children refused and, when the relatives insisted, Tuvia announced that he would leave school and run his father's shop to earn some money, becoming in effect the breadwinner and head of the family.

On 23 July a different team of judges heard an appeal on technical grounds – as a result of which Dvorah's lawyer came to tell her that her sentence had been reduced to seven years and Yitzhak's conviction had been quashed, so that he would shortly be released. As to the 'hard labour' that had to be performed by her in prison, she never spoke about it, but the prison conditions for an Israeli spy in Arab hands were inevitably harsh. Another indicator of Tuvia's calibre came when the same abusive wardress refused to allow Dvorah to receive a food parcel at Passover 1964. He was so furious that he laid siege to the office of the Minister of the Interior and refused to leave until an aide had formally recorded his complaint. A cable was sent to the prison authorising the food parcel, after which the thought of Dvorah having 'friends in high places' so terrified the wardress that she ceased victimising the Israeli spy in her keeping, and was eventually herself sentenced to two years in prison for abusive treatment of prisoners.

On 5 June 1967 the powerful Cairo radio station Voice of the Arabs announced that the United Arab Republic, Jordan and Syria were at war with Israel and had already won a number of important battles. This was a lie. Egyptian troops massing on Israel's southern border in preparation for an invasion had triggered a pre-emptive Israeli air strike against the Egyptian air force, destroying most of its aircraft on the ground and also destroying most civilian planes of the Lebanese company Middle East Airlines. Anti-Israel riots erupted outside the prison and Dvorah's cellmates became so hostile that she was placed in solitary confinement at her own request. After six days the war ended with a series of Israeli victories against the combined armies of their Arab neighbours, which had suffered 20,000-plus deaths against Israeli casualties of less than 1,000 for the conquest of the Sinai Peninsula and the formerly Jordanian territory known as the West Bank. While grateful for the victory, Dvorah was personally depressed. Her lawyer had been talking about an early release, but how could Lebanese president Hélou afford to show lenience to an Israeli prisoner after such a humiliating defeat of his country's allies?

About one month after the Six Day War, as it was already being called, Dvorah was summoned to the governor's office to meet Alain Modoux of the International Red Cross, who informed her that he had been instructed by his Israeli counterparts to discuss her release with the Lebanese government. As she later learned, many Lebanese citizens had been imprisoned in Israel during the war and considerable construction equipment belonging to a rich Lebanese contractor was captured by Israeli forces on the Golan Heights. Jerusalem was offering to swap these in return for a pilot who had ejected and landed in Lebanon and a soldier who had mistakenly crossed the frontier. At the last minute, someone in Mossad had added Dvorah's name to the list of prisoners required in the exchange. Negotiations dragged on for several weeks, but on 23 August she was awoken early from a fitful sleep and dressed herself in some clothes that no longer quite fitted. In the governor's office she met – of all people – the senior man of her interrogation team. Now courteous and smiling, Joseph Barody had been appointed to give her a tour of Beirut and then accompany her to the hand-over at Ra's an-Naqurah on the Lebanese–Israel border. As he drove her around the city, the tour became increasingly unreal: the Lebanese capital had greatly changed during her six years behind bars. Given a choice of where to eat lunch, she chose The Pigeon's Cave – a restaurant where she had often met Georges. Obviously knowing why, Barody seemed amused. But Georges was far away across the Atlantic. Afterwards, Barody drove her to Ra's an-Naqurah, arriving exactly at the appointed time, and said farewell. A Lebanese customs officer carried Dvorah's suitcase across no-man's-land to the border, where an Israeli Army officer saluted her and welcomed her home.

On 12 May 1959 the author shared this experience. Released from solitary confinement in a Stasi political prison that morning, he was escorted across the border between two hostile states – the so-called German Democratic Republic and the Bundesrepublik – by an elegant lady in the uniform of the International Red Cross. His imprisonment was nowhere near the trial that Dvorah Dror had endured, in either duration or harshness – but he still recalls the sense of unreality. At one moment, one is still liable to be returned to prison after a mysterious last-minute phone call. Then, one is walking for what seems like a long time away from armed men in a hostile state until, suddenly, one is 'home'. It is very disorientating.

Yet, on the thirty-minute drive to Haifa, the first major city on the route south, Dvorah was not in a daze. Catching sight of herself in the rear-view mirror – there were no mirrors in the prison – she asked for the car to stop at the small town of Nahariya[163] so that she could find a hairdresser to cut and style her prematurely greying hair. This, so that her family would not immediately see the effects of her long imprisonment. With Yitzhak and the children who had flown to Israel via Cyprus, she tried to settle down to the life of a respectable mother and grandmother in Jerusalem. It was not easy. In 1975 she became manageress of an antiques shop in the tourist area near the King David Hotel, where neither staff nor customers knew she was the formerly famous spy from Beirut. In January 1979, at the age of 59, she was invited to meet President Yitzhak Navon, who handed her a citation recording the nation's gratitude for her work in Lebanon.

15

Dutch Courage

The expression 'Dutch courage' meaning bravery after drinking alcohol, may be a slur from the time of the now largely forgotten Anglo–Dutch wars of the seventeenth and eighteenth centuries, implying that Dutch sailors had to be given a ration of Genever gin before every battle. Although most people have heard of Anne Frank and her family being sheltered by ordinary Dutch neighbours risking their own lives, it is not generally appreciated how many other Dutch civilians showed exceptional courage to save other people's lives during the German occupation of 1940–45.

Corrie Ten Boom was 48 years old when it began. She and her sister, Betsie, were the unmarried daughters of a watchmaker in Haarlem. All the family were members of the Protestant Dutch Reformed Church, which regarded the Nazi persecution of the Jews as a defiance of divine authority. Using a secret room built behind a false wall in her house that could just accommodate six or seven adults for short periods, she was instrumental in saving the incredible figure of about 800 Dutch Jews, young men seeking to escape conscription for labour service in Germany and Resistance agents on the run.

On 28 February 1944 a Gestapo raid during a religious meeting in the house failed to find any illegal refugees but the searchers suspected the existence of a secret hiding place, and arrested the family so they could conduct a more thorough search of the premises. Failing to find anyone, they staked the house out in the belief that hunger would eventually force anyone hiding in there to come out. In fact, it was a piece of bad luck that did the trick. A man reported to the Dutch police that his grown son had disappeared and a friendly detective entered the house, calling out to the young man by his family nickname – at which the refugees emerged.

Corrie and the other members of her family were driven to the Dutch concentration camp at Vught, near Hertogenbosch. The only concentration camp not on German territory – Natzwiller was in Alsace, annexed into the Reich – it had been sited there in order to provide slave labour in the nearby factories, including those of the electrical giant Philips. With most of the Philips family having fled abroad, the enterprise was headed by family member Frits Philips, who had stayed in post so that the Germans would not take over completely. Although forced to work with the SS, who supplied thirteen prisoner groups to work outside the camp, he managed to save the lives of 382 Jews by stating that they were essential workers. Arrested on 30 May 1943, he was afterwards hailed as 'Righteous among the Nations' at the Yad Vashem holocaust memorial in Israel.

Arriving at Vucht, Corrie and Betsie immediately began evangelising other prisoners. A particular inspiration for everyone they met was their cheerful endurance of the hardship and humiliation of camp life, even when Corrie's 85-year-old father died after one month there. On 6 September, she and Betsie were transported to Ravensbrück women's concentration camp in Germany, where Betsie died in December 1944. As a result of what seems to have been an administrative error, Corrie was freed on 31 December and devoted herself to preaching forgiveness after the German surrender in May 1945. In 1947 she gave the evangelical message a personal twist after coming face to face with one of the most brutal female guards from Ravensbrück.

Although Corrie wrote a series of devotional booklets, she did not want to write an autobiography that might be seen as self-aggrandisement. She did, however, give an account of her family's life before and during the war to American authors John and Elizabeth Sherrill. First published in 1971, *The Hiding Place* was translated into several languages, with a Dutch version entitled *De Schuilplaats*. A film based on the book was made in 1975. Two years later, at the age of 85, Corrie went to live in Orange County, California, for six troubled years, during which she suffered several strokes. She died there on her 91st birthday, 15 April 1983, and is also remembered as one of the Righteous among the Nations at the Yad Vashem memorial. Her family house in Haarlem is open as a museum to her work and life.

Also honoured at Yad Vashem, Geertruida Meijer, known to family and friends as Truus, was 44 years old when the Wehrmacht marched into Holland on 10 May 1940. Her family had a quiet record of philanthropy. After the First World War, in which Holland was neutral, they welcomed into their home a number of malnourished and ill Austrian children. At the age of 18, Truus went to work in a bank, where she met her husband, J.F. Wijsmuller, but the couple did not marry until nine years later, when Truus changed her surname to Meijer-Wijsmuller. Unable to have her own children, after Hitler came to power in 1933 she involved herself in the Kindertransporte movement, which helped an estimated 10,000 children, whose parents would allow them to flee from Nazi persecution, to travel out of Germany by many different routes to Britain and elsewhere.

Officially, the British government only allowed these children to enter the country for the purpose of completing their education. Some went on to relatives in North and South America; others stayed in Britain all their lives. In 1946 the author attended Bunce Court school in Kent, founded and run for refugee children by Anna Essinger. Although Jewish, she had worked with Quakers running soup kitchens in Germany after the First World War. She accepted a handful of English pupils for money, which was always in short supply. Almost all the German-speaking pupils had been saved by the *Kindertransport*. After the German surrender, a trickle still arrived, fresh from concentration and death camps. Many were very traumatised by their experiences and had lost all their close relatives. Some children stole clothing, others hid food, stolen from the kitchen, in their beds. Inevitably, although all lessons were in English, children would relapse into German or Yiddish among themselves, at which Tante Anna would ring a little bell and say, 'English, please!' Apart from that, there were no rules.

In Holland, with a women's group called the Association for Women's Interests and Equal Citizenship, known as VVGS,[164] Tante Truus and her friends rescued children from Austria and Germany, using bribery and charm in dealing with Nazi officials. Her greatest single success was with Adolf Eichmann in Vienna, who told her she could have 600 Jewish children, providing she took them immediately. He was probably amusing himself in the belief that this was impossible. By breaking all the rules, it was accomplished, with 500 of the children travelling straight to the Hook of Holland, and from there to Britain, while the others were temporarily accommodated in The Hague.

The logistical and emotional problems of simultaneously handling so many children at once forced the VVGS women to limit future transports to 150 at a time as the maximum manageable number, but so many parents were desperate to save their children that Truus travelled back and forth into the Reich several times each week, shepherding the groups. She was in Paris when the *drôle de guerre* stopped being funny in June 1940 and the Wehrmacht marched into Holland. Hurrying back to Amsterdam, she was begged to take a last group of seventy-four children to Ijmuiden, for the final boat to Britain. Having embarked them, she returned to her husband but the children, being technically 'enemy aliens', were not allowed to set foot on British soil for several days, until the ship reached Liverpool.

Once the German occupation authorities were installed, the rescue operations became illegal, but smaller groups were escorted to Vichy France en route to neutral Spain. Working with the Dutch Red Cross, Truus was one of a small team delivering extra rations to the transit camp at Westerbork in Holland and Theresienstadt concentration camp in Czechoslovakia. Once, in 1942, she was briefly arrested by the Gestapo, but released for lack of evidence. A little known episode in Holland's war was the winter of 1944, known as *de hongerwinter* because the Germans still occupied most of the country and requisitioned almost all food supplies. Many people, especially the elderly and young children, actually died of starvation, so Tante Truus tried to move city youths to country areas where peasants could conceal some of their harvest. After the Allied liberation of Holland in 1945, she spent twenty years in local government and philanthropy.

She died at the age of 82 in Amsterdam on 30 August 1978. In 2011 a monument commemorating the 10,000 children who passed through the Hook of Holland was erected, designed by a sculptor who had been one of those children. A statue of Tante Truus also graces the Bachplein in Amsterdam.

Star of films such as *Breakfast at Tiffany's* and *My Fair Lady*, the elfin-faced Audrey Hepburn grew up in Britain, Belgium and Holland, having a British father and Dutch mother. After their separation, it was her mother who decided in 1939 to bring Audrey from her English boarding school back to live with her at Arnhem. The decision was based on the grounds that, having been neutral during the First World War, Holland might escape occupation in the coming conflict. During the occupation, Audrey lost an uncle, had one brother hiding from the Gestapo and another in a German labour camp. In addition to dancing – she was an accomplished ballerina – to raise funds for the Resistance, Audrey also acted as a courier on occasion, trusting to her innocent looks to keep her out of trouble. During the *hongerwinter* of 1944 the main enemy was not so much the Germans as starvation. Although ill and malnourished like most of the Dutch population – Audrey was too weak to continue her dancing lessons – she so appreciated the relief workers who saved her life after that terrible time that in 1989 she renounced her film career for good and became an ambassador for UNICEF. She died in 1993 at the relatively young age of 63.

Not Dutch, but a Flemish-speaking Belgian, Maria de Meersman was 19 when the Germans invaded Belgium in 1940, less than twenty-two years after they had been driven out at the end of the First World War. Living in Brussels, she immediately joined a Resistance group, her sweet and innocent looks enabling her to talk her way out of trouble on numerous occasions. The following year she was asked by the leadership of her network to have an affair with a Gestapo officer, to get inside information, which she did.

In the summer of 1944 she discovered that a Resistance hero nicknamed 'King Kong' because of his large build was actually working as a double agent for German counter-intelligence in the hope of saving his brother's life. Real name Christian Lindemans, he betrayed more than 200 Resistance members, including agents sent by SOE from London. Realising that Maria was on his track, Lindemans arranged an attempt on her life, after which she fled to Vienna. There, she was arrested by the Gestapo and, probably because she was having a miscarriage, underwent a sterilisation, apparently without anaesthetic. Because no evidence against her was found by the Vienna Gestapo, she was released and managed to make her way through the chaos of the German collapse to forward troops of the US 101st Airborne Division, later made famous by the TV series *Band of Brothers*, acting as their interpreter and guide.

Returning to Belgium in 1946, her affair with the German officer saw her accused of collaboration, instead of being hailed as a heroine. Determined to get on with her life, she married and opened a successful shop in Elsene. Sixty years after her unmasking of Lindemans, she gave an account of her war in the book *Spionne in der Derde Rijk* – A Woman Spy in the Third Reich – which went into eight editions.[165] Two years later she was awarded six medals for her Resistance activities and in 2011 another book, *Fatale Opdracht*[166] – Fatal Assignment – was published, making her even more famous at the age of 90. Despite her age, Maria's ghost-writer, Dominique Vandekerchove, said afterwards, 'She still has an impeccable memory for facts, faces, names and places.'

After enduring great suffering from Parkinson's disease, Maria made the headlines again in February 2015 when, at the age of 94 and weighing only 49kg, she requested and was granted permission to undergo assisted suicide.[167]

Born during the German occupation of Belgium, Rita Aussenaert grew up with her grandparents, only learning at the age of 15 that they were not her real parents and that her 'older brother' was really her uncle. She is included here because her book, *En toen kwam de vijand* – meaning 'And then came the Enemy' – tells something of the suffering of the families of those caught up in espionage. Rita's mother was active in the Belgian Resistance. After being badly wounded in an air raid during 1943, she was ordered – similarly to Maria de Meersman – to marry a Flemish man, twenty years older than herself, who was working for German counter-intelligence. Born in 1944, Rita was their daughter.

In January 1945 her mother died after a long illness. Her father sentenced to life imprisonment after the liberation, the grandparents adopted his 1-year-old daughter. Learning the truth from them fourteen years later, she began visiting her real father in prison, and continued until he died in 1962. Dik Musschoot, the Belgian journalist who co-authored her book, with its cover photo of Rita's mother showing a pretty, blonde girl-next-door, made the point that Rita's mother became a spy by force of circumstances rather than passionate conviction, and by that act unwittingly but effectively orphaned her unborn daughter, as has happened to so many children of spies, male and female.

An even more distressing tale is that of Dutchwoman Adrienne Minette Boissevain van Lennep, known to friends as Mies. Born in 1896, she was 44 at the time of the German invasion of Holland, running her own beauty salon and living with her husband and five children in one of the fine houses that line the canals of central Amsterdam. Before the war, she too had been an active member of the VVGS with an especial interest in child welfare. If that sounds rather do-gooder, she was also quite famous for her witty limericks published in a weekly paper, one of which mocked a government minister who announced publicly that it was unnatural for women to work because it took jobs away from unemployed men.

A woman of conscience, starting in 1933 Mies took an active part with Truus Wijsmuller-Meijer in helping Jewish refugees from Nazism and getting Jewish children from Germany to safety. By the end of 1939 her home was already an important centre of resistance in preparation for the inevitable German invasion the following summer. Disguises and false papers were obtained for people who would be targeted by the Gestapo and SS. In 1941 her husband, Jan, was arrested, released and re-arrested, spending three years in concentration camps in Holland and Germany before dying in Buchenwald of starvation and disease, like thousands of other inmates. His two eldest sons, Jank and Gideon, belonged to an active Resistance group known as CS6, which stockpiled arms and ammunition in the cellar of the family home. All these activities inevitably attracted attention of German counter-intelligence. In August 1943 Mies, her three sons and seventy other Resistance fighters were arrested. Fortunately her two daughters were not at home at the time. On 1 October nineteen of the arrested men, including Jank and Gideon, were executed by firing squad, with Mies and her other son, Frans, locked up in Vucht concentration camp, where she worked in the sick quarters, known to her patients as Sister Mammie.

In September 1944, with the Allies pushing east from the Normandy beachheads, the camp was evacuated and Mies despatched with the other women to Ravensbrück, where she narrowly missed being selected for gassing. Although ill herself, Mies continued nursing other inmates, knowing nothing about the fate of Frans, who had been deported to Dachau with the other male prisoners from Vucht.

By the time of the German surrender in April 1945, Mies was a wreck of the woman who had been arrested nearly two years earlier. Weighing just 33kg (or 72lb), she was evacuated by the Red Cross to Sweden, where it took several months' convalescence before she was fit enough and had regained sufficient body weight to travel back to Holland. Her spirit unbroken, she rejoined her daughters and Frans. It was not long before she decided that Dutch society, traumatised by the occupation and the starvation of the winter of 1944, needed cheering up with some of the women's solidarity that had been so important for survival in the camps. At a time when it was impossible to buy new clothes or even the material to make them, she formed an organisation entitled Festrock, meaning 'party frock'. Just as, in the camps, women had stitched rags together to make clothes, each woman now made a unique and colourful dress from bits of material with special memories of lost friends and loved ones, with their names embroidered on the border of the skirt. The dresses were worn on special occasions such as national holidays. It may seem like a strange idea today, but it was an important morale-lifting idea, which Mies introduced also in other countries recovering from the occupation.

She died in February 1965.

16

Condemned for Mercy

The United Kingdom of Belgium was created after Napoleon's defeat at Waterloo in 1815 by joining some Flemish-speaking provinces and some French-speaking ones, plus a small area where German was the first language, to make a buffer zone between France, Germany and Holland. At the time, this was intended to prevent future *French* expansionism. Yet the threats to Belgian independence came from Germany, first united as a nation under Bismarck in 1871 – notably in two brutal invasions that brought the otherwise often squabbling French- and Flemish-speakers together in resistance to the occupier.

Once Field Marshal Alfred von Schlieffen drew up his plan for invading France in 1905, it was a foregone conclusion that German armies would pass through Belgium to attack France sooner or later. In the summer of 1914, when it was increasingly obvious that a European war was imminent, the Belgian government called up reservists and mobilised its armed forces on 31 July – not to attack Germany, but to defend its own neutrality. German Chancellor Theobald von Bethmann-Hollweg anticipated Hitler by declaring the 1839 non-violation treaty 'just a scrap of paper'. So, on 1 August the government of Kaiser Wilhelm II sent an ultimatum to Brussels, demanding the right for its armies to march through Belgium in order to attack France.

Two days later, Brussels rejected the terms of that ultimatum, perhaps believing Great Britain's somewhat unrealistic guarantee of military support in case of invasion. On 4 August the German government declared war on neutral Belgium and its armies crossed the frontier in a modified Schlieffen Plan, advancing with a disproportionate savagery that they themselves called *die Schrechlichkeit*[168] and the world called 'the rape of Belgium'. Great damage was inflicted on towns and cities; thousands of Belgian soldiers and civilians were killed; at least 25,000 homes were destroyed, plus many historic public buildings; an estimated 1.5 million people fled across the frontier into neutral Holland. Stocks of food and strategic materials were looted and sent into Germany. Fearing a massive uprising from the remaining civilian population of occupied Belgium and north-eastern France, the German occupation authorities in Brussels deported some 15,000 important people as hostages to Germany and conducted massacres of men, women and children in several towns. On August 25 the city and university of Leuven were ravaged, with the university's collection of 300,000 medieval books and manuscripts deliberately burned, 248 residents killed and the entire population forced to leave their homes.

Pushing back the army of France's Third Republic and the ineffectual British Expeditionary Force, in places the Germans advanced up to 120 miles into French territory before they were stopped – more by inadequate logistics than the defenders' prowess. Deportations and other repressive measures imposed on the thus occupied territory proved counter-productive because no organised uprising had been planned; it was the invaders' heavy-handedness that provoked widespread resentment. Most men of military age were either fighting on the other side of the lines or locked up in German POW camps, so it was women who played the major part in this. Most English-speakers will have come across the name of executed British nurse Edith Cavell, but may never have heard that more than 4,000 Belgian and French civilians – mainly women – braved horrific punishments actively to resist in various ways the German occupation of their homelands in 1914–18.

In August 1914 many hundreds of French, Belgian and English soldiers found themselves trapped behind the rapid advance of the Kaiser's armies. Since attempting to cross the lines and rejoin their units carried the risk of being shot at by both sides on the heavily militarised front, they hid out in isolated farmhouses and forests, waiting for a chance to get back to Britain or unoccupied France via still neutral Holland. Once the Dutch frontier was wired off, that was impossible without a lot of help. Hiding for weeks or months in remote farms, isolated châteaux and the forests, these men also needed food – which was a big problem because it was now strictly rationed in the occupied territory. After the announcement of meat rationing, one Belgian joke was that the Germans would issue free magnifying glasses to everyone so that they could see their meat on the dinner plate. A harmless joke? Not if one was overheard repeating it by the wrong person.

If the soldiers on the run were caught without resistance, they were sent to a POW camp, but the consequences for their helpers were far more serious. In both French and Belgian armies there was a tradition of 'godmothers' who adopted soldiers at the front and sent them letters and small gifts. These 'godmothers' now undertook secretly to supply the men in hiding with food and civilian clothing, and performed small services such as regularly washing the underwear of men in forest hideouts where there was scant water. Slowly networks formed with printers, local government officials and women working as secretaries in town halls supplying both false and genuine identity papers. If caught, they risked heavy fines and harsh imprisonment.[169]

Running a training college for nurses in Brussels, Edith Cavell was 48 years old at the time of the invasion and considered by her students as a strict disciplinarian and efficient administrator – in other words, a no-nonsense person, like most matrons and senior nursing staff. Although given the chance to flee home to Britain when the Germans crossed the frontier, she chose typically to stay at her post, supervising the care of sick and wounded men, and training a new generation of nurses, desperately needed in Belgium with all the war-wounded to care for. In November 1914, she undertook to hide two British soldiers on the run and arranged for them to have false papers and be escorted to the Dutch frontier. This one humanitarian operation led to her realisation that a nationwide network of helpers was required to handle the hundreds of men trying to make a home run. By February 1915 an 'underground railway' had been set up by Edith and some forty helpers, mostly women. Headquartered at her training college in Brussels, it stretched from the front lines in France all the way to Holland.

The four most important members of the network were Edith, Princess Marie de Croÿ, Countess Jeanne de Belleville and schoolteacher Louise Thuliez. Thanks to their aristocratic titles, the princess and the countess were paid some respect by the German troops in their areas and took advantage of this to hide men in their châteaux. By November of 1914 so many soldiers were hidden in her home that Princess Marie tried without success to persuade them to surrender to the Germans. Then she discovered that her friend the countess of Belleville was equipping other men on the run with papers and clothing, and arranging for them to reach Edith Cavell in Brussels. Marie used the same methods to get her protégés to Brussels. It was a system that worked from November 1914 to July 1915. Alerted by the number of men entering the nursing school to be hidden and, in some cases, nursed back to health, German counter-intelligence searched the premises on 14 June, but came away empty-handed.

A golden rule of clandestine life is not to mix activities because this increases the likelihood of being detected. Edith's most important male courier was architect Philippe Baucq, who also printed and distributed a resistance tract under the banner *La Libre Belgique*. Six weeks after the search of the training college, Feldgendarmerie (German military police) officers arrested one of Baucq's accomplices, whose confession led them to his house on 31 July. After the Germans arrived, Baucq's 13-year-old daughter tried to hide some copies of *La Libre Belgique* on a window ledge, but they either blew away in the wind or fell off, to be found by the searchers.[170] Baucq and Louise Thuliez were arrested and locked up in St Gilles prison in Brussels. Less than a week later, on 3 August, Edith Cavell was arrested in her turn and questioned in connection with the escape network, which had by then saved some 200 men.[171] Within the two weeks following her arrest, she signed three admissions of guilt. Whether she was tortured or confessed in the hope of taking all the blame and saving her accomplices is unknown. If the latter, it was in vain.

The Countess de Belleville was arrested on 24 August, Princess Marie de Croÿ on 6 September. At the trial of the group, in the second week of October in Brussels, five death sentences were handed down. Three were commuted, due to the protests of the King of Spain and Pope Benedict XV, but

Cavell and Baucq were shot on the morning of 12 October. In all, thirty-five members of the network were captured, with another, named Marie Henriette, entering the Order of Redemptorists and dying as a nun two months before the Armistice. Louise Thuliez wrote to her at the convent once, using the name of another woman so that the censors would not make a connection. She received a cool reply, from which she deduced that Marie Henriette's superiors in the Order wished to terminate a possibly compromising correspondence.

At this time, there was little equality between aristocrats and working class women, or indeed between them and the middle class. Yet Louise Thuliez wrote of her time at Siegburg prison, near Cologne:

All classes were represented in the prison, from the humble working-woman to the aristocrat, from the peasant who had never before left her native village to the city lady accustomed to a life of luxury and ease. There were even some nuns. The prisoners came from all parts of occupied France and Belgium. Sometimes there were whole families in prison. Madame Ramet, a Belgian whose son had been shot, was there with her two daughters, Mme Denoël with four children. Our common misery created bonds of affection that survived the war.[172]

That 'common misery' covers a lot. Daily rations per prisoner were 175g of black bread and a dish of what the women called 'insect soup' until the Western Allies arranged for them to be treated as prisoners of war in 1917, after which they received also a ration of hard tack biscuits. But the rations were still inadequate, cells were unheated and the prison doctor was called 'Dr Sortez' because his customary words to any woman reporting sick were, 'Get out!' In these conditions, some women giving birth had to do so alone while locked in their cells. In the final months of the war, an epidemic of typhoid in Siegburg prison caused the withdrawal of the German staff, leaving the prisoners to run the infirmary, do what little nursing was possible and act as coffin-bearers and grave-diggers for the dead.[173]

Far from hushing up the October executions, Governor-General Moritz von Bissing did the same as his successor in the post of *Oberbefehlhaber Belgien* was to do during the German occupation of 1940–45. He had posters printed and displayed all over the occupied areas, announcing the executions as being effected on his authority and warning that anyone caught sheltering, feeding, clothing or otherwise helping any enemy of Germany would be sentenced to death or hard labour. The news of Edith Cavell's death set off a shock wave of horror, capitalised on by the Allies as proof that the ungodly Hun – symbolised as a soldier with spiked Pickelhauber helmet dashing a child's brains out or in some way abusing a defenceless woman – was an inhuman monster.

Sentenced to ten years in prison, Marie de Croÿ arrived on 5 November 1915 in the woman's prison at Siegburg. In the first two weeks of her imprisonment, because she was ill, Marie was prescribed a walk in the prison yard every afternoon with a young German girl criminal to support her. There was another woman in solitary exercising at the same time, but it was forbidden for prisoners to speak to each other so they whispered brief messages when passing, taking care not to alert the wardresses.

Very fortunately, Marie later wrote a book about her experiences, from which the details below are drawn.[174] On her second night at Siegburg, the terrible groans and coughing of the woman in the next cell to hers were intermingled with pleas to the wardress on night duty to leave her cell door open, so she could breathe. In the morning Marie asked the prison doctor to let her nurse this poor woman. He replied that she was a German criminal in the final stage of tuberculosis. Marie's protestation that even a sick dog merited some care were ignored. A little later, two porters came with a stretcher to remove the suffering woman, who died later that day. Her cell was roughly cleaned and left open for forty-eight hours, after which Marie was transferred into it as punishment, the bedding and the walls still stained with blood the woman had coughed up. Marie's later tuberculosis was probably due to this exposure.

Another neighbour was a French girl of 17, who had been arrested for the 'crime' of hiding the father of her unborn child. Heavily pregnant, she cried all the time for her mother, who was far away, to help her with the birth. In principle, a midwife was called to the prison for births, but often arrived too late to help. When the babies were removed from the mothers at the age of 9 months, they were sent to wet nurses outside the prison, who brought them in one Sunday a month for their birth mothers to see. With so little contact, the cruellest thing for these young women was to realise that their infants were gradually failing to recognise them.

Conditions in Siegburg were deliberately harsh. Woken at 7 a.m., the prisoners received a cup of unsweetened black ersatz coffee. The midday meal consisted of black bread and vegetable soup with a small piece of meat in it or salted cod, sometimes dried fruit such as figs or prunes. In the terrible winter of 1917 when food shortages were biting hard all over Germany due to the Allied shipping blockade, the prison soup was made from unpeeled swedes or turnips cooked with their leaves and stalks. Finally the prisoners received what they called 'mouse soup', made from a powder of ground up peelings from the vegetables sent to soldiers at the front. This tasted so rancid and gritty that many prisoners could not swallow it, despite their pangs of hunger.

At 4 p.m. there was a cup of something hot and, for those on work details, a piece of cheese, salted cod, pickled cabbage or maybe half a pickled herring. This they had to eat with their fingers because the cutlery had been removed for the night. The evening meal was a cup of gruel made from oats or barley, which the countrywomen among them thought disgusting because these were normally fed to their chickens.

There were seldom any potatoes because the Germans requisitioned these to make alcohol needed in the manufacture of explosives; those that did arrive at the prison were often rotten, due to being stored too long. As Marie de Croÿ pointed out, the rations were approximately the same for the wardresses as the war ground on and the allied blockade caused shortages of just about every foodstuff in Germany, but a limited selection of additional food could be purchased in the canteen by those who had the money and occasionally women would receive a parcel and share the contents. For the prisoners in Siegburg, the two worst problems were the cold in winter, which many found cruel for their undernourished bodies, and the lack of lighting after dusk, especially during the long winter nights. All mail was, of course, censored – both incoming and outgoing. Although her book was written without bitterness, Marie de Croÿ commented that a number of women had to be removed to mental hospitals. She was asked one day to counsel a woman on the verge of losing her reason, who told her that she had once seen her husband in the distance at another prison, but been unable to speak to him. Several weeks later she learned that he had been shot the day after she saw him.

Prisoner Anne-Marie L'Hotellier had been condemned to death for helping to feed twenty-two wounded soldiers trapped behind the German lines after the battle of Cambrai, where she was the matron of the civilian hospital. This was commuted to ten years' hard labour. Knowing that she was a trained nurse, the wardresses would send for her to come and nurse women who were obviously critically ill.

The punishment cells in Siegburg were narrower than the others and had only one small window high up in the exterior wall, which allowed little light to pass. When von Bissing received from the Countess of Mérode-Westerloo a protest about the conditions under which Marie de Croÿ was detained, he expressed a profound astonishment that a 'princess of German origin' dared to criticise measures taken by the German authorities. After what he called 'a thorough investigation', he replied that Marie was being treated with all possible care.[175] By that time she had lost a third of her body weight and her jaws were so decalcified that her teeth were falling out, making it difficult and painful to eat.

Despite her emaciated condition, during a tour of inspection of German prisons by a senior civil servant, Marie de Croÿ asked him whether he considered it appropriate for the Belgian and French women to be detained alongside German female criminals, some violent and infected with venereal diseases. Her courage and ability to harangue a German in his own language resulted in the criminals being transferred elsewhere and some relaxation in the conditions for the other prisoners. The measure most appreciated was permission to take exercise in the prison yard in twos, which enabled them to converse during the exercise. Marie wrote:

The six cells allocated for sick women were on the first floor above the admin offices. North-facing and looking out onto the kitchens and boiler room, they received little daylight and

no direct sunlight at all. What heating there was came from a
narrow cast-iron tube along the base of the wall, which might
have given some heat for those who could bear to keep the
window completely closed. Throughout the winter, the temperature in my cell was around 9 degrees Centigrade, but on
Sundays and national holidays when the ground floor offices
were not in use, the boiler was not lit at all. Strange to relate,
not moving about much in a low temperature, without ever
going near a fire, some of us got used to the cold. It's the
same with hunger, except for those who have nothing else to
worry about.[176]

When Marie received a birthday book as a present from an old
friend, she circulated it around the cells for each woman to write
in it her name and the reason why she was there. These were
some typical entries:

Marie Guéant – My husband is away in the army. I was condemned on 19 September 1916 to three years in prison for
supplying food to a French airman, and had to leave three
small children and my aged mother behind.
Marthe Flavigny – condemned on 1 July 1915 to three years
for having hidden my son aged eighteen.
Marguérite Bertholet – my husband is dead. Arrested in
Verviers on 28 November 1916, I was tried by court martial in
Liège and given six months for feeding a Belgian soldier. I had
to leave five small children at home.
Emilie Flament – Schoolteacher at Laon, I was sentenced to
two years' imprisonment for 'anti-German feelings' because I
failed to denounce a neighbour who had hidden a bicycle. My
husband is in prison at Wittlich on the same charge. We left
our two small children to be looked after by strangers.

Sister Victoire, a nun – I was condemned to three months for telling schoolchildren that the Germans were rude.

Louise Paroche – condemned in 1916 to five years in prison for giving food to two Russian POWs.

Germaine Bael – given a nine months' sentence for not betraying my husband in hiding.

Marie Wauters – death sentence commuted to hard labour for helping my husband collect information. He was executed for espionage.

Madame Lemnaire-Lerche – aged seventy-five, for hiding a English soldier I was sentenced to fifteen years' hard labour, together with my daughter and two friends.

Jeanne Merckx – I was condemned to death for espionage. Sentence commuted to hard labour for life. My brother has been shot, my husband and sister given ten years each. Two other brothers are [fighting] in the Belgian army.

Madame Aubry – I was condemned to three years' prison, together with my unmarried daughter, for the crime of keeping and hiding the weapons of my husband, who died in combat in 1914.

Madame de Laminne – Accused of helping young men to evade capture, I was condemned to five years' imprisonment with a fine of 10,000 marks.

Rose Boisard – I was arrested in 1916 for feeding four hidden soldiers during eighteen months. My husband was shot, my son condemned to death – but this was commuted to hard labour for life. A second son was sentenced to three years. My third son is a POW in a German camp.

17

Death Behind Bars

At the time of the German invasion of Belgium in 1914, Gabrielle Petit was 21 and had been raised in an orphanage run by nuns after her mother's death. It was from them that she learned a passionate love of her country that is difficult to imagine today, but she was far from being a contemplative. One of her tutors described her as, 'An adorable little mischief.' When war broke out, Gabrielle volunteered as a nurse and was immediately persuaded to join an espionage network, collecting intelligence for the Allies. Her method was simple: writing everything she heard from her German patients on cigarette paper, she slit postcards in two, inserted the paper and re-gummed them to post across the lines. The last of these, dated 31 January 1916 and describing the crash of a Zeppelin at Mainvault, was still in her possession the following day when she was arrested by the Germans and incarcerated in the prison of Saint-Gilles, in the south of Brussels.

There, she refused to divulge any information during her interrogations and was condemned to death, refusing to sign a plea for clemency. On the day prior to her execution, her younger sister Hélène was allowed to give her the news that she had only hours to live. Interviewed for Belgian state television in March 1966, she recalled that last meeting so long before:

> I said to her, 'Gaby, it's tomorrow.' She understood and blushed bright red. I was too upset to say any more, but she told me that the others arrested with her had been taken away that morning, so she knew that her time could not be far off. She was not afraid of dying, but I did not believe she would really be killed. I kept on thinking and hoping that somehow she would survive.[177]

Gabrielle was shot by a German firing squad at Schaerbeek on 1 April 1916, just 23 years old. Consoled by her Catholic faith, she faced the men pointing rifles at her with courage, her youth and spirit making her a symbol of Belgian patriotism. In 1919 she was given a state funeral and there are still statues of her to be seen in Tournai and Schaerbeek. Whether or not she actually said in the execution yard, 'I shall show them that a Belgian woman knows how to die', that is what people believe.

Louise de Bettignies was born French in 1880 at Saint-Amand-les-Eaux, north of Lille and very near the Belgian border, the seventh of eight children in an aristocratic but impoverished family. With few work opportunities in those days for an educated young woman, she was employed as a private tutor by noble families in several European countries, acquiring fluent English, German and Italian, with some Russian, Czech and Spanish.

During the German invasion of 1914, she volunteered to nurse German and Allied wounded at Saint-Omer. Hearing her chatting with wounded German POWs in their own language and writing last letters home dictated by dying men, an officer of

French military intelligence – le Deuxième Bureau – suggested she become an active agent in her occupied home territory, but 34-year-old Louise decided to work for British Intelligence. It was thought by some that this was because it had a larger budget, but it was probably because she thought it would be more secure. She crossed the Channel to Folkestone, where the Bureau Inter-Allié de Renseignement (Allied Intelligence Bureau) was headed by Major Cecil Aylmer-Cameron, whose job was to co-ordinate intelligence-gathering in the German-occupied territory for both French and British high commands.

Brought up in a devout Catholic family – her brother had become a priest – Louise had been intending to take holy orders before war broke out – possibly after a disappointment in love. Unusually for a young educated woman of the time, she was athletic and loved walking, riding and swimming, and her ability to eavesdrop on the unguarded conversations of German soldiers made her an excellent undercover agent. Her motivation lay in the way her strong Catholic religious feelings translated into a sense of mission to drive out 'the godless Hun' – those soldiers of the Protestant Kaiser who carried the motto *Gott mit uns* on their belt buckles.

Immediately impressed with Louise's linguistic knowledge, her calm intelligence and her unflinching motivation, Aylmer-Cameron arranged for her to have a brief but intensive course in espionage techniques including the use of codes and preparation of accurate maps. Louise was allotted a 40-mile stretch of the lines, with a map of it divided into squares, each identified by a letter and a number. This enabled her to pass over the exact co-ordinates of German gun batteries, ammunition and supply dumps and tactical railway lines – which, even if camouflaged, became immediate priority targets for Allied shelling or aerial bombardment.

Instructed to select a *nom de guerre* to conceal her true identity, she chose Alice Dubois and was given a cover job with a grain import-export company based in the Dutch port of Flushing, which would account for her needing repeatedly to cross the Dutch–Belgian frontier, ostensibly on business. Thus prepared, she returned to Lille via Holland to set up the Alice network. Among her first recruits was a nurse named Marie-Léonie Vanhoutte, who took the cover name Charlotte Lameron, and the boss of the De Geyter chemical company, whose photographic laboratory was equipped to make false papers. By the summer of 1915, she had eighty agents working for her all along the crucial stretch of front Lille–Roubaix–Tourcoing. Of all ages from children to grandparents, they included doctors and priests, who were by profession discreet, as well as postal workers and railwaymen, who were ideally placed to note German troop movements and whose jobs gave them passes to travel on duty in this high-security area behind the front. Intelligence was also collected by people renting rooms overlooking railway lines and by children playing on bridges, under which troop trains and munitions transports had to pass.

There was no doubt in the minds of Louise and her volunteers about the risks they were running. During the four-year occupation twenty-one death sentences were imposed by German courts martial in this area alone, plus many prison sentences and punishment by forced labour. To stop smugglers bringing meat, eggs and other food across the Dutch–Belgian frontier, Governor-General Moritz von Bissing erected a heavily patrolled triple fence of barbed wire stretching 300km, all the way from the coast near Knocke to the Dreieckpunkt, where the borders of Belgium, Holland and Germany met near Aachen. On the Belgian side of the new barrier was a free-fire zone, where any civilian was liable to be shot without warning, but the main deterrent was the middle fence, electrified with 2,000 volts of direct current. In country areas little was known of electricity in those days and many people were killed trying to crawl between or under the wires.

Von Bissing's other big idea was to crush the power of Belgium forever by separating politically and physically the Flemish-speaking eastern provinces from the French-speaking Walloons of the western and southern parts of the country. He died before the end of the occupation, so his 'Belgian divorce' plan never came to fruition, although it is an idea that still surfaces from time to time as a result of the friction between the two main linguistic groups.

To cross into Holland with her reports for Major Aylmer-Cameron, Louise had to use one of the heavily guarded official crossing points. Travelling to Britain fifteen to twenty times to deliver her reports to Folkestone,[178] she inevitably attracted the scrutiny of Feldgendarmerie officers checking papers at the crossing points and of plainclothes counter-intelligence officers. Her biggest coup was to alert the Allies to a secret visit of Kaiser Wilhelm II to the front. Just outside Lille, two British aircraft machine-gunned the imperial train without harming the Kaiser, after which his visit was called off. Her last major coup was a warning that the Germans were planning a huge 'push' against Verdun in early 1916. Although this was passed on to the French High Command, it was disbelieved, with the result that the French were pushed back with heavy losses when the attack opened on 21 February.

It is possible that Louise de Bettignies' downfall was due to her belief that she was doing God's work and under some divine protection; on one occasion she spent a night in a 'blown' safe house where Marie-Léonie had been arrested by German military police on 25 September 1915. But luck was with Louise that night. For whatever reason, the house was not under surveillance, although German counter-intelligence officers were actively seeking the reason why what they called 'this accursed stretch of front' was suffering such high losses from the accurate artillery and aerial bombardments that indicated the presence of a large and efficient spy network.

Louise's luck could not hold. Two plain-clothes counter-espionage officers arrested her on 20 October 1915 near Tournai. During a scuffle, she managed to swallow the intelligence material she was carrying, but several different identity cards were found on her, which was enough to prove her guilt. She spent six months in the Saint-Gilles prison at Brussels under pressure to make her confess. On 2 March 1916 she was condemned to death by a court martial for espionage, but this was commuted to forced labour for life, largely due to international protests at the German executions of Edith Cavell and Gabrielle Petit. Transferred with Marie-Léonie to the prison at Siegburg on 21 April, Louise eventually found herself one of 300 similar women, including several of Cavell's surviving agents.[179]

After her very active life before arrest, Louise could not settle down to be a 'good prisoner'. She was frequently punished for insubordination and stirring up trouble. The prison was situated near several factories producing armaments for the German forces and the only work allowed to break the prisoners' boredom was assembling fuses for artillery shells. It has been said that this was contrary to the Hague Convention, but these women were not technically prisoners of war, so the Convention did not apply. However, Louise and another woman organised a strike to put a stop to Belgian and French women making munitions to be used against their own people. Although other, non-war-related, work was found for other prisoners, the two ringleaders were placed in solitary confinement on a bread and water regime as punishment.

In solidarity, several other women went on hunger strike. On the third day of this, a young prisoner named Blankaert jumped up on her bench in the chapel after Mass, so that she could be seen by all the other women in their partitioned stalls, and made a passionate appeal for all the prisoners to refuse to work against their own countries. She ended, 'Let us accept together every punishment, rather than do something that may harm our soldiers.' Taken by surprise, the wardresses fought their way through the surrounding stalls to pull her down. Mlle Blankaert was put into a punishment cell, but since she had already been sentenced to death and had this commuted to lifelong imprisonment, it was difficult to worsen her conditions. In her solitary suffering, she had the satisfaction of learning from a note slipped under her cell door that orders had been given for prisoners no longer to be obliged to do war work.

Marie de Croÿ recorded how the health of Louise de Bettignies declined rapidly after she was placed in one of the damp, unheated punishment cells. Weakened by the poor food, inadequate clothing and the cold and damp, Louise collapsed with pleurisy and had to be removed to the prison hospital. There, it became evident that she and Jeanne de Belleville urgently required operations to remove tumours on their lungs. Talking about this with Marie de Croÿ, they all agreed that such an operation in the insanitary prison hospital was tantamount to death. Yet there was no precedent for a prisoner with a life sentence being allowed to go outside, even for urgent medical care. Jeanne nevertheless made the request, which was supported by the prison governor and the chaplain. The surgeon also refused to operate under prison conditions. Three precious weeks elapsed in negotiations before Jeanne de Belleville was taken to a hospital in Bonn for a successful operation. But Louise de Bettignies, exhausted by the delays imposed on her due to the trouble she had caused during incarceration, eventually agreed to be operated on in the prison. Evidently impressed by her personal qualities, after the operation some of the wardresses brought her flowers, as did prisoners who had picked them in the grounds of the prison. A post-operative infection saw her removed to the St Mary Hospital in Cologne, where she died on 27 September 1918, less than two months before the Armistice. In February 1920, her remains were reinterred in Lille and she was posthumously awarded the cross of the French Légion d'Honneur and the Croix de Guerre. She was also made an officer of the Order of the British Empire.[180]

On Christmas Eve 1916 the cell doors were left open so that the women could stand in the doorways listening to the prisoners' choir singing in the central hall of the prison. In the next 'sickness cell' to Marie de Croÿ was Madame Ramet de Verviers, whose son had been shot and whose daughters' death sentences had been commuted to hard labour at Siegburg. Being very ill, Marie and her neighbour were allowed to sit on stools during the concert, and managed to exchange some conversation without attracting the wardress on duty. When Madame Ramet died a few weeks later, her daughters were not allowed to follow the coffin as that was against the regulations. At the end of the war, the elder daughter was released with broken health and died after much suffering, so that only the younger daughter survived.

There was no logical reason why the prisoners in Siegburg should not speak to each other; the enforced silence was just part of the punishment. Marie recounted how, in Mass one Sunday, the woman in the pew in front of her passed back a slip of paper torn from a prayer book, with her name and address on it. Marie furtively squeezed her hand as they filed out of the chapel, but was observed by a wardress. The punishment for the other woman was to be sent away to a more distant prison, where she became ill – eventually surviving to become a nun after the end of the war. Transportation to distant prisons was also used to separate mothers and daughters as additional punishment.

When the German armies rapidly overran Belgium in late summer of 1914 Marthe Cnockaert, a 22-year-old medical student at Ghent University was on holiday at the family home, a prosperous farm near Roeselare in south-west Belgium with her father and mother – her three brothers were absent, fighting with the Belgian Army. The farmhouse had been roughly fortified by French troops hacking firing slots in the outer walls before their withdrawal. Believing that her father had done this with intent to resist them, the Germans announced that the farmhouse was to be burned down with him inside. Unknown to them or anyone else, he escaped through a cellar window, but the house was destroyed. Despite this, Marthe and her mother joined forces with three nuns from Passchendaele to convert a large house nearby into an emergency hospital for German wounded but it was not long before field security officers became convinced that the five women were spies, signalling information to the enemy. The nuns were compelled to leave or be shot, but Marthe had to stay, her linguistic knowledge – she spoke Flemish, French, English and German – and her medical expertise being too useful in the hospital. With her mother and eleven women from the village, they were the only civilians in the forbidden zone, close to the front lines.

In January 1915 a temporarily successful Allied advance in this sector of the front convinced the Germans that Marthe must be a spy, so she was ordered to report for nursing duties further back from the lines at the German military hospital in Roeselare town. There, she was reunited with her mother and had the great joy of seeing again the father she had believed dead. Unknown to them, she was in touch with a network of

Belgian women who were servicing what later came to be called dead letter drops as a way of passing on to the Allies information she gleaned from chatting with the doctors and wounded officers in the hospital. Using the code name Laura, she left digests of what she learned about troop movements and plans in collection boxes and other safe places in churches. It was quite usual at the time for a woman to pop into a church to offer a prayer for a husband or other relative in the army, so the sight of women visiting churches did not arouse suspicion. In this way, her reports of troop movements, location of arms dumps and the first gas attack at Ypres were passed via other female members of the network, for forwarding to British HQ on the other side of the lines. The churches were also sometimes used as safe houses in which to hide Allied soldiers on the run.

Life in the war zone was not much fun. When a neighbour decided to sell his café, frequented by German soldiers, and move his family to a safer place, Marthe persuaded her parents to buy it in March 1915, and served in it during her free time. The hostility towards them of most Belgians made her very popular with the German clients, since she could speak their language and seemed friendly. One way and another, she was able to warn the Allied high command that drums of chlorine poison gas were being stored in the area and two German chemists were staying in rooms above the café and making ascents in observation balloons to map wind currents. On 22 April 1915, the first chlorine gas attack was launched against the Allied lines near Passchendaele.

In May 1915, for outstanding services as a nurse, Marthe was awarded a medal by Duke Albrecht of Wurttemberg, Commander-in-Chief of German IVth Army.[181] This was later to save her life. In a change of management at the hospital, the new matron took a personal dislike to Marthe and sacked her, which gave her more time to devote to her espionage activities. These apparently included exposure of a priest behind the Allied lines who was spying for the Germans, the assassination of a Feldgendarmerie officer and arranging for dynamite to be placed under an arms dump through a disused sewer. It is difficult to know how much of this to believe, yet it was apparently at the site of the sewer that she lost a gold wristwatch engraved with her initials. In November 1916 German counter-intelligence cunningly advertised a list of personal property supposedly recovered from a thief's haul, including the watch. When Marthe dropped her guard and went to collect it, she was confronted with the details of where it had been found – and arrested.

After two coded messages were found hidden in her bedroom, she was charged with espionage. At her court martial held in the prison at Ghent, Marthe refused to name her accomplices in return for leniency, and was found guilty and sentenced to death. Testimony by doctors with whom she had worked in Roeselare of her excellent work with the German wounded and the award of her German medal saw this commuted to life imprisonment. She was released after the Armistice in November 1918 and awarded the Belgian Herinne-Ringsmedaille and the Overwinnings-medaille, and in the *London Gazette* of 26 August 1919 it was announced that Field Marshal Haig had personally thanked her for her 'gallant and distinguished conduct in the field'.

For once, there was a happy ending. After the war, Marthe was tracked down by a Dublin Fusiliers officer named John McKenna, who had analysed her reports at British Intelligence headquarters. In October 1921 she married him and the couple settled down in her home town. Her first book, co-authored by McKenna, with a foreword written by up-and-coming British politician Winston Churchill, was entitled *I Was a Spy*. This book went through eighteen editions, becoming a best-seller in Britain and the US, with the royalties enabling the couple to pay for the building of a comfortable home. After film rights were bought by the Gaumont cinema company, an all-star cast made Marthe even more famous, so that on all her promotional tours she was hailed as both author and heroine.

Sixteen more spy books flowed from McKenna's pen. While none had the blockbuster effect of the first one, they were all successful. In May 1940, when it was obvious that the Germans were about to invade Belgium again, the couple fled to Cheshire, where McKenna volunteered for non-combatant war work and Marthe was a housewife. She died in Roeselare in February 1966.

Strangely, since the First World War ended long before most European women had the right to vote, the Germans also had a spymaster known as 'Fräulein Doktor'. Elsbeth Schragmüller was 27 at the start of the war. She came from an old Prussian military family and, as an exceptionally bright girl, was admitted to the first grammar school for girls in Germany, at Karlsruhe. Obtaining the all-important Abitur certificate with ease, she went on to study political science at Freiburg University, becoming one of the first female graduates in all Germany. Having fluent English and French, learned from native speakers, she was at first employed on the staff of Governor-General Colmar von Goltz in Brussels, intercepting mail from Belgian POWs. After that was realised to be far below her potential, she was transferred to Lille, where she was appointed to Abteilung IIIb of military intelligence.

This was where she came into her own, being promoted to oberleutnant and receiving the Iron Cross for her work, recruiting and training many deserters from the French Army and organising the systematic collection of military intelligence by

contacts throughout the Allied countries, even as far away as
America, given training in secure communication methods to
pass their information to the German Supreme Headquarters.
In 1929 Hans-Rudolf Berndorff's book *Spionage!*[182] included
a female master-spy said to be based on Elsbeth Schragmüller,
whose fantastic James Bond-ish adventures must have given
the real Fräulein Doktor a few hollow laughs, if she bothered
to read it. It was thought that the real female German master-
spy was recalled to service in 1939, presumably to work for the
Abwehr, but she died the following year from bone tuberculosis.

18

Women in the Cold War

As the years pass, the period known as the Cold War (1945–89) seems to shrink in perspective for most who lived through it in fear of nuclear annihilation. For those born since in the increasingly federalised Europe, it may seem like ancient history to be told that the populations of Czechoslovakia, Hungary, Poland, East Germany and the Baltic States were locked for four decades into Stalin's prison empire, separated from their European neighbours by the Iron Curtain. In the West, we had the US-dominated North Atlantic Treaty Organisation (NATO) and in the East the Soviet-dominated Warsaw Pact, each controlling millions of men and women in uniform poised for nuclear, biological, chemical and conventional war to the death. Paradoxically, spies working for both sides did much to defuse the tension by revealing the true state of affairs in the enemy bloc.

In researching *Daughters of the KGB*,[183] the author came across thousands of soul-wrenching personal histories of women caught in the crossfire between the two political blocs. One of the

most unlikely was 26-year-old Daphne Maines, who was working in a safe job as a secretary at the British Embassy in Prague.
On 15 December 1951 – at the height of the Korean War – she
volunteered to go for an evening drive with Second Secretary
Robert Neil Gardner, who thought that a couple seated in his
car would be less suspect than a man alone to the KGB-cloned
state security organisation Státní Bezpečnost (StB), whose officers shadowed every journey by Western embassy staff, especially
in embassy cars with giveaway diplomatic number plates. These
were early days in the Cold War, so it is possible that Gardner
thought James Bond-type driving techniques could shake off
unwanted followers.

In the event, the Cold War turned hot as the two British
diplomats drove out of the Czech capital, heading into a forbidden military zone, where foreigners were not allowed. Prague
Radio claimed next day that they were caught red-handed in
an espionage operation, exchanging money for secret military
information. It was a set-up. Gardner was observed by hidden
guards digging up a tin containing allegedly secret military
documents and a written promise of more information to come
from the same source. In payment for this, he secreted a bis-
cuit tin containing notes to the value of 40,000 Czech crowns
– approximate value US $1,000 – in a cavity in a nearby wall.
Meanwhile, Daphne was standing lookout beside his car, and
noticed nothing wrong. The swap accomplished, they both got
into the car to make a quick exit from the forbidden zone, but
were almost immediately intercepted by several converging StB
vehicles. Gardner pumped adrenalin, switched off the head-
lights, gunned the engine and chicaned white-knuckled between
them in what was described as a cloak-and-dagger chase. When
the British Embassy car was stopped by gunfire, it may have
crashed because both occupants were injured, in Daphne's case

with a bullet wound bad enough to require immediate hospitalisation. Gardner was described as just shaken and bruised.

Arrested, but enjoying diplomatic immunity, he realised he had fallen into an StB entrapment. The Czech Foreign Ministry handed to the British Embassy a note demanding that he leave the country before 6 p.m. Prague time the following day, but gave an assurance that Daphne would be allowed to leave the country as soon as she was discharged after treatment for her wounds in a Prague hospital, where she was guarded around the clock by Czech secret police. It is probable that British Ambassador Sir Philip Broadmead KCMG, MC was not aware of Gardner's moonlighting for SIS, since most ambassadors preferred to be able to say they had no knowledge of SIS clandestine operations undertaken by their staff. British newspapers reported that Gardner had been 'called home' by the Foreign Office and Daphne had been due for reassignment. A cover story alleged that the incident was unwarranted and yet another case of Czech harassment of Western diplomats at roadblocks all over the country. The absence of any subsequent high-profile trial of a Czech citizen charged with supplying the documents Gardner dug up in the zone confirmed that Gardner had been set up by an StB officer posing as a traitor willing to supply secrets for cash. West German frontier guards noticed as Gardner was driven out of Czechoslovakia on 16 December that he had wounds on his face resembling cuts from shards of glass from the shattered car windows.

That the whole madcap operation was SIS-sanctioned became clear when Daphne returned safely to Britain and was subsequently rewarded with a posting to the Washington Embassy, where she met chess master Norman Alasdair Macleod. Gardner disappeared into the wilderness of mirrors, his erstwhile accomplice marrying Macleod in Cheshire in October 1956 and becoming the mother of two daughters.[184] When and if they learned that their mother had come close to death on the wrong side of the Iron Curtain in December 1951, is unknown.

Nine years later one of the oddest espionage plots was hatched by Maureen Bingham, the 30-something wife of Sub-Lieutenant David Bingham. He was serving as a weapons electronics officer aboard HMS *Rothesay*, a recently commissioned modified Type 12 frigate. Aged 31 and married with four children, he was not thought a security risk. The risk was his wife, a shopaholic who was also addicted to gambling. Thinking she had found the ideal way to augment her husband's salary, she knocked on the door of the Russian Embassy during a trip to London and offered his services to the KGB. The Naval Attaché, Lory Trofimovich, suggested she should return for a tea party under the cover of researching a book on housewives of the world. At their second meeting she was taught the use of dead letter boxes so that she would not need to visit the embassy again.

With her husband totally ignorant of all this, she photographed pages from a notebook he used at home, later claiming that she deliberately induced camera shake so that the prints – this was before digital photography – would be illegible. Before she could receive any payment from the Russians, her gambling debts led to her selling the family car without the knowledge of the hire purchase company and the first payment via the dead letter box of £2,800 bailed her out for the time being. When Sub-Lieutenant Bingham learned that the money was from a scam his wife had perpetrated on the Russians, he realised that Maureen and he were now vulnerable to blackmail if they did not feed some genuine information. At his trial, the court was told that one document he had supplied was extremely important.

At his trial, Bingham said that he took his son, Karl, with him to meet a Soviet handler in some woodland and when he refused to continue supplying material the Russian pointed a gun at him and said, 'What about your children's lives?' Whether or not he was so threatened, Bingham shortly afterwards told a senior officer what he had been doing. For whatever reason, no action was taken, so he also told the police, and was arrested. At his debriefing by Royal Naval Intelligence his account of leaving empty cigarette packets in country telephone boxes and posting church notices to KGB safe houses was likened to a badly written spy novel. At the time of his trial in September 1971, Prime Minister Edward Heath had just declared 105 Soviet diplomats, presumably including Trofimovich, *personae non gratae*. Bingham was sentenced on twelve counts at Winchester Crown Court to 126 years, to run concurrently, therefore lasting twenty-one years.

The situation was hardly clarified by Maureen taking reporters to the Soviet Embassy and declaring that Moscow had treated the couple better than the Royal Navy. Assessed as being a pathological liar, she was sentenced to two and a half years in prison. The couple's children had to be taken into care and placed in foster homes. After serving seven years, Bingham was released and changed his name to Brough, rebuilding a life running a small hotel in Bournemouth and re-marrying. He died in a presumably accidental car crash in February 1997, aged 56.

Mothers probably always will be taken for granted by their children. Sometimes, finding old diaries listing wartime duties can be a shattering revelation to their offspring, wondering, 'Why did she never tell us?' Martha Peterson is now a respectable suburban grandmother living 'somewhere in America' whose children were amazed to learn that she and their father had both been CIA officers. When younger, she was an

attractive, blonde, just-married embassy wife in Laos, where
her first husband, a former Green Beret, was involved in infil-
trating CIA-trained Laotian guerillas to harass supply convoys
travelling down the Ho Chi Minh trail during the US war in
Vietnam. After he was killed when his helicopter was shot
down over jungle, the young widow was repatriated in shock.
Coming to terms with her loss, she volunteered for an active
role with the CIA to avenge her husband's death and was posted
to Moscow, where female embassy staff were not trailed everywhere because at the time KGB counter-espionage officers did
not consider Western women dangerous. It is a Russian char-
acteristic, despite all the female agents employed by Soviet and
Russian spy agencies over the years. From 1975 to 1977 Martha
worked in the embassy as a low-grade clerk, popular with
her colleagues, who had no idea of her CIA work. In her free
time, she collected increasingly important material from dead
letter drops, leaving in exchange espionage equipment such
as preset-focus, ultra-miniaturised cameras concealed inside
harmless-looking lumps of concrete – all this to service a source
inside the KGB code-named Trigon, real name Alexander
Ogorodnik, recruited while posted abroad.

KGB officers arrested Peterson after watching her make
one of these dead drops near the Krasnoluzhskii Rail Bridge.
Slightly roughed up when she resisted arrest, she was held for
three days in the Lubyanka before being released under her
diplomatic immunity, unaware that Ogorodnik was also in the
prison but lying dead in the morgue. Before being posted back
to Moscow, he had persuaded his CIA case officer to give him
a cyanide pill so that he could end his life on his own terms if
caught. This was hidden inside an expensive Montblanc foun-
tain pen. At his first interrogation, he slipped the pen out of his
pocket and bit through the specially weakened casing to release

the poison. From then on, it became KGB routine not only to handcuff suspects with hands behind their back at the time of arrest, but also to remove any personal possessions immediately.

As Martha Peterson later said, case officers and cut-outs under diplomatic cover are usually at little risk, but their agents have no such protection and pay a high price if all goes wrong.[185]

A very different story is that of US citizen Elizabeth Bentley, one of the most important figures in Cold War espionage. Born in 1908, she emerged from Vassar, the top American women's college, in 1930 with a degree in English, Italian and French. Three years later, at Columbia University she won a scholarship to the University of Florence, where she flirted with a Mussolini-era student fascist movement before falling in love with her communist tutor there and doing a political U-turn under his influence. Back at Columbia University to complete her Master's Degree, she joined the Communist Party of the USA (CPUSA) headed by Earl Browder[186] in March 1935. In 1938, with war looming in Europe, she was working for Mussolini's US propaganda bureau, passing intelligence gleaned there to Browder, who passed it on to Soviet agents. It must have been useful because Russian émigré Jacob Golos, a long-time naturalised US citizen involved in the assassination of Leon Trotsky, became both her lover and case officer, although she later said she had no idea he was an agent working for NKVD until the US Justice Department obliged him to register as an agent of the Soviet government in 1940. Subsequently under FBI surveillance, Golos refrained from direct contact with his network of spies, using Elizabeth as a cut-out and promoting her to the very well-paid position of vice-president of United States Service and Shipping Corporation, a Comintern cover organisation, where Moscow Centre allocated her the code name *umnitsa* – clever girl.

After the USA and USSR became allies following Hitler's invasion of the USSR in summer 1941 and the US entry into the war following the Japanese attack on Pearl Harbor on 7 December, her network of politically committed spies was swollen by a number of basically loyal Americans who wanted to help what they saw as 'the gallant Russian victims of German aggression'. This led to a confusing situation when the senior NKVD illegal agent in the USA, named Ishhak Akhmerov, tried, with Moscow's support, to take over Elizabeth's networks and she fought him off with support from Earl Browder, both believing that direct contact with a Soviet agent would frighten off many of their highly placed sources in the political and administration establishment. Moscow's eventual approval of her work was evident when Golos died of a heart attack in 1943 and Elizabeth was promoted in his place. She had for years had a drinking problem and the stress of her work and the death of her lover sent her into a severe depression, where alcohol became her only relief, as it was, and is, for many in the clandestine world.

After D-Day in June 1944 Browder crumpled under Akhmerov's pressure and handed many agents over to him directly. Elizabeth said later that this capitulation made her see Browder clearly, not as the head of an important political party, but as a craven yes-man following Moscow's orders. Using Elizabeth's breakdown as justification, Akhmerov kept up the pressure, taking over all her agents and firing her from her well-paid sinecure job with US Service and Shipping. At a meeting with his successor she was plainly drunk and threatening to 'spill the beans' to the FBI, which she afterwards realised could easily have earned her a fake suicide – the favourite Soviet method of silencing an untrustworthy agent. An unhappy love affair did nothing to stabilise her when she came to suspect that her new lover was probably a Soviet agent trying to entice her to the USSR, where she could be disposed of more easily. As an insurance policy, in November 1945 Elizabeth followed up exploratory talks with the FBI by offering up 100–150 names of highly placed US citizens in her former networks, some of whom were already under suspicion after debriefings of previous Soviet defectors. Given the code name Gregory, she was placed in a witness protection programme with the vague idea that she could be used as a double agent.

Fortunately for her, the FBI advised the British SIS representative in New York of the situation and the news reached Kim Philby in London. Warned by him, Moscow Centre cut all contact with Elizabeth's former agents so they could not lead watchers to their controllers. This in turn prevented the FBI finding any 'smoking gun' leads to named agents, who were thus able to plead innocence or refuse to testify under the Fifth Amendment to the US Constitution, which makes it legal for any witness to refuse to testify if doing so would possibly incriminate him or herself. Subsequent decoding under the Venona programme of deciphering encoded radio transmissions from agents in America to Moscow Centre confirmed Elizabeth's long-running and important role and substantiated her story.

Forced by the Justice Department to testify to a grand jury, Elizabeth afterwards decided to tell her own story to the media, causing a sensation as the beautiful blonde spy. Some of the Democratic political bigwigs she revealed as having been her wartime sources called in favours, President Truman even labelling her testimony as a Republican smear operation despite fellow ex-spy Whittaker Chambers corroborating much of what Elizabeth said to the House Un-American Activities Committee and in law cases. Another unhappy affair with a physically violent lover did nothing for her stability, and her drinking continued, although always under control when on the witness stand. To support herself she took office and teaching jobs, earning extra money from occasional lectures to Catholic groups about the reality of Soviet espionage. She died of cancer at New Haven in Connecticut in December 1963, aged 55, the event causing only the faintest ripples in the press, but those who had access to the full Venona decodes being broken at Arlington Hall in Virginia never lost their appreciation of her importance.

Venona really began in May 1945 when US military intelligence officers were hastily going through German Foreign Office archives in Saxony, on territory about to be handed over to the Red Army. They discovered a partly burned codebook that the Germans had recovered in June 1941 from the Soviet consulate in Petsamo, Finland. A second Soviet codebook was recovered about the same time in Schleswig by an officer from Arlington Hall. Over the following thirty-five years, until the programme ended on 1 October 1980, Venona decrypts were instrumental in identifying many Soviet spies.[187]

Readers with memories long enough to recall the scandal of the atom spies will recall the most famous name from that scandal. Ethel Rosenberg was executed in the electric chair at Sing Sing prison in the early evening of 19 June 1953, either just before or just after her husband, Julius. The hour of execution had been advanced to before sunset in order not to infringe the Jewish Sabbath. Both born in New York City, Ethel and Julius met at meetings of the Young Communist League and married in 1939. They were the only people among all those rounded up by the FBI to die for the capital crime of espionage. The Venona decrypts of encoded Soviet cables did identify Julius as the head of one Soviet spy ring, who recruited his brother-in-law David Greenglass, then employed as a machinist on the Manhattan Project at Los Alamos, but Ethel was convicted largely on Greenglass's evidence. He later stated that he had falsely named her in order to save his wife, Ruth, who had collaborated. He did this, he said, 'because Ruth is the mother of my children.'

Apparently, while Julius Rosenberg died after the first electric shock, doctors determined that Ethel's heart was still beating after three shocks. Two more were administered, witnesses reporting that her hair was smoking after the final shock. That weekend her sons were taken by the Jewish Childcare Association of New York, which found suitable foster homes for them. They both spent years trying to clear their parents of any wrongdoing.

Ethel Elizabeth Gee was a 44-year-old spinster working as a filing clerk in the Admiralty Underwater Weapons Establishment (AUWE) at Portland, Dorset, who devoted her free time to caring for three elderly relatives. When a colleague, ex-Chief Petty Officer Harry Houghton, started courting her in 1958, she was a pushover for his Romeo approach, which included taking her to pubs for a few drinks, while he downed many more. She seems to have been unaware that his marriage was on the rocks and he was a chronic alcoholic, drinking away money received from agents of Polish State Security Urząd Bezpieczeństwa (UB), to whom he sold whatever material he came across at AUWE. Later he was passed on to a KGB handler.

Several years earlier, in 1951, Houghton had been a Royal Navy master-at-arms, posted as a civilian assistant to the office of the naval attaché in the British embassy in Warsaw. It apparently passed unnoticed by the embassy security staff that he was an alcoholic financing an extravagant lifestyle by selling on Warsaw's black market Western goods and medical supplies, which made him vulnerable to blackmail by Służba Bezpieczeństwa (SB) – the Polish counter-intelligence service. When Houghton's wife complained to his superiors about domestic abuse, he was posted back to Britain in 1952 and assigned to the secret research establishment at Portland. Warnings by his wife that he brought restricted documents home for an unknown purpose were treated as the bitter allegations of an abused wife, although it should have been obvious Houghton was again living well beyond his means, buying a series of expensive cars and a new house. After, or maybe before, his divorce in 1956 Houghton observed that, although she was a low-grade employee, Ethel Gee had access to a safe in which top secret documents were kept.

She was so bowled over with his attentions that, apparently without major qualms, she 'borrowed' these documents for him to photograph at home and then replaced them before anyone had noticed their absence. Once a month she was rewarded when they both travelled to London, spending the night in a hotel as a married couple. The purpose of the trip was to deliver the monthly haul to a Soviet contact. Unbelievably, in July 1960 Houghton actually introduced Ethel to a man he said was a US Navy commander named Johnson tasked with checking how the Royal Navy was safeguarding secret information received from the US Navy. This was a classic false flag operation for her benefit. How long this might have gone on is anyone's guess had not Houghton and Ethel already been under surveillance by MI5, which warned the base security officer to keep clear and do nothing.

The reason for this was Mikhal Goleniewski, born in 1922 in an area of eastern Poland that is now Belarussian territory, who rose to the rank of lieutenant colonel in the Polish Army in 1955. Receiving a doctorate in political science at the University of Warsaw in 1956, he was appointed head of the Technical and Scientific Department of Ministersvo Bezpieceństwa Publicznego (MBP) – the Polish Ministry of Public Security – from 1957 to 1960. In this position, since MBP was controlled by the KGB, he was required to report to Moscow Centre; in 1959 he became a triple agent, feeding both Polish and Soviet material to the CIA under the code name Sniper without revealing his true identity by using anonymous notes left in dead letter boxes. In April 1959, the CIA informed British counter-espionage agency MI5 that 'Sniper' had revealed the existence of an SB informant in the Royal Navy, with a name that he had overheard just once. It sounded to him like 'Huiton'. 'Sniper' also passed over some copies of documents procured by 'Huiton' which made it obvious that his place of work was AUWE.

In addition, 'Sniper' reported a top-level Soviet penetration of MI6 – which turned out to be the mole George Blake. Fortunately, the rank of 'Sniper' was so high that he learned just in time when the KGB first heard of a mysterious CIA source inside SB and was able to make his well-prepared escape with his mistress to West Berlin at the end of 1960. Once in the West, they were immediately flown to the CIA's Ashford Farm in Maryland for debriefing, in which he revealed a number of other UB or KGB sources inside NATO forces and intelligence agencies. After his defection, Golienewski was sentenced by a Polish court to death *in absentia*. He brought no documents with him, but had already established his bona fide with the stream of leaks while he was still in place, and also revealed the whereabouts of several caches of photographic and other material left behind for eventual retrieval by CIA agents. Given US citizenship, he was placed in a witness protection programme.

On 6 January 1961 Ethel Gee passed to Houghton details of the latest sonar devices for the detection of enemy submarines, which the couple then took to London on the following day. On previous contacts, their MI5 watchers had been able to identify Houghton's controller, using the identity of a Canadian businessman named Gordon Lonsdale, who ran a successful business importing jukeboxes. In a quick brush pass, Houghton would hand him an envelope and receive a different envelope in return. On this occasion, however, all three were arrested on the approach to a bridge over the Thames. The actual arrest was carried out by Special Branch Inspector George G. Smith because, rather oddly, MI5 did not have the authority to arrest anyone. Ethel's shopping bag was found to be stuffed with film, photocopies of classified documents and plans of Britain's first nuclear submarine, HMS *Dreadnought*.

The previous MI5 surveillance of Lonsdale must have been very good because, although trained in fieldcraft, he had not spotted it. His watchers had noted how, after the meetings with Houghton, he would pay a visit to a bungalow in Ruislip, West London. This was the home of Peter and Helen Kroger – a couple posing as antiquarian booksellers. They too had been placed under discreet surveillance. Immediately following the arrests of Lonsdale, Houghton and Gee, Inspector Smith and two colleagues drove out to the house in Cranley Drive, Ruislip, and knocked on the door, pretending they were from the local CID and investigating a spate of burglaries in the neighbourhood. Having gained admittance without alarming the Krogers and giving them time to destroy any evidence, they arrested them. Helen Kroger asked permission to stoke the boiler of the central heating system before leaving the bungalow. The request was transparent to Inspector Smith, who confiscated her handbag, in which was a number of microdots that were to have been pasted into antiquarian books posted abroad, disguised as punctuation marks – and which she had been intending to burn in the boiler.

The MI5 searchers found the bungalow to be a veritable spies' nest, with false passports, large sums of money, microfilming equipment and a burst transmitter[188] for communications with

Moscow Centre. So much material was there that it took more than a week for searchers in the crawl space under the house and in the loft to discover the state-of-the-art transmitter. Later residents' building work continued to reveal more hidden espionage equipment years after these events.

Two days after the arrests all five were charged with espionage at Bow Street Magistrate's court, where Houghton tried unsuccessfully to turn Queen's evidence and claimed that he had been forced to do what he had done because a woman with whom he had been having an affair during the posting to Warsaw would otherwise have been thrown in jail and that, after his return to Britain, threats of violence against Ethel and his ex-wife compelled him to continue his treachery.

At the trial starting on 13 March 1961 Ethel seemed at first to believe that what she and her lover had been doing was innocent because Lonsdale was an American naval officer. She and Houghton were sentenced to fifteen years' imprisonment each. Lonsdale was given twenty-five years and the Krogers were each sentenced to twenty years. In 1969 they were exchanged for a British teacher named Gerald Brooke, who had served four years in a hard regime labour camp for unwisely smuggling anti-Soviet material into the USSR. The longest terms were actually served by Gee and Houghton, released in May 1970. They married the following year, Ethel dying in 1984.

At the trial, in true KGB fashion, neither the Krogers nor Lonsdale said a word, but in a statement he tried to clear them by claiming that he had hidden all the espionage equipment in the bungalow while house-sitting there during their absences. Given the contents of Mrs Kroger's handbag there was no chance of that being believed. In any case, fingerprint evidence had already shown that the Krogers 'had previous form' as Morris and Lona Cohen, who had acted as couriers for material stolen from the Manhattan Project – the crime for which Ethel and Julius Rosenberg had been executed – after which they had simply disappeared. Lonsdale's past remained a complete blank, prior to his fictitious identity, starting in Canada in 1954. Even personal letters to his wife and child in the USSR, enlarged from some of Mrs Kroger's microdots, gave little away. Not until his release was negotiated with the KGB three years later did Moscow Centre identify him as Konon T. Molody. On 22 April 1964 he walked across the 'bridge of spies' – the Glienecke Bridge between Berlin and Potsdam – in a swap for British businessman and part-time spy Greville Wynn, who was ill after being held in the far less comfortable conditions of a Soviet labour camp,

As to the Krogers, Mrs K was born Leontine Petke in the USA to a family of Polish immigrants, joined the CPUSA and met Morris Cohen, US-born of Polish–Lithuanian parents, at a party meeting after he returned wounded from the Spanish Civil War in 1938. While in Spain, he had been recruited by Soviet spy Amadeo Sabatini and, in turn, recruited Leontine as a Soviet agent, code-named Vogel, while he was designated the code name Volunteer. After the US entered the war, in 1942 Morris was conscripted, leaving her to set up a network of sub-agents spying in aircraft and armaments factories near New York. She also couriered secret material from Los Alamos to the Soviet embassy in New York, for forwarding on to Moscow.

The defection of Elizabeth Bentley in 1945 caused them and many other Soviet spies in the USA to be ordered to lie low for a while, but they were back on active service by the beginning of 1949, working with Rudolf Abel aka Emil Goldfuss, aka Martin Collins and true name William Fischer. Ordered by Moscow to return home in 1950, they travelled via Mexico back to the USSR, reappearing in the West four years later with New Zealand passports as Mr and Mrs Kroger, antiquarian book dealers. It was a brilliant cover identity: nobody would think New Zealanders would spy on the mother country and dealers in old books are almost the last people to be suspected of espionage.

On 19 July 1985 the British Secret Intelligence Service 'lifted' KGB mole Colonel Oleg Gordievskii by spiriting him across the Soviet–Finnish border in a split-second operation that would only work once. Gordievskii having been the *rezident* in the Soviet embassy in London it is likely there was a connection between his arrival in the West and the apprehension one month later of a 'typically suburban' couple using the names Reinhard and Sonja Schulze, although some sources aver that the tip-off came from West Germany's Bundesnachrichtendienst (BND). Whichever is true, they were arrested at their rented home, 249 Waye Avenue in Cranford, near London's Heathrow Airport. The husband was a talented kitchen designer, highly valued by his employer and popular with his clients; his wife worked as a technical translator. Reinhard had come to Britain with a West German passport in 1980, concealing the fact that he also held papers in the name of Bryan Strunze, the British-born son of a German father and English mother, who had disappeared on a visit to the GDR. The false Schulze rented an apartment for a few months and followed a postal course in interior design. Although without visible means of income, he seemed to have plenty of cash. After leaving the country briefly, he returned with Sonja posing as his fiancée, whom he said he had met while on holiday in Ireland. They married in Hounslow Registry Office, where he gave his age as 32; she stated hers as 29 and gave her maiden name as Ilona Hammer.

After renting the house in Cranford, they were an unre-markable couple to the neighbours and a pair of grey ghosts to monitors in GCHQ recording undecipherable Morse code blocks of five-figure groups from a short-wave transmitter sited somewhere near Berlin giving the newly-weds their instructions. When the house in Waye Avenue was raided by Special Branch officers a large collection of detailed maps was found, especially focusing on flight paths into Heathrow and other important British airports, together with many British town plans. Various agencies took the house to pieces, the most incriminating find being inside a can of aerosol in the garden shed, where partly-used one-time pads were concealed. These had served to decipher the incoming Morse transmissions picked up in Cheltenham. Whether they permitted the deciphering of the recorded transmissions by staff at GCHQ was not revealed, but it would have been usual procedure to destroy the used sheets associated with those transmissions. A short-wave receiver and tape recorder were also found, but no transmitter. Well secreted in the lining of a holdall was what appeared to be an escape kit containing false passports for the couple under different names and a supply of cash.

Although one HVA agent had escaped the net just before arrest in 1984, these were the first satellite country spies to be caught red-handed in Britain since the Lonsdale–Houghton–Kroger network was broken up in 1961. Several of their trips abroad were followed by large cash deposits in their bank accounts. Under routine questioning, Reinhard was tripped up by his ignorance of the British family of the real Reinhard Schulze, after which, although refusing to talk about their real activities, they admitted using false papers on entry into Britain.

According to a BBC newsflash dated 28 August 1985, the couple appeared before Horseferry Road magistrates court in London, did not request bail and were remanded in custody. Identified as GDR citizens, they were duly charged under the Official Secrets Act with 'possessing documents detrimental to the public interest'. Both then and during their subsequent nine-day trial at the Old Bailey, they refused to answer any questions about what they had been doing in Britain and the investigating officers were said to be so baffled by the trail of false identities that they had no idea who the couple really were. Yet Schulze requested that the GDR Embassy be informed of their arrest and, after they were each sentenced to ten years' imprisonment for preparing an espionage operation for an unidentified foreign power, the Third Secretary at the embassy visited them every week in jail. Under a swap of which the details were not disclosed, they were released and deported from Britain in 1991.

19

Women in the
War Between the States

The American Civil War, fought between 12 April 1861 and 9 May 1865, was caused by the secession from the United States of America of eleven southern states, known collectively as the Confederacy, which clashed with the determination of the dominant, industrialised northern states that they had no right to do so.

In America, the Confederate Army eventually numbered 1 million men, against Union armies totalling 2.1 million men. Included in that rough figure were reputed to be some hundreds of women disguised as men, who joined up to keep an eye on their conscripted menfolk or to avenge their deaths. The usual images of the conflict are of exhausted soldiers in uniform at camp, on the march, standing to before an attack and – in Matthew Brady's iconic glass plate photographs – lying dead where they fell. And fall they did by the thousand, after the invention by the Frenchman, Captain Minié, of the more accurate bullet that bore his name and was fired from rifled gun barrels, which replaced the spherical balls fired from smoothbore muskets. According to the record, 620,000 men died in the war, roughly in the ratio of one in battle to two from disease and other causes. A small number of women, inspired by mothers, grandmothers or aunts who had given birth in covered wagons on the long trail west, considered that one more pair of hands to hold a rifle was neither here nor there, and chose a more dangerous way to support the side they favoured by spying for it, some writing books about their experiences later when it was safe to do so.

Quakers have been active in human rights in many theatres of war – none more so than Elizabeth Van Lew of Richmond, Virginia. Born in 1818 into a slave-owning family, Elizabeth attended a Quaker school, where she was taught that slavery was evil. After her father died in 1843, her brother, John, took over the family hardware business and emancipated the family's nine slaves, employing some of them as paid servants. John also attended Richmond's slave market, frequently purchasing whole families in danger of being split up by sale to different buyers – and freed them all. Elizabeth's inheritance of $10,000 – a considerable sum in those days – was spent buying and freeing relatives of her family's former slaves. When the war began with the attack on Fort Sumter on 12 April 1861, Elizabeth wrote in her diary how the outburst of war fever made her think of the mobs in the French Revolution. Describing this in her diary, she quoted from Luke 23:34 'They know not what they do.'

Early in the war, with many Union soldiers locked up in makeshift prisons around Richmond, she and her mother took food and clothing to them, which earned much local ill feeling for them. Elizabeth also helped some prisoners to escape and sheltered them as well as Confederate deserters in a secret room between the walls of the family mansion. Setting up a spy ring to pass Confederate war plans to the North, Elizabeth bribed civil servants and politicians. She also managed to place one of her emancipated slaves named Mary Bowser as a servant in the Confederate White House, to use her photographic memory and eavesdrop on strategy conferences for Elizabeth's reports to the Union leader, General Benjamin Butler.

When Union forces captured the burned out ruins of Richmond in April 1865, the Van Lews raised a Union flag and invited General Ulysses S. Grant to tea. Discretion would have been a better policy as cosying up to the victors brought home to all her neighbours the extent and importance of Elizabeth's espionage during the war. As a result, the family was ostracised. There is a belief that she managed to obtain from Washington the records of her spy ring, in order to destroy them, but no proof is available. Elizabeth never married and died at 81 years of age in 1900 after three and a half decades of being despised by her neighbours as a traitor to the Southern cause. Shortly before her death, her nieces dug up the old wartime diary she had buried in the garden, but much was missing.

It is impossible to tell – perhaps it always was – whether more women spied for the North or the South because most agents tend to keep silent after hostilities have ended. In May of 1843 or 1844 a girl was born in Martinsburg – some 90 miles north-west of Washington DC and now in the state of West Virginia. She was given the names Maria Isabella Boyd, but nicknamed Belle Boyd. No known relation of the author, she was a strong-willed and spirited tomboy, whose idea of arriving at a party given by her parents, which she had been told she was too young to attend, was to ride into the house during it on her pony, declaring boldly that her pony was surely old enough to attend, and she was merely riding it.

Her father was a prosperous merchant, who paid for his several children to have good classical educations. At Mount

Washington Female College in Baltimore, Belle acquired some Latin and Greek. Having enjoyed a 'coming out' ball as a debutante, when the civil war broke out in 1861, Belle and her family defied pro-Union Martinsburg by sympathising with the Southern cause. Belle's father volunteered for the 2nd Virginia Infantry under General 'Stonewall' Jackson as a common soldier so that a less prosperous man, whose family might suffer hardship during his absence, could claim an officer's pay and emoluments.

However, on 3 July 1861 Union troops occupied the town. On the following day, some soldiers entered the Boyd family home searching for Confederate flags reputed to be hidden there. One of the men insulted Belle's mother in very coarse language. As the daughter of the house explained, 'All our men being with the army, we ladies were obliged to go armed to protect ourselves as best we might.' Belle whipped out her pistol and shot the man, who died shortly afterwards. Given her youth and the circumstances – these were early days in the war, when gallantry still governed officers' attitudes to women – the Union commander pardoned her action, but sentries were posted around the house and officers kept close track of her activities. Typically, Belle took advantage of this contact, charming at least one of the officers into revealing military secrets that she sent across the lines in a hollow watch case carried by her slave, Eliza Hopewell. On this first attempt at spying they were caught and told they could be sentenced to death, but were pardoned.

Perhaps that gave Belle a sense of invulnerability because she started systematically eavesdropping on the occupation forces and writing down what she heard of the Union Army's plans. These notes were carried through the lines by Eliza to General Jackson's camp, which was only 7 miles away. When one of the letters was intercepted and the slave questioned, Belle was in trouble again, but played the card of her youth and was merely warned not to do it again. The warning had no effect. Before her 18th birthday, Belle crossed the lines to nurse wounded Confederate soldiers of General Jackson's army after the first major battle of the war at Bull Run in July 1861, in which the Confederate victory was largely due to her information. She was out riding with two young officers after this, when her horse bolted and carried her back into Union territory. In the book she wrote afterwards about her adventures, she was careful to explain to her English readers that for a girl of her age to ride unchaperoned with young gentlemen in America was not considered a breach of decorum.

The Confederates being dubbed 'rebels' by the North, her exploits made her notorious as *la belle rebelle*. This publicity led to her being tried and imprisoned, but the inability of her all-male Unionist judges to believe a young girl capable of independent action in wartime saw her released after a week. She next hit the headlines in May of 1862, when she sneaked into a hotel at Front Royal to listen in while a Union general was briefing his officers. That night, she used false papers to ride through the lines and report what she had heard, which enabled the Confederates to take Front Royal next day. Arrested on 29 July 1862, she was locked up in Washington's Old Capitol Prison for a month. She was released on 29 August and exchanged for Union POWs at Fort Monroe. In the following year, she would be locked up in the same jail for five months. Also incarcerated there was D.A. Mahoney, editor of the *Iowa Herald*, who wrote:

Among the prisoners in the Old Capitol prison when I reached there was the somewhat famous Belle Boyd, to whom has been attributed the defeat of General Banks, in the Shenandoah Valley, by Stonewall Jackson. Belle, as she is familiarly called by all the prisoners, and affectionately so by the Confederates, was arrested and imprisoned as a spy.

Belle was put in solitary confinement, but allowed to have her cell door open, and to sit outside of it in a hall or stair-landing in the evening. Fronting on the same hall or stair-landing were three other rooms, all filled to their capacity with prisoners, mostly Confederate officers. Several of these were personally acquainted with Belle. In the evenings these prisoners were permitted to crowd inside of their room-doors, whence they could see and sometimes exchange a word with Belle. When this liberty was not allowed, she contrived to procure a large marble, around which she would tie a note, written on tissue-paper, and, when the guard turned his back to patrol his beat in the hall, she would roll the marble into one of the open doors of the Confederate prisoners' rooms. When the contents were read and noted, a missive would be written in reply, and the marble, similarly burdened as it came, would be rolled back to Belle. Thus was a correspondence established and kept up between Belle and her fellow-prisoners, till a more convenient and effective mode was discovered.

Belle's situation was a peculiarly trying one. If she kept her room, a solitary prisoner, her health, and probably her mind, would become affected by the confinement and solitude; and if she indulged herself by sitting outside her cell door, she became exposed to the gaze of more than a hundred prisoners, nearly all of them strangers to her, and many of them her enemies by the laws of war.[189]

Released, Belle realised that she had made herself too well known to continue her line crossing. Using the alias of 'Mrs Lewis', she volunteered to take dispatches to neutral Britain by ship in May 1884, when the war still had one more terrible

year to run, but the *Greyhound* – the Confederate vessel on which
she was travelling – was intercepted by the USS *Connecticut*, a
Union blockade ship. Before the Union prize crew came aboard,
Belle managed to cast overboard the dispatches she was carrying.
The Union officer taking command of the prize was Lieutenant
Samuel Wilde Hardinge, who fell in love with his charis-
matic prisoner on the voyage north to New York and Boston.
Although it has been said that Belle was just trying to seduce
him to change allegiance to the Confederate cause, in her book
she states that they were both in love and determined to marry.
It was this episode that gained her another epithet: the Cleopatra
of the Secession. Her gallant suitor was court-martialled, not
for his attentions to Belle, but for allowing the captain of the
Greyhound to escape at Boston.

For some time, Belle's fate hung in the balance as the Union
authorities debated whether to incarcerate her again or have her
escorted to neutral Canadian territory under sentence of death
if she should ever return to the United States. The Canadian
solution won, but Belle's spirit was unbroken. Travelling via
Toronto and Quebec, she again took ship for England. On
contacting a Confederate agent in London, she learned that
Lieutenant Hardinge had been looking for her there, and gone
on to Paris, thinking she might be in France. That problem
resolved by the new-fangled telegraph, they were married in
London on 25 August 1864 but, after the bridegroom returned
to America, he was arrested as a deserter from the Union navy
and harshly imprisoned, for part of the time in shackles. Some
time in 1865, he died, leaving Belle to describe herself as 'a war
widow with one child' – a daughter by Hardinge. Apparently
in dire financial straits, Belle set to and wrote a two-volume
book entitled *Belle Boyd, in Camp and Prison*.[190]

How much Belle received from sales of her book is moot. Even Charles Dickens had difficulty, dunning publishers for his dues. What is known is that, after the war, Belle began a new career on the stage, where her notoriety as the daring Confederate girl spy stood her in good stead, both in England and on her return to America. In 1866 another former Union officer named Hammond fell in love with Belle and married her in 1869. After she bore him four children in fifteen years, that marriage ended in divorce. Her third marriage to a younger fellow-actor named Nathaniel High in 1885 seems not to have prospered because she returned to the stage the following year, both acting and giving lectures about her spying career to members of the Grand Army of the Republic, a veterans' organisation for former Union soldiers. During a performance in Wisconsin, she died on stage on 11 June 1900, aged 56 or 57, a trooper to the last.

When the war between the states broke out in April 1861 Rose O'Neal Greenhow was no impulsive teenager like Belle Boyd, but a mature 48-year-old mother of four daughters who had moved to Washington from the Maryland plantation of her slave-owning family after her father was murdered when she was only 4 years old. The Greenhows moved in the best political and social circles in Washington, which enabled Rose to cull important military information from her contacts and pass these to Union Captain Thomas Jordan.

Disapproving of Union policy, he resigned his commission and headed south to enlist for the Confederacy. Before leaving Washington, he asked Rose to take over his team of Confederate sympathisers in Washington and gave her a simple code in which to encipher her despatches sent to the Confederate armies. Exposed as a spy in August 1861, Rose was placed under house arrest, but managed to continue running her spy ring despite surveillance after sending her three older daughters away so that they should not suffer if she were arrested.

She was right to do so. The founder of the soon to be famous Pinkerton detective agency, Allan Pinkerton, was on her trail. Watching the comings and goings at her home, he concluded that she belonged to a circle of Southern sympathisers. Searching the house, he found evidence of her spying in the form of confidential documents and drafts of coded messages to Captain Jordan. Placed under house arrest, Rose continued compiling and sending reports to Jordan, unaware that Pinkerton was intercepting them and introducing misinformation. However, leaving Rose in her own home made people suspect that she was being too leniently treated, so in January 1862 Rose was locked up in the Old Capitol Prison. As a special concession, her youngest daughter – aged 8 and known as Little Rose – was allowed to stay with her. At the end of May, Rose and Little Rose were released without trial and deported to Confederate territory, travelling on to Richmond, Virginia, where President Jefferson Davis hailed her as a heroine for the Southern cause. In 1863 Rose volunteered to travel to France and Britain, canvassing support for the South. The outward leg went well, with her ship successfully running the Northern blockade.

While in France, Rose was received by Emperor Napoleon III and in London by Queen Victoria. While in London, to raise funds, she completed a memoir she had been preparing, which was published under the title *My Imprisonment and the First Year of Abolition Rule at Washington*.[191] On 19 August 1864 Rose set sail on a British blockade runner that on 1 October ran aground near Wilmington, North Carolina, while being chased by a Union gunboat, the USS *Niphon*. Whether Rose's panic was a fear of being reincarcerated or that she would be robbed of all the proceeds of the sales of her book, which amounted to $2,000 and was secreted in her clothing, is unknown. She persuaded some sailors to take her in a rowing boat to the shore, where her pursuers dared not set foot, but a wave overturned the boat. Weighed down by her clothes and the gold, Rose drowned. When her body was recovered, also on her was a copy of her book – perhaps for publication in America, and a note for her daughter. She was buried with military honours at Wilmington.

The most bizarre account of a female agent spying in the civil war is that of 20-year-old Canadian citizen Emma Edmonds, who volunteered for the Union Army as a male nurse named Frank Thompson, wearing men's clothing. When a Confederate sniper shot dead Lieutenant James Vesey, with whom Emma was in love, she determined to avenge his death. Still dressed as a man and identified as Frank Thompson, she was grilled by a panel of Union officers to assess her suitability to spy and also had to pass a firearms test. Accepted, she bought some old clothes, stained her face, neck, hands and arms black with silver nitrate, had her own hair shaved off and purchased a wig to give herself the appearance of a black male slave, in which disguise she infiltrated the Confederate lines, armed with just a small revolver.

Joining a group of slaves building fortifications for the Confederates, she copied plans of the defences on a paper hidden inside a shoe. She also recognised a pedlar who frequently travelled in Union territory, and realised that he was spying there for the Confederates. In her book *Nurse and Spy in the Union Army*,[192] she alleged that he was the man who enabled the sniper to kill Lieutenant Vesey. Her first mission lasted only three days because the silver nitrate began to fade in sunlight, but she returned eleven more times under various other disguises. Falling ill with a bout of malaria, she finally abandoned this work, fearing that any hospitalisation would result in her sex being discovered by the enemy.

After treatment for the malaria, she discovered that her alter ego Frank Thompson was wanted for desertion, which was a capital offence, and reverted to woman's dress, working as a nurse in a hospital for wounded soldiers at Washington. Incredibly, after all these adventures, in 1867 Emma settled down to married life with a mechanic who was a fellow Canadian and bore him three children. In 1886 she was awarded a pension of $12 a month for her service to the Union cause and given an honourable discharge as Frank Thompson. In September 1898, one year after being admitted as the sole woman member of the Grand Army of the Republic, she died in Texas and was buried in Houston.

20

'Intrigues Best Carried
On by Ladies'

Two clear centuries before the American Civil War – in the time when European settlers in North America numbered only a few thousand and New York was a Dutch colony called Nieuw Amsterdam – England was itself in the throes of a civil war that raged, off and on, from 1642 to 1651 and was just as bitterly contested. Indeed, the vengeance of King Charles II on those he considered responsible for the execution of his father, Charles I, produced the biggest manhunt in English history, with the new monarch's agents tracking down fugitives all over Europe and in North America, to kill them.[193]

Most images we have of the English Civil War are of flamboyant Cavaliers and unsmiling Roundheads, as in the Victorian tear-jerker painting of the little royalist boy being menacingly interrogated, with the question, 'And when did you last see your father?' This was an age ruled by maleness and privilege. Cromwell's men were fighting against royal privilege, but they shared their enemies' unquestioning assumption of male superiority, with which some women were beginning to disagree. One of these political pioneers was Katherine Chidley, a Leveller or proto-democrat, who in 1649 led a demonstration of several hundred women to Parliament, protesting successfully against the continued imprisonment of Leveller activist John Lilburne despite him having been cleared of charges of treason. Their petition justified their activities thus:

> The Humble Petition of divers well-affected women of the citis of London and Westminster, etc, Showeth that since we are assured of our creation in the image of God, and of an interest in Christ equal unto men, as also of a proportional share in the freedoms of this Commonwealth, we cannot but wonder that we should appear so despicable in your eyes, as to be thought unworthy to petition or represent our grievances to this honourable House.[194]

When Lilburne was tried a second time in 1653, another petition, signed by 6,000 of these women, evoked the reply that Parliament could not take notice of it because they were 'women and many of them wives, so that the Law took no notice of them.'[195] This can have come as no news to the petitioners, some of whom realised during the civil war that they had a decided advantage in clandestine activity, because most men would 'take no notice of them'.

That women chose to fight in this conflict with weapons in their hands is evident from King Charles I's ordinance of 1643 forbidding them from disguising themselves as men in order to take up arms. Yet some women defied this ordinance – on both sides. A famous example is that of Jane Ingleby of Ripley Castle in North Yorkshire, who is said to have charged with the king's cavalry at the battle of Marston Moor. Many other women travelled with the armies to accompany their husbands or as camp followers and took up arms when hard pressed.

Wars have done more to liberate women than all the peace-time politicking. During the Crusades many a noble wife took command of her husband's fief while the men were away in Outremer, many never to return. Similarly, during the English Civil War, numerous aristocratic women took command of home or castle while their husbands were away fighting with the royalist armies. Lady Mary Bankes held the important Corfe Castle in Dorset for the king throughout a three-year siege, she and her household women hurling rocks and burning coals down on the attacking besiegers, causing 100 casualties. On 2 May 1643, during his absence 'on the king's business', Baron Thomas Arundell charged his 61-year-old wife, Lady Blanche Arundell, to defend Wardour Castle, near Salisbury, with twenty-five trained men and the household servants. On 2 May 1643 a parliamentarian force of 1,300 men under Sir Edward Hungerford arrived with artillery and sappers to undermine the walls. Hungerford demanding to enter the castle and search for royalists hidden there, Lady Blanche refused and held out with the help of her domestics and the handful of trained men for about a week,[196] at the end of which time the castle was so damaged by the besiegers' artillery as to be uninhabitable. Lady Blanche agreed to surrender, was taken prisoner and confined in Dorchester. Her husband having died of wounds after the battle of Lansdowne, it was her son, Henry, who returned to besiege his own castle, causing much further damage and forcing the parliamentarian garrison to surrender in March 1644.

French-born Lady Charlotte Stanley became a legend for her very hands-on defence of her home, Lathom House near Ormskirk, in the absence of her husband, Earl Stanley. This was the last remaining royalist hold-out in Lancashire at the time: an impressive fortress, with eighteen towers [197] and outer walls 6ft thick. Commanding 300 men inside the walls, Lady

Charlotte refused to surrender when surrounded by General Sir Thomas Fairfax's force of 500 cavalry and 1,500 foot soldiers in February 1644. Displaying considerable generalship, she divided her defenders into guardians of the walls day and night and a corps of sharpshooters, sniping at the besiegers, to demoralise them.

On 27 May Prince Rupert of the Rhine arrived with a superior force to lift the siege, Lady Charlotte and her household afterwards taking refuge on the Isle of Man, of which Earl Stanley was the lord. With him in parliamentarian hands, she offered to exchange the island for his life, but he was beheaded at Bolton and she found herself facing an uprising of the Manx people, who had no wish to become English as payment for a foreign overlord's life. At this point she surrendered, perhaps the last royalist commander to do so in the first phase of the civil war.

Born into a very cultured family, Jane Cavendish was both poet and playwright in her own right. Her father having fled to France after the royalist defeat at Marston Moor, she and her sisters surrendered Welbeck Abbey to the parliamentarians in August 1644. After it was recaptured by the king's army, they had the honour of entertaining Charles I there twice in the following year. Following Charles' execution, their father being considered a traitor, the sisters were placed under house arrest and closely watched, which did not stop Jane conducting clandestine correspondence with other royalist sympathisers.

Lady Anne Dalkeith served King Charles I in a traditionally feminine, but politically very important way. Being a godmother to Charles' youngest daughter, Princess Henrietta, and with Queen Henrietta Maria having fled to safety in France, Anne regarded the royal, but not very healthy, infant as her personal responsibility. In April 1646, after being besieged in

Exeter by parliamentary forces, she refused to escort the princess to house arrest in London, instead disguising herself and the girl as peasants to make their way to Dover, there to take ship to France and safety. On the way, the princess innocently blurted out that she was not accustomed to being dressed in such shabby clothes, which nearly gave the game away. Once in France, and appointed governess to Princess Henrietta, Anne lived in the émigré court at St-Germain-en-Laye for the following five years, despite wagging tongues alleging that she was one of the king's mistresses.

Lady Anne Halkett was instrumental in arranging the escape from parliamentarian London of Charles I's 15-year-old son, James, Duke of York – who later came to the throne as James II. Fortunately, Lady Jane was a great writer and keeper of diaries. In her manuscript autobiography she records this dangerous deed after royalist Colonel Bampfield, referred to as 'C.B.', confessed that he was still under the king's orders and:

> Att this time hee had frequentt letters from the King, who imployed him in severall affaires, butt that of the greatest concerne which hee was imployed in was to contrive the Duke of Yorke's escape outt of St James (where his Highnese and the Duke of Glocester and the Princese Elizabeth lived under the care of the Earle of Northumberland and his lady). The dificultys of itt was represented by C. B.; but his Majestie still pressed itt, and I remember this expresion was in one of the letters: – 'I beleeve itt will bee deficult, and if hee miscary in the attempt itt will bee the greatest afliction that can arive to mee; butt I looke upon James's escape as Charles's preservation, and nothing can content mee more; therfore bee carefull what you doe.'
>
> This letter, amongst others, hee showed mee, and where the King aproved of his choice of mee to intrust with itt, for to

gett the Duke's cloaths made, and to drese him in his disguise.
So now all C. B.'s busynese and care was how to manage this
busynese of so important concerne, which could not bee performed without severall persons' concurrence in itt, for hee
beeing generally knowne as one whose stay att London was in
order to serve the King, few of those who were intrusted by
the Parliament in puplicke concernes durst owne convearse
or hardly civility to him, lest they should have beene suspect
by there party, which made itt deficult for him to gett accese
to the Duke. Having comunicated the designe to a gentleman
attending his Highnese, who was full of honor and fidelity,
by [this] meanes hee had private accese to the Duke, to whom
hee presented the King's letter and order to his Highnese for
consenting to act what C. B. should contrive for his escape,
which was so cheerfully intertained and so readily obayed,
that being once designed there was nothing more to doe than
to prepare all things for the execution.

I had desired C.B. to take a ribban with him and bring mee
the bignese of the Duke's wast and his lengh, to have cloaths
made fitt for him. When I gave the measure to my tailor to
inquire how much mohaire would serve to make a petticoate
and wastcoate to a young gentlewoman of that bignese and
stature, hee considered itt a long time, and said hee had made
many gownes and suites, butt hee had never made any to such
a person in his life. I thought hee was in the right; butt his
meaning was, hee had never seene any woman of so low a
stature have so big a wast; however hee made itt as exactly
fitt as if hee had taken the measure himselfe. Itt was a mixed
mohaire of a light haire couler and blacke, and the under-pet-
ticoate was scarlett. All things beeing now ready, upon the 20
of Aprill, 1648, in the evening, was the time resolved on for
the Duke's escape.[2]

Itt was designed for a week before every night as soon as the Duke had suped hee and those servants that attended his Highnese (till the Earle of Northumberland and the rest of the howse had suped) wentt to play hide and seek, and sometimes hee would hide himselfe so well that in halfe an howers time they could not find him. His Highnese had so used them to this, that when hee wentt really away they thought hee was butt att the usuall sport.

A litle before the Duke wentt to super that night hee called for the gardiner, who only had a treble key besides that which the Duke had, and bid him give him that key till his owne was mended, which hee did. And after his Highnese had suped, hee imeadiately called to goe to the play, and wentt downe the privy staires into the garden, and opened the gate that goes into the parke, treble locking all the doores behind him. And att the garden gate C. B. [Colonel Bampfield] waited for his Highnese, and putting on a cloake and periwig huried him away to the parke gate, where a coach waited that caried them to the watter side, and, taking the boate that was apointed for that service, they rowed to the staires next the bridge, where I and Miriam waited in a private howse hard by that C. B. had prepared for dresing his Highnese, where all things were in a readinese.

C. B. had desired mee, if they came nott there precisely by ten a'clocke, to shift for my selfe, for then I might conclude they were discovered. Though ten a'clock did strike, and hee that was intrusted offten wentt to the landing place and saw noe boate coming, asked mee what I would doe. I told him I came there with a resolution to serve his Highness, and I was fully determined nott to leave that place till I was outt of hopes, and would take my hazard.

Hee left mee to goe againe to the watter side, and while I was fortifying myselfe against what might arive to mee, I heard a great noise of many as I thought comming up staires, which I expected to be soldiers to take mee, but it was a pleasing disapointmentt, for the first that came in was the Duke, who with much joy I took in my armes and gave God thankes for his safe arivall. His Highnese called "Quickely quickely dress me;" and, putting of his cloaths, I dresed him in the women's habitt that was prepared, which fitted his Highnese very well, and [he] was very pretty in itt. Affter hee had eaten something his Highnese wentt crose the bridge to the staires where the barge lay, C. B. leading him; and imediately the boatemen plied the oare so well that they were soone outt of sight, having both wind and tide with them.[198]

Anne had taken a potentially mortal risk, and was to wait many years for her reward. Keeping herself in the meantime by practising medicine and acting as governess to a noble family, she was eventually awarded a pension when the prince she had saved came to the throne as James II in 1685.

Described as a tall, well-fashioned and well-languaged gentlewoman with a round, pockmarked face, Jane Whorwood was a red-haired and very spirited woman who carried to extremes her loyalty to King Charles I. The wife of an Oxfordshire squire who had fled to the Continent, she lived with her son and daughter in his family property, Holton House, near Oxford, where Charles I's court was established. She was of mixed English–Flemish–Scottish stock, the last blood perhaps accounting for her loyalty to this Scottish king precariously seated on an English throne. As uninhibited as she was courageous, in all the turmoil of besieged Oxford in 1643, 31-year-old Jane took as her lover Sir Thomas Bendish,[199] later to be Charles II's ambassador to Turkey.

Executing what Charles II's Lord Chancellor Edward Hyde, Lord Clarendon, called in his history of the civil war 'intrigues which, at that time, could be best managed and carried on by ladies',[200] she smuggled funds to Charles I at his wartime headquarters in Oxford and later twice arranged his escape from imprisonment, coming within an ace of saving his head from the block by spiriting him away to the Continent. In these enterprises, Jane collaborated with another Scottish lady, Kate d'Aubigny, who used her feminine advantages to plead she needed to wind up her husband's business affairs in London in order to carry to the capital Charles' mandate for a rebellion there during the spring of 1643. Grand ladies travelling in their private coaches were known to obtain passports to go between royalist Oxford and London without much difficulty, aided by the fact that they were women and thus not suspect – and also by the illiteracy of the parliamentary sentries, impressed by any document with a seal held in an imperious, gloved hand. However, Kate was caught in the act and sentenced to a year in the Tower, after which she was released to return to Oxford.

One ruse that Jane Whorwood employed to smuggle funds into Oxford was to persuade a laundress to secrete gold in barrels of soap that passed through the Parliamentary blockade outside Oxford. Quantities of soap were required because the inadequate diet inside the siege lines produced widespread constipation and the soap was used as a laxative. The gold came from Sir Paul Pindar, made immensely rich by his interests in the East India Company and mining in Africa. In 1644 alone, Jane brought £77,000 worth of his gold to Oxford for the king's war chest in this way. Historian John Fox calculated that this shipment was 2,073 pounds *troy*, which translates to more than $25 million in current value.

When Charles I was locked up in Carisbrooke Castle on the Isle of Wight in the summer of 1648, she managed to have access to his chamber for what he referred to as 'swiving' in their private correspondence,[201] where he addressed her as 'sweete Jane Whorwood' and she signed her enciphered messages to him as 'N', '390', '409' and '715'[202] The king wrote to their accomplice William Hopkins, 'You may freely trust Whorwood in anything that concerns my service, for I have had perfect trial of her friendship to me. I cannot be more confident of any.' In addition to sharing his bed, Jane was actively planning and arranging his escape, spending five weeks aboard a ship moored on the tidal flats of the River Swale, daily expecting his arrival, to spirit him away to Berwick or Holland. However, his escape from the castle on a dark night when the guards had been given an allowance of wine went awry because news of the plot had leaked to his jailors, who moved him from a ground floor room to an upper floor, from which there was no easy egress. There was also a mutiny in the navy and unrest throughout Kent at the time, which would have complicated the hell-for-leather cross-country ride necessary for the king to reach Jane on the Swale.

On the night of 29 May, Charles was dripping smuggled nitric acid on the lead sealing the bar of his window into the stone sill, in the hope of loosening it and making his escape anyhow, when the commander of Carisbrooke, Colonel Hammond, entered the room and offered 'to take leave of Your Majesty, for I hear you are going away'.[203] The conspirators waiting for the king below with horses were chased off with musket fire and the whole delicate fabric of the enterprise collapsed, the Marquess of Hertford writing to Jane's brother-in-law, Lord Lanark: 'Had the rest done their parts as carefully as Whorwood, the king would have been at large.'[204]

Several more rescue plans fell by the wayside as pressure in the parliamentary camp for Charles' execution built up. Shortly before the now forbidden festivity of Christmas he was moved under heavy security to Windsor Castle, a scheme of Kate d'Aubigny's to smuggle him out of Bagshot Park en route also failing. From Windsor, Charles was ferried down the Thames to London and shuttled between house arrest under armed guard in the former St James's Palace[205] and Westminster, which made rescue virtually impossible. After his trial, he was executed at Whitehall on 30 January 1649.

For her services to the dead monarch, the House of Commons voted on 25 June 1651 to fine Jane the enormous sum of £600, with her to be held in prison until the fine was paid. In November 1645 Jane's husband returned to England and took as his mistress a servant girl called Katherine Allen, living at Holton House in an uneasy *ménage à trois*. Household servants later testified that for the following five years he 'beat and abused' Jane so that her face and breasts were frequently black and blue. For some time he kept her locked in the tower of the house, referring to her in public as 'whore, bitch and jade'.

After the Restoration of the monarchy, Charles II returned to London and his father's throne on his birthday, 29 May 1660. Jane was then rewarded by him with a generous pension of £1,000 per annum and a gift from Parliament of £1,000 in recognition of her past services to the new monarch. After marrying Sir Clement Fisher in December 1663, Jane seems, like so many royal pensioners, to have suffered non-payment of her pension. She died aged 72 in 1689, leaving a personal estate worth just £10.

Not all women were for the king. In late 1642 hundreds of London women helped dig trenches around the city to keep the royalist cavalry at bay. Ironically, the Dorset town of Lyme, given the honorific 'Regis', meaning 'of the king', by Edward I in 1284, was also pro-Parliament. In the seven-week siege of Lyme by royalist forces (April–May 1644) more than 400 towns-women took over the civil defence, fighting the fires caused by flaming arrows while the men were manning the town walls. The royalists being on high ground outside the walls, a number of women were killed or maimed by sharpshooters as they fought the flames. The intensity of the incoming fire is evidenced by the large collection of leaden musket balls in the municipal museum and private collections. The women also took turns as sentries on the town walls, reloading muskets for their menfolk and, on occasion, firing them at the besiegers. During one lull in the fighting, they also made a sortie to level some of the enemy earthworks with picks and shovels.

The Puritan Lady Brilliana Harley defended Brampton Bryan Castle in Herefordshire against the royalists during a three-month siege in the absence of her husband, Sir Robert Harley, who was an MP and Secretary of State. The castle had not been attacked for the first eleven months of the civil war but, being situated in a largely royalist region, Lady Brilliana's tenants were obliged by the sheriff of Hereford to pay their rents to him on pain of being sent to jail if they refused. Neighbours and troops of parliamentary soldiers drove off livestock and destroyed crops in a campaign of harassment that climaxed on 26 July 1643 when 700 soldiers surrounded the castle itself.

Refusing all offers of surrender, Lady Brilliana conducted a competent defence with three of her children and 100 men, about half of them civilians, in conditions that deteriorated daily. All outlying buildings were destroyed and the castle roofs shot away by the besiegers' cannon. Despite musket fire at anyone showing himself on the battlements, the defenders' lost only one man killed and a few wounded while the enemy suffered the better part of 100 casualties. The siege was lifted on 9 September when the royalist troops departed to reinforce the attack on Gloucester. Brilliana ordered her tenants to level the abandoned siegeworks and rather provocatively despatched forty men to attack a nearby royalist camp. She died shortly afterwards and thus never saw the return of the royalists in the following year, resulting in almost complete destruction of the castle in the second siege.

Jane Lane – later Lady Jane Fisher – anticipated Fiona MacDonald's rescue of Bonnie Prince Charlie nearly a century later after the rising of 1745. A sister of Colonel John Lane, she was 25 years old and described as highly intelligent but not pretty when Charles II was on the run after the battle of Worcester in 1651 with a reward of £1,000 on his head – and the loss of her head, had she been caught. Taking refuge in the Lanes' family home, Bentley Hall near Walsall, Charles was more than 6ft tall and very recognisable, so to disguise him as a woman would have been impossible. It was also forbidden for Catholics such as Jane to travel more than 5 miles from their homes without a pass from the sheriff of their county. Jane had such a pass, permitting her and a servant to travel to Bristol to visit a relation who was having a baby. It seemed to the king's close advisers that this would enable him to take ship there, so the monarch was dressed as a servant, given the alias William Jackson and off they set, apparently both riding the same horse.

Perhaps because of that, at Bromsgrove the horse needed to be re-shod. In the guise of servant, Charles took it to a farrier, who chatted while shoeing the horse, obliging Charles to agree that all royalty needed their heads cutting off, as his father's had been. After a series of unnerving encounters with parliamentary troops en route, they reached the outskirts of Bristol on 12 September, staying for three days with friends of Jane. In the house was a man who had been at the battle of Worcester and presumably recognised the king, but stated that he was taller than Jane's 'servant'. Finding a ship for Charles proved impossible because the Bristol port authorities were too vigilant, so he and a companion headed south in the hope of finding a vessel in Lyme Regis or Weymouth. Jane's friend having miscarried, she was obliged to forge a letter urgently requiring her to return home and departed northwards in the hope that she had not been detected by parliamentary spies. Learning on 14 October that Parliamentarian agents were coming to arrest her, she disguised herself as a simple countrywoman before they arrived and walked cross-country to Yarmouth, finally making it to Paris that December. Made welcome at the émigré court in St-Germain-en-Laye by both Charles and Queen Henrietta Maria, she was appointed lady-in-waiting to Charles' sister, Princess Mary.

The most famous female agent of the period was the playwright, novelist and poetess Aphra Behn, born in Kent, possibly near Canterbury. Her early life is a confusion of conflicting stories, not helped by her use of several aliases, including Ann Behn, Mrs Bean and Agent 160. She claimed to have travelled to the Dutch East Indies, possibly as an English spy, before her marriage in or just after 1664 to a German or Dutch merchant named Johann Behn. Although he soon disappeared from her life, she continued to use her married name, even when the second Anglo–Dutch war broke out in 1665. This was also the year in which 100,000 Londoners died of bubonic plague. As one of the first women to earn a living by writing in England, she rose from obscurity to be noticed by Charles II after the Restoration and, being fluent in Dutch, was despatched to Antwerp by his spymaster, Joseph Williamson, to seduce William Scot, an officer of the English regiment in the Dutch Army, and with whom

Aphra had enjoyed an affair two years before when they were both in the East Indies. Williamson gave her the code name Astrea, which she used in her reports to him and also as a *nom de plume* with which she signed several of her subsequent works. In July 1666 – the year of the Great Fire of London, following so soon on the plague – she was in Bruges, tasked with enticing this former lover to turn double agent.[206]

When he informed the Dutch authorities that she was an English agent, it was time for Aphra to leave in a hurry, but her troubles were just beginning. Having received little or no money from Charles II, she was reduced to pawning her jewellery for food and borrowing the fare for her return to Britain, where things looked up. She took to writing for the stage and enjoyed the friendship of notable poets and aristocrats. During the political troubles of the Exclusion Crisis 1679–81, which was caused by Parliament's desire to prevent Charles II's Catholic brother, James, succeeding him to the throne, Aphra wrote a work that brought her much legal trouble. Having learned discretion, she thereafter devoted her writing skills to politically anodyne prose and translation work. Remaining a staunch supporter of the Stuart line, after the arrival in Britain of the Protestant William of Orange, Aphra refused to write a paen of praise for the new monarch. She died shortly afterwards and was buried in Westminster Abbey, where there was plenty of room beneath the flagstones, the remains of Cromwell and so many of his favourites having been disinterred by Charles II and dumped in a mass grave elsewhere as posthumous punishment.

21

Strange Ladies Indeed

To exploit the advantages women enjoy in clandestine activity, men have many times disguised themselves as female – and continue to do so. That most unladylike veteran TV reporter Sandy Gall dressed himself and his two-man camera crew in outsize *burkas* to be smuggled from Pakistan into Afghanistan on one visit. The ruse worked, with none of the hundreds of armed men met on the entire journey bothering to look at the three robed 'women' sitting in the back of a pick-up van bumping along the dusty roads. The disadvantage, of course, was that they had to sit in the open space behind the cab since, as women, they were not important enough to sit inside it.

A number of spectacular espionage coups have been carried out by male agents adopting female dress for a mission or, in the case of the Chevalier d'Eon, habitually. His father, Louis d'Eon de Beaumont, was a rich lawyer who made a fortune in the wine business and was then entrusted by King Louis XV with managing the royal vineyards. Louis' wife, Françoise de Charanton, gave birth on 5 October 1728 in Tonnerre, a town in the Burgundy region of north-eastern France, to a baby entirely enveloped in a caul and whose sex could not be determined by the doctor present. Christened with a mixture of masculine and feminine names – Charles Geneviève Louis Auguste André Timothée d'Eon de Beaumont – the child was raised as a girl and destined for great things.

In 1743, at the age of 15 and belatedly recognised as male, due to considerable prowess as a swordsman and outstanding equestrian skills, young d'Eon was sent to continue his studies in Paris. He gained degrees in civil and canon law at the age of 21 and followed in his father's footsteps, becoming a lawyer attached to the Parlement de Paris. As proof of intellect, he published several works of politics and history, so well received that Louis XV's cousin Prince Conti gave him his first royal appointments. Throughout this stage, d'Eon oscillated confidently, but confusingly for other people, between male and female dress.

In June 1756 he was appointed secretary in the French mission despatched to Russia with the aim of persuading Tsarina Elizabeth I to conclude an alliance with France in the Seven Years' War. Once in the Russian capital, d'Eon reverted to his female identity, which intrigued the empress. Of slender build and pretty of face, he took the name of Lia de Beaumont, and so amused Elizabeth that he was appointed her unofficial companion, to read aloud to her in the evenings. On one occasion at least, Elizabeth tried to seduce her pretty young companion, but was unable to arouse an erection. It was, however, her custom to hold balls at which the noble ladies were obliged to dress as men and the men as ladies. At these events, Lia naturally outshone all the other guests, to the empress' evident pleasure.

The result of this strange intimacy was a draft treaty between Russia and France. Switching gender again, d'Eon changed skirts for breeches and turned horseman, arriving in Paris with the draft two days before the Tsarina's official despatch riders clattered over the cobbles of the City of Light. Louis XV rewarded this combined feat of diplomacy and horsemanship with the brevet of a captain of dragoons, fighting as which d'Eon was wounded in one of the last battles of the Seven Years' War. Returning to civilian life, he was despatched as a secretary in the peace embassy to London, where his constant gender-swapping was one of the reasons the French ambassador fell out with this insubordinate subordinate. Matters worsened until each was suing the other for libel in the English courts, d'Eon appearing at his court appearances one day in a dress and another day in breeches and boots, with sword and spurs. When questioned, he insisted firstly that he was a hermaphrodite, then that he had always been female. The result was that he was widely taken as being slightly mad, which was an excellent cover for his intelligence activities. Without the ambassador's knowledge, but acting on orders from *le secret du roi* or French royal intelligence service, he was reconnoitering the southern coastline of mainland Britain to select the most suitable site for a French invasion.

His work was so appreciated in Paris that this strange spy was awarded the high distinction of the Order of St Louis, patron saint of France. Having no illusions by this stage about the fickleness and mortality of monarchs, d'Eon decided to keep copies of his clandestine correspondence with *le secret du roi*. With the accession to the French throne of Louis XVI, the new king despatched to London a lawyer to acquire from d'Eon the copies of the embarrassing correspondence with his predecessor, including the plans for the French invasion. Playing the gender cards confusingly, as was his wont, d'Eon dragged out the negotiations for fourteen months until a twenty-page pact was finally agreed, under which all the compromising documents were handed over and 'le chevalier d'Eon' became officially 'Mademoiselle d'Eon', and was awarded a royal pension for life.

D'Eon nevertheless returned to the French court dressed as a captain of dragoons. This infuriated Louis XVI, who forbade him dressing in male clothing anywhere on French soil. Narcissism overcoming prudence, d'Eon returned to court on 23 November 1777 in a gorgeous corset dress made by Rose Bertin, the top Paris couturier, who dressed Queen Marie-Antoinette. As to how the dress was paid for, there was gossip that this celebrity dressmaker had managed to procure the physical reaction in her new client that had eluded the Tsarina. Whether that was true or not, everywhere Mlle d'Eon went, she was greeted as a star.

Disaster came when d'Eon defied the king again by resuming the uniform of a dragoon officer once more to volunteer for combat in the American War of Independence – fighting against the British. Louis XVI therefore had him arrested in March 1779, exiled from the court and from Paris, and confined to his family property in Tonnerre. In 1785, for reasons unknown, the king relented and, thinking to rid the court for good of this confusing courtier, granted d'Eon a passport permitting him to return to England and thus avoid settling the considerable debts he had built up in France. With the outbreak of the French Revolution, in which mobs of women played their part and *les tricoteuses* sat knitting as heads rolled off the guillotine, the indomitable d'Eon enthusiastically proposed to the National Assembly that he should form and lead an army of Amazons – a proposal that was treated with appropriate lack of interest in revolutionary Paris.

Debt-ridden on both sides of the Channel by now, d'Eon scraped a living by giving exhibition bouts of fencing in London, always dressed as a woman. Despite becoming somewhat portly with age, he still displayed great agility and superior swordsmanship. In one bout a broken foil pierced a lung, which could have been a mortal wound. As if that was not enough, he was sent shortly afterwards to a debtors' prison, from which he was liberated after promising to write his memoirs, which would have been a best-seller. However, a stroke and a heart attack confined him to bed, after which he died in poverty on 21 May 1810, aged 81.

At last the mystery of his true sex could be resolved. A post-mortem in the presence of seventeen witnesses resulted in a surgeon's report, which read:

> I (name of surgeon) hereby certify that I have examined and dissected the body of the Chevalier d'Eon in the presence of (names of witnesses) and that I have found on the body perfectly formed male sexual organs.

No anomalies noted, then. After a life in which forty-nine years were spent as a man and thirty-two years as a woman, the Chevalier d'Eon was buried in St Pancras cemetery, London. But the grave was not to become a pilgrimage site for later generations of transgendered persons because the construction of the Midland Railway in 1860 involved destruction of that part of the cemetery. D'Eon's remains were disinterred and dumped in a common grave, leaving as the sole legacy of this extraordinary person the words 'eonist' and 'eonism' as the prettiest euphemisms for male-to-female cross-dressers and their practice in any language.

Spying is always deceit, but sometimes on so crass a scale that outsiders can only wonder at the gullibility of the victims. One of the most famous such cases involved Bernard Boursicot, a 20-year-old accountant posted to the French Embassy in Beijing shortly after it was opened in 1964 as the first Western diplomatic mission to China since the Korean War. Boursicot's homosexuality was known to colleagues, but it was thought that there would be no opportunity for illicit liaisons in the strictly disciplined society of the Chinese capital. A major error!

At embassy receptions and other diplomatic functions, the young accountant from a working-class family felt awkward and out of place. The female staff even mockingly changed his name to Bourricot, meaning a small donkey. At one party he met a charismatic Chinese person dressed as a male in the obligatory Mao suit and a leather jacket, who was employed to teach Mandarin to foreign diplomatic staff in Beijing. A fluent French-speaker, Shi Pei Pu was a 26-year-old semi-professional actor, specialising in the shrill soprano female roles of traditional Peking opera.

So began a twenty-year affair. Boursicot's first indiscretion was to invite Shi for a dinner date at a restaurant chosen by his new friend. This was at a time when *any* contact between foreigners and Chinese was automatically monitored by the counter-espionage service of the Ministry of Public Security. At a subsequent tryst, Shi told Boursicot about the traditional opera *The Story of the Butterfly*, in which he claimed to have performed his most famous role as the heroine. He also claimed to have studied under a great master of Peking opera, which the singing master's family later denied.

The *Butterfly* plot concerns a beautiful girl who is unable to attend an imperial school, open to boys only, so she swaps clothes with her brother and enters the school using his identity – leading on, of course, to tragedy when she falls in love with a fellow student. Summoned back to her family home, where a marriage has been arranged, she goes, but her boyfriend dies of a broken heart. Instead of going to her wedding, she goes to his grave and dies there. Realising what has happened, her parents

bury her beside her sweetheart and the two souls turn into but-
terflies, which fly away together.

This chat between Boursicot and Shi led to Shi's confession
that 'she' had been born a girl in Yunnan province, but raised as a
boy because her father already had two daughters and wished for
a son. Shi claimed to have graduated from Kunming University
at age 17 with a literature degree and afterwards written both
plays and operas, mainly about workers and industrial issues,
which conformed to Maoist communist ethics. Shi also claimed
that he was taking male hormones, to look more masculine
although, like many Asian males, he grew no beard.

Boursicot had had sex with boys at school, but said later that
he was desperate to find out what sex was like with a woman,
so Shi's confession that 'she' was really a woman sparked an
immediate chemistry between them – at least on Boursicot's
side. Eventually Shi was forced by the Ministry of Public
Security watchers who kept all Westerners under close scrutiny
to admit an ongoing affair with the young French diplomat. At
least, such was the story later given in court, although it is more
likely that Shi was working for the Ministry from the start.
At the lovers' infrequent meetings in Shi's home, theatrical
female garb was the order of the day, or rather, night. It would
have been dangerously bourgeois to wear any feminine clothing
in public at this time. At their meeting in December 1965, after
Boursicot had been told he was being posted back to France, Shi
told him that 'she' was pregnant.

The Chinese were playing a long game, for Boursicot's
lowly status on the first posting to Beijing was unlikely to
have given him access to many secrets that could be betrayed.
When Boursicot returned to the Beijing embassy in 1969, the
relationship was resumed after Shi produced a photograph of a
4-year-old mixed-race boy and said that their child, Shi Du, born

in August 1966, had been sent to live in far away Xinjiang province for safety during the unrest of the Cultural Revolution. In fact, the boy had been purchased from his mother there.

Boursicot's new duties were in the embassy archives, which made him a much more interesting target for the Ministry of Public Security, so Shi was ordered to intensify the relationship. At a meeting with two public security officials in Shi's house, Boursicot's concern for his alleged son's welfare led him to admit that he had access to the diplomatic pouch and reports from other embassies. He thereafter furnished several hundred documents, which the two security men photographed before he returned them to the archives. After the end of that posting, in 1977 Boursicot volunteered for and was appointed to the embassy in Ulan Bator, the capital of Mongolia, where embassy security was non-existent. He took the train to Beijing every six weeks, where Shi Du was now living with his 'mother'. Boursicot no longer had any sexual interest in Shi, but felt great affection and responsibility for the boy, purchasing his continued safety by handing over more classified documents. It was said at his trial that between 1969 and 1972 and in the years 1977–79 he had disclosed some 500 diplomatic papers in this way.

Meetings between the two former lovers in these years were infrequent, and ceased completely after Boursicot's return to Paris in 1979. Yet, concern about his 'son' led him in 1982 to arrange a three-month tourist visa for Shi and the boy, now aged 16, to come to Paris, where they both moved into the apartment Boursicot shared with his long-term male lover. The Parisian glitterati making Shi a celebrity after a couple of television appearances singing Peking opera female roles, Boursicot was able to arrange a twelve-month extension of the visa on cultural grounds.

On 30 June 1983 officers of French counter-intelligence organisation La Direction de la Surveillance du Territoire made a routine check after being informed that two Chinese nationals were sharing an apartment with a Foreign Service officer. Bit by bit, the story came out, although Shi refused to admit having known anything of Boursicot's meetings with the two public security officials, alleging they must have taken place while 'she' was absent. The investigating magistrate was, however, able to clear up one ambiguity by insisting on a medical examination, in which Shi revealed to the doctor how 'she' had duped Boursicot in bed. By tucking away his testicles, pulling his penis tightly back between the legs and using the loose skin of the scrotum to provide the simulacrum of a vulva, Shi had been able to provide an intercrural orgasm for Boursicot.

All this time, Boursicot remained convinced that Shi was female and Shi Du his biological son. On remand awaiting trial, he was so horrified to hear on the radio in his cell how his ex-lover had concealed 'her' true sex successfully throughout their long, if irregular, period of intimacy, that he slashed his throat with a safety razor blade. The injury was minor.

After a long investigation, both Boursicot and Shi were accused of conspiring to communicate confidential information to a foreign power. In court, Boursicot claimed he had only fed low-grade trivia to the Chinese, and was obliged to listen as Shi explained to the prosecutor that they had had *des rapports sexuels* only rarely, rapidly and in the dark, which the young Frenchman had believed was traditional Chinese feminine modesty. Side by side in the dock, with Boursicot looking imperturbable and Shi, having suffered a heart attack, looking wretched and very unlike his glamorous stage persona, they were both sentenced to six years' imprisonment. Shi was pardoned by President Mitterand in April 1987 as a gesture in the *détente* between Paris and Beijing. Four months later, Boursicot was also pardoned.

The whole intriguing honeytrap episode was made into a successful Broadway play in 1988 under the title *M. Butterfly* and filmed five years later with Jeremy Irons playing Boursicot. Shi meanwhile had returned to the stage, singing female roles occasionally and writing some libretti. Although they both lived in Paris, Shi met Boursicot rarely, although always telling 'her' old paramour that 'she' still loved him. On 30 June 2009 at the age of 70, Shi died.

Boursicot had suffered years of ridicule in public and in private for not discovering the sex of 'the mother of his child' and made no comment, except to say that he was now free – whatever that meant.[207] As so often in espionage, the ripples did not stop with Shi's death. To explain his mixed race appearance, Shi Du said that he came from China's Uighur minority people and had been sold by his mother to Shi Pei Pu, not because his mother did not love him, but because the family was starving. It is more likely that he was procured by the Ministry of Public Security, which would be well aware that many women of the Uighur Muslim minority race living in the far north-west of Xinjiang autonomous region – which has common borders with Kazakhstan and Russia – bore children by Russian men, and that this was regarded as a disgrace, with the baby to be got rid of as early as possible.[208]

22

Sex and the Secretary of State

During the Cold War many Western diplomats and business-men fell victim to KGB honeytraps in Warsaw Pact countries, being filmed with a prostitute or, if gay, with another man by a concealed camera and microphones. It seemed in 1963 that this 'sexpionage' so beloved of fiction writers had actually occurred in London after a series of uncovered Soviet spy operations in Britain: the Portland spies (see pp. 186–191), George Blake, the KGB mole inside MI6 and the homosexual Admiralty clerk John Vassall. Secretary of State for War Stephen Profumo and Captain Yevgeni Ivanov, the naval attaché at the Soviet Embassy in London, had been taking turns in the bed of a prostitute, so it was widely assumed that she must have been wheedling secrets from the Secretary of State to pass on to the Russian spy.

The girl was 21-year-old Christine Keeler, who shot from the shadows to the front pages. She was not beautiful, but had a good body, exuding sexual availability and feminine vulner-ability when in the presence of a possible client. The catalyst in this tangled web was a middle-aged society osteopath named

Stephen Ward, who procured girls for affluent male clients – and for MI5 when it wanted sexually compromising photographs of foreign diplomats and VIPs for blackmail purposes.

After meeting Christine in a Soho cabaret club, where she was working as a topless dancer, Ward offered to paint her portrait.[209] She had dreams of becoming a fashion model, so her vanity was piqued and shortly afterward she moved into his luxurious house in Wimpole Mews, Marylebone. From the shop work and waitressing of her past life, this was a leap into another world. Although she afterwards said they never had sex and Ward behaved like a good father to her, she did have sex for money with other men. Some of his rich patients knew Ward also arranged discreet sado-masochistic orgies for himself and friends, but very few knew that he, most improbably, had been a communist for several years and was particularly friendly with Ivanov, with whom he enjoyed all-night sex-and-drink sessions. This being at the height of the Cold War, Ivanov was under routine surveillance by MI5 after being 'outed' by KGB mole Oleg Penkovsky as an agent of Soviet military intelligence Glavnoe Razvedyvatelnoe Upravlenie (GRU).

From time to time, Ivanov pressured Ward to prove his communist leanings by wheedling out of his politician patients any military intelligence of interest to the USSR. Ivanov swiftly became Christine's most frequent client in an already long line that included a black US serviceman two years previously – after she left home to avoid her stepfather's physical advances at the age of 17 – and by whom she had a baby that died shortly after birth. There was also a longer relationship as mistress of the infamous slum landlord Peter Rachmann, whom she passed on to another dancer from the cabaret club named Mandy Rice-Davies, known to her friends as Randy Mandy. These two girls' faces would become known to everyone in Britain and many other countries who ever saw a newspaper. Opening it was not necessary because they were usually on the front page.

Over the weekend 8–9 July 1961 Keeler was staying with Ward and some of his friends at the riverside cottage, for which he paid a peppercorn rent or none at all, on the Cliveden estate of Lord Astor in Buckinghamshire. In the main house on the estate, Astor was playing host to a large party of personalities from the arts and political worlds in honour of Pakistan President Ayub Khan. Among the guests were John Profumo and his wife, the popular film star Valerie Hobson. On the Saturday evening, when Ward's group was mingling with the larger party around the swimming pool, 19-year-old Christine stripped off to display her wares, swimming in the illuminated pool directly in front of Astor and Profumo. Seeing her naked body, the 46-year-old Secretary of State was immediately infatuated. Educated at Harrow and Oxford University and rising to brigadier rank in the Second World War, Profumo's successful political career and marriage to Valerie Hobson had survived many other extra-marital affairs.

Introduced to Profumo while trying skilfully not to cover herself too well with a towel, Christine had no idea who he was but, hearing he was married to a film star, thought they might in her words, 'have a bit of fun together'. The bit of fun developed into an affair, if one can call it that, shortly after the meeting at Cliveden. Presumably in one of their routine meetings, on 12 July, Ward told his MI5 contact, whose cover name was Mr Woods, that Ivanov and Profumo had met at Cliveden and that the latter had clearly been turned on by Christine. Ward also stated that he had been asked by Ivanov for information about the supply of nuclear weapons to West Germany. MI5 regarded it as normal for a Soviet naval attaché to ask such questions, but Profumo's interest in Christine complicated a plan to use her in a honeytrap for Ivanov. Ward's news was therefore referred to MI5's director-general, Sir Roger Hollis.

Profumo's visits to Christine at Ward's home had to be carefully choreographed, so that he did not bump into Ivanov.
Sometimes there were only minutes between one of them leaving and the other arriving. Christine later said that Profumo
made love to her unromantically. He complained that her
conversation consisted of make-up, hair styles and pop music
– which was fair enough, since he was not seeking intellectual
stimulation. Usually, they met at Ward's house in Wimpole
Mews, but once Profumo took her back to his home in Regent's
Park when his wife was absent. On another occasion, he indis-
creetly took her for a drink with a former Secretary of State, the
only possible reason being to show off his young 'conquest'.

On 9 August the Cabinet Secretary, Sir Norman Brook, who
had been told by Hollis of Profumo's closeness to Ward's circle of
friends, advised him that this was unwise. Profumo's guilty conscience made him think that it was his new affair with Christine
that had triggered the rather vague warning and unwisely wrote
her a letter, beginning, 'Darling ...', in which he told her they
had to end their liaison, although she later maintained it continued for several months, perhaps more discreetly than before.
Christine, in turn, passed this news on to Ward, whose complicated lifestyle gave him many reasons to be alarmed that his
name was being mentioned in this context.

In October 1961 Ward took Christine slumming in Notting
Hill, where she met Aloysius Gordon, a Jamaican jazz singer
with a record of petty crime and violence, who became her
regular client. He was extremely jealous of other men she was
seeing, which included another Caribbean figure named Johnny
Edgecombe, a former merchant seaman and underworld figure
from Antigua. Edgecombe and Gordon had a knife fight, presumably to establish who had the first call on Christine's services.
As a result, Gordon required seventeen stitches in his face. On
14 December 1962 Mandy was also at Ward's house in Wimpole

Mews when Edgecombe arrived, demanding to see Christine. Fed up with his violent behaviour, she would not open the front door, at which he fired five shots.

On 22 January 1963 the Soviet government recalled Ivanov to Moscow. Up to this point, the whole Profumo–Keeler affair might have been hushed up but, after police were summoned following Edgecombe's attack, Christine accused Gordon of the shooting and – perhaps hysterically – talked of Ward's procuring of girls for important men and asking her to obtain information from Profumo. Seeking to disengage himself, Profumo made a personal statement to the House of Commons that he did not know her, and would issue writs for libel and slander if any accusations were made. Given his past dalliances, few MPs can have believed him. His subsequent confession that he had lied was followed by Profumo resigning his ministerial post and his parliamentary seat on 4 June 1963. The resulting scandal was considered to be a contributory factor in the Conservative government losing the 1964 general election. At the time, that sober periodical *The Economist* printed a picture of Christine under the headline 'The Prime Minister's Crisis'.

At his trial Gordon maintained that he had an alibi, of which the two witnesses could apparently not be found – at least, not by anyone wearing a uniform. He was pronounced guilty, largely on Christine's evidence, and sentenced to three years' imprisonment. The media were kind to the two girls, describing Christine as a freelance model and Mandy as an actress. Possibly to deflect media attention from an ex-minister and restore confidence in the government, it was believed that police were pressured by Home Secretary Sir Henry Brooke to ignore the MI5 protection Ward had enjoyed and take the opportunity to investigate his vice activities. They interviewed 140 of Ward's friends and patients, kept a twenty-four-hour watch on his home, and tapped his telephone, which required direct authorisation from Brooke. Among those who provided statements was Keeler, who confirmed her sexual relationship with Profumo by describing details of the interior of his home in Regent's Park. To break her silence, Mandy was arrested on two minor charges and twice locked up briefly in the grim Victorian building that was Holloway women's prison.

Christine attempted to sell her story to several national newspapers, but the best offer she received after handing over Profumo's letter addressing her as 'Darling' was £200 from *The Sunday Pictorial* with the promise of £800 on publication. After Ward told the *Sunday Pictorial* that Christine's story was a tissue of lies, and that he and others would sue the paper if it was published, the offer was withdrawn, so Christine was left with only £200. When Profumo's lawyers attempted to buy her silence, the sum she demanded was so high that they considered prosecuting her for blackmail.

Ward was put on trial on 22 July 1963, charged with living off the immoral earnings of Christine, Mandy and two other prostitutes, and with procuring women under 21 to have sex with other persons.[210] In court, Christine tried to protect Ward by testifying that any money she had given him was to cover household expenses when she was living in Wimpole Mews and for the repayment of loans he had made to her. The only light moment in the trial was when Mandy – who was 'as bright as a button', as the saying went – replied chirpily to counsel's statement that Lord Astor denied ever having met her. She reduced the entire court to laughter with her riposte: 'Well, he would, wouldn't he?'[211] Facing a certain guilty verdict after a very hostile summing up by the judge, Ward took an overdose of sleeping pills on 3 August 1963 and died later in hospital.

After Gordon's conviction was quashed by the Court of Appeal when his witnesses reappeared to testify on oath that Christine's evidence at his trial was false, she received a nine-month sentence – not for espionage but for perjury. When Edgecombe's trial began, Christine was a key witness for the Crown but was hiding in Spain, afterwards claiming that she had forgotten the date. Edgecombe was found guilty of possessing a firearm with intent to endanger life and sentenced to seven years in prison.

And so London's great sexpionage scandal fizzled out like a very damp squib. In those inhibited days before kiss-and-tell, Christine's ghost-written book was not a success, nor was a film in which she played the part of herself. Most of her income from these went to pay her lawyers. She married twice, but neither husband stayed the course, despite the two sons born to her during this time. At the time of writing, she lives alone with a cat and says she never enjoyed sex. Profumo was cleared of any breach of security by an official inquiry headed by Lord Denning, but subsequently attempted to expiate his guilt by working as a menial volunteer for an East End charitable trust. He did not return to politics and died after receiving several honours for his charity work in March 2006, aged 91. After his recall to Moscow, Yevgeny Ivanov resumed his naval duties in the Black Sea Fleet. In 1992 his partly-ghosted version of the Ward–Profumo–Keeler scandal was serialised in *The Sunday Times*, but some material had to be removed from the English book edition[212] after lawyers acting for John Profumo challenged certain events. He died in Moscow in January 1994, aged 68. Of them all, Mandy Rice-Davies came out best. She married an Israeli citizen and became part-owner of restaurants, bars and hotels in Israel. Two marriages later, with her self-confidence and sense of humour intact, she was living with a millionaire acquaintance of Denis Thatcher, whose wife Margaret found her an amusing holiday companion, by all accounts. Mandy died of cancer in December 2014 at the age of 70, being survived by her third husband and a daughter.

23

The KGB is Dead.
Long Live the SVR!

During the four decades of the Cold War, the initials KGB signified terror all over the world. They were even more feared by citizens of the USSR, since the Komitet Gosudarstvennoi Bezopasnosti – or Committee of State Security – also controlled draconian internal security and locked up to 5 million Soviet citizens *at any one time* away from society in the Gulag camps. Spying on the rest of the world was the task of its First Chief Directorate which, after the collapse of the USSR, was given a facelift and rebranded Sluzhba Vneshnei Razvedki (SVR) – the foreign intelligence service. In case anybody thought Moscow had stopped spying – and many people did, but espionage will always be with us – on 27 June 2010 the FBI mounted a synchronised series of arrests across the USA. Ten arrested people pleaded guilty in a Manhattan court to the charge of acting as undeclared agents of a foreign power, an offence that merited five years' imprisonment under federal law. Other charges not pressed included money laundering, which carried a sentence of twenty-plus years on conviction.

The FBI obviously wanted to wrap up the whole business swiftly, because on 9 July the ten prisoners were at Vienna International Airport, walking from a chartered American aircraft to a Russian one, due to fly them to Moscow's Domodedovo Airport, while four Russians, who had spied for Britain and the US, were walking in the opposite direction in the biggest spy swap since the Cold War. End of story? Not quite. There was a mysterious eleventh agent, in Greek Cyprus at the time, using the Hellenic-sounding name Christopher R. Metsos. Whatever his real identity – it was reportedly Pavel Kapustin – the bespectacled mid-50s Metsos was the bagman for the swapped agents and provided their illicit funds, totalling several million dollars over the years – which would amply have justified the withdrawn charge of money laundering. He was arrested under an Interpol mandate by police at Larnaca airport as he was about to take a flight to Hungary. Why was he in Cyprus? It has a considerable Russian population; many shares in the Bank of Cyprus are owned by Russians; immense Russian oil and gas companies such as Lukoil and Gazprom send billions of dollars to the island each year; its Russian-educated president Demetris Christofias is the only communist head of state in the European Union; and the island's drugs and prostitution are controlled by Russian mafias. It is probably the best place in the world to launder Russian money. Not surprisingly, Metsos was released on bail and allowed to slip secretly out of the country on the following day, suffering only the minor inconvenience of having his false Canadian passport revoked by Ottawa.

The backstory to all this, however, is fascinating. Many of the SVR agents in the US had been under surveillance for several years, being filmed and video-recorded by FBI followers exchanging material or money in identical bags during brush passes in busy places and also monitored using temporary Wi-Fi links, short-wave radio, invisible ink and other espionage tools. More sophisticatedly, some of them also inserted encrypted messages in digital photograph files posted on Facebook, to be decrypted by SVR. Exactly what intelligence the ten had collected was never made clear. Their declared tasks to report on US policy in Latin America and Washington's attitude to Russia and fears of the internet being used by terrorists, do not require even a presence in the States, let alone the enormous planning that went into this complex of missions. For example, it was revealed that most of the arrested agents had been paired in Russia as couples by SVR, with the women even bearing children by their espionage partners. So, they had dual roles as active spies who also made their partners' cover seem more legitimate.

Who were these extraordinary women? Anna Vasilyevna Kushchenko, aka Anna Chapman, who held a British passport; Lydia Guryeva, aka Cynthia Murphy; Vicky Peláez, a Peruvian journalist with US citizenship; Natalya Pereverzeva, aka Patricia Mills; and Yelena Vavilova, aka Tracey Lee Ann Foley.

At the time of her arrest, Anna Chapman was a 28-year-old with the looks and figure of a model, but also the ability to look sweetly shy and demure, as in her US Marshals' mugshot. Born in Volgograd, the daughter of Vasili Kushchenko, a serving KGB officer, she earned a master's degree in economics in Moscow and met a British businessman named Alex Chapman at a London disco rave in 2001, marrying him shortly afterwards. Aged just 20 and in possession of a British passport, she showed little interest in her new husband, spending most of her time with the young Russian *novyrichi* set partying in London. In the daytime, she worked for Barclays Bank, the aircraft-sharing firm NetJets and other companies, but never for very long. Her public face was on LinkedIn, Facebook and a Russian classmates' site – all apparently normal for a young woman of her age and type.

The couple divorced in 2005. After Anna returned to Russia the following year, her husband believed that she attended an SVR spy school. She next surfaced in the West living with a rich American businessman in Manhattan, where she set up an international Internet property agency. After two years with little business to show, she suddenly seemed to hit it rich, describing herself as CEO of a company named Propertyfinder that, she claimed, had fifty employees. At the time of her arrest, she was in a relationship with a fashionable restaurateur.

The *modus operandi* used by Anna to communicate with her SVR handlers might have been foolproof, had she not already been under surveillance while sitting in a Barnes and Noble bookshop or a Starbucks coffee shop every Wednesday, tapping away on a laptop that looked like any other but had a neat modification that enabled her to use a temporary discrete Wi-Fi connection to pass material to an employee of the Russian consulate sitting in a car parked nearby. It was therefore most unusual when an FBI agent, posing as a member of the Russian consulate in New York, asked for a face-to-face meeting with her in a Manhattan Starbucks and handed over a false passport to pass on to another member of the group, which she agreed to do. Suddenly alarmed, Anna bought a new mobile phone and SIM cards to call her ex-KGB father in Moscow and another person in New York, both calls being monitored by the FBI. Advised to get rid of the passport swiftly, she did so by handing it in to a local police station on the following day, but was arrested shortly thereafter. During a refuelling stop on the spy-swap flight to Vienna, Anna may have been interviewed by MI5 with an offer to revalidate her British passport, revoked by the Home Office on 13 July, in return for information about her activities during her years in Britain. If that offer was made, it was turned down.[213]

Earning the comfortable salary of $135,000 p.a., 39-year-old Lydia Guryeva/Cynthia Murphy lived in a middle class suburban home that cost nearly $500,000 dollars in Montclair, New Jersey, with her 43-year-old husband Vladimir Guryev, who went under the name of Richard Murphy. Since arriving in the US some time before the collapse of the USSR, she had been awarded two university degrees and a master's in business administration, establishing herself as vice-president of a financial services company, apparently to gain insider information about the world gold market. The couple had two daughters, aged 9 and 11 at the time of the arrests.

If Lydia could pass as an American citizen – she claimed to have been born in New York City – that could not be said for her husband, who was a bizarre choice for this mission, having a strong Russian accent and what acquaintances considered very Russian behaviour patterns. He had been under surveillance for at least six years, on one occasion travelling to Moscow and bringing back a modified laptop computer, on another handing over a large amount of cash to another member of the group. Supposedly the Murphy/Guryev couple was gathering intelligence on Washington's policy vis-à-vis the SALT treaty[214] negotiations and other high-level policy issues, but it seems that Lydia did not think highly of her husband's performance.

Aged 55, Vicky Peláez already had a 38-year-old son before this mission, and a second son aged 17 by her partner Mikhail Vasenkov, aged 66, who was using the identity of Juan Lazaro,[215] a Uruguayan child who had died at the age of 3. To muddy his trail, Mikhail applied for Peruvian citizenship, which was granted in 1979. He married Vicky in 1983 and, posing as an anthropologist in the US, was employed in 2003 as a university lecturer for just one term before being sacked for expressing

overtly anti-American opinions to his students – a strange thing
for a deep cover agent to do.

Throughout her television journalistic career in her native
Peru before coming to the US, Vicky Peláez consistently
expressed anti-US views – not unusual in Latin America, but
very indiscreet for a future deep cover spy. She married 'Lazaro'
in 1983 and was allegedly kidnapped by a communist guerilla
group the following year, but showed no animosity towards her
captors and was thought to have been instrumental in the kidnapping of a group of journalists. They were released after she
negotiated with her employers to broadcast a propaganda film
about the Sendero Luminoso – Shining Path – terrorist movement. In 1985 she moved to suburban New York with 'Lazaro'
and her adult son.

The 36-year-old Natalya Pereverseva/Patricia Mills lived in
Seattle on the West Coast – home to many hi-tech companies
– with her 41-year-old partner, Mikhail Kutsik, aka Michael
Zottoli. He appears to have entered the US in 2001; the first trace
of her dates from 2003. In Seattle they both obtained degrees
in business administration, meanwhile receiving and decoding
encrypted shortwave radio transmissions from SVR. Although
there are many different accents in the US, neither could pass as
North American-born. Natalya did not have paid employment,
but stayed home to look after their two sons. In 2009 Mikhail
lost his job, prompting a move to Arlington in Virginia for purposes not revealed, except that it is very near to Washington and
several government agencies. There, the couple lived on money
passed to Mikhail by Guryev/Murphy and were once observed
by an FBI surveillance team digging up a stash of money that
Metsos had buried in a field months earlier.

When arrested, 47-year-old Yelena Vavilova and her 49-year-
old partner, Andrei Bezrukov, aka Donald Heathfield, confessed

their Russian nationality and admitted that they had been spying in the US. Yelena had a job with a property agency in Massachusetts, where the couple lived. Although claiming she was Canadian, she travelled on a British passport. What they were doing before this mission is a mystery because they had two sons, aged 16 and 20 at the time of the arrests, so were patently a couple before the mission commenced. The older son, studying in Washington, was reportedly being groomed by his parents for a career in espionage. Out of the country at the time of the arrests, he was barred from re-entry into the US. Also pretending to be a Canadian citizen, Yelena's partner had a degree in public administration from Harvard, which was revoked after the arrest because he had used a false identity to register. What exactly he did remains a mystery, although he was a member of several scientific organisations and attended conferences where he met scientists in government employment, none of whom apparently had a high security clearance.

Of the others in the group – it was not, strictly speaking, a network – 28-year-old Mikhail Semyenko used his own name and lived in playboy style, driving an expensive sports car although he was employed in a travel agency. He also openly spoke Russian in public and had been observed in Wi-Fi communication from a modified laptop with a Russian consular official known to have funded illegal agents, who was sitting in a car parked in the vicinity.

On 13 July another illegal agent was named as Alexei Karetnikov, who had been working at Microsoft. A 23-year-old geek, who was said to have little knowledge of English, but know his way around the IT world, he too was expelled, and another illegal, out of the country at the time the FBI swooped, was denied re-entry.

The *quid pro quo* for allowing the eleven agents arrested in the US to walk free was revealed by a Reuters correspondent

in Moscow. In Cold War spy swaps, Western nationals imprisoned in the USSR were freed, but Soviet citizens were not. In
2010 the price for the return of the ten Russian agents and Vicky
Peláez was the release of four Russians caught spying for Britain
and the US, and detained in very harsh conditions – one at least
in a Gulag camp somewhere in the Arctic, although the Gulag
is no longer supposed to exist. No women here. Their names
were Alexander Zaporozhsky and Igor Sutyagin, convicted of
spying for the US; Gennady Vasilenko, who was sentenced to
three years for possession of illegal weapons; and Sergei Skripal,
a former Russian Army colonel, who had been sentenced at his
trial in 2006 to thirteen years for betraying to MI6 the identities
under which a number of Russian agents were spying in Western
Europe. He got off the aircraft when it landed at RAF Brize
Norton airfield on the homebound leg; the others continued to
the US.[216] The swap was done in a very calm and gentlemanly
manner, with the children left behind in the States escorted
'home' to be reunited with their parents in Russia, where some
of them had never lived.

As to who broke the cover of the illegal agents, on 3 May 2011
a Moscow court martial blamed 59-year-old SVR Colonel
Alexander Poteyev, deputy section head of department 'S', controlling illegals in America. He was found guilty on the charge
of spying for the CIA since 1999, when he was posted to the US
under diplomatic cover, and sentenced *in absentia* to twenty-five
years' imprisonment. Evidence was given by Anna Chapman to
the effect that only Poteyev could have given the FBI the password uttered by the undercover agent who gave her the false
passport. In true master-spy fashion, Poteyev had left Moscow
on a train to Belarus to avoid airport security after telling colleagues he was making a private visit to a mistress who had
just given birth. It was not illogical because he had been born

there. Some thought the mistress was in Ukraine. From Belarus, he entered Ukraine and then travelled to Germany, texting his wife, left behind in Moscow, to stay calm although he was not coming back, ever.

Strange? Well financing a group of spies costs money. 'Metsos', as was known, had made many trips to the US, transporting funds. Since Poteyev and his colleagues in department 'S' were able to arrange this as part of their work for SVR, it seems that one of them had the idea to use the same channels to launder in the West illicit cash belonging to *siloviki* – members of the new Russian super-rich. Even stranger was that Poteyev's adult son and daughter lived in the US, having possibly grown up there, and were allegedly involved in the racket. Under the old KGB regime, no officer was allowed to have relatives abroad; they were effectively held hostages for his good behaviour. Do times change that much?

It is usually the case that blown spies, once repatriated, fade from view, but not all these five women did that. Natalya Pereverzeva, with her degree in business administration, was employed as an adviser for foreign economic relations to the president of the Transneft oil conglomerate in January 2011. Vicky Peláez surfaced in February 2011, attending her father's funeral in Peru. Her child by Vasenkov/Lazaro was not with her. Nothing is known about Yelena Vavilova, but her husband Bezrukov/Heathfield works as an advisor to Russia's largest oil and gas company, Rosneft. When giving him the job, the president of the company said, 'I don't know if he was a spy. He's a normal guy with a knowledge of international affairs.'

During the group's debriefing by the SVR, they were not held *incomunicados*, but allowed family visits – which implies very low security – after which they were awarded medals in October by then-President Dmitry Medvedev. Not too much should be read into this because many Russians sport a chestful of medals, awarded for all sorts of reasons. In December then-Prime Minister Vladimir Putin – himself a former KGB officer – warned ominously that the traitor who had betrayed this group would come to a bad end.

Anna Chapman wasted no time starting a new career as the 'beautiful girl spy' – *shpionka* in Russian – appearing at fashion shows in April 2011 and June 2012 on the catwalk modelling expensive clothes, doing a photo-shoot in scanty lingerie for the November 2010 issue of Russian glamour mag *Makzim*, in which she tried to look sultry or sexy and was interviewed playing the part of a femme fatale who had set a honeytrap for a senior member of Obama's White House. She was dubbed Agent 90-60-90, the figures describing her figure in centimetres, which won her a place in the magazine's list of 100 most beautiful Russian women. According to the news agency Interfax on 1 October 2010, Chapman was then employed as an adviser on investment and 'innovation issues' to the president of FundserviceBank, a Moscow bank that handles payments on behalf of Russian companies in the aerospace industry. Her fame spread even further when January 2011 saw her hosting her own weekly television programme called *Secrets of the World* for REN TV. Six months later, she was said to be editor of *Venture Business News* magazine, according to Bloomberg News. Really? Well, anyone with a Cyrillic keyboard can browse through hundreds, possibly thousands, of Russian-language sites devoted to her, one of which plays on the title of a James Bond film. Entitled *Iz Rossii bez liubvy* – which translates as From Russia *Without* Love, it includes her announcement that she married Alex Chapman to get a passport, nothing more.

So, what are we to make of this bizarre episode? On 9 July 2010, US Attorney General Eric Holder said none of the accused had passed *any* classified information to a foreign power, which was the reason why no one was charged with espionage. If that is true and this was a serious espionage operation, what did it achieve? What spymaster trained in the KGB/SVR would choose such an obviously Russian person as Vladimir Guryev to be a deep cover agent in America? Both Vicky Peláez and Vladimir Vasenkov were publicly anti-American; at the age of 66 he was fit for retirement in any case. Neither Natalya Pereverseva nor her partner Mikhail Kutsik could pass as the native-born Americans they claimed to be. Since Yelena Vavilova and Andrei Bezrukov had a 20-year-old son, what had they been doing since he was born? Semyenko lived habitually beyond his apparent means and made no secret of his Russian origin. Karetnikov could not even speak English fluently. And the glamorous Anna was hardly the archetypal 'grey person' who makes the ideal spy: she constantly courted attention both in Britain and the US. Whatever SVR training she may have had did not stop her calling her father in panic after the meeting with the undercover FBI agent. Listening in to that conversation must have been a laugh-a-minute for the snoopers at NSA Fort Meade, GCHQ Cheltenham or wherever.

All in all, the operation cost many years in preparation and a lot of money, yet apparently achieved nothing. Old KGB hands – both in Russia and defectors under protection programmes in the West – were rightly scornful. But in what James Jesus Angleton, former CIA counter-intelligence guru called the 'wilderness of mirrors', there is also smoke. Smoke and mirrors? This whole SVR scenario, largely made possible by the women involved, who were prepared to get pregnant and bring up children in a society they were trying to destroy, can only be seen as a scenario so flawed that it was *designed* to be uncovered after burning up manpower of the FBI and other US agencies for years, to deflect attention from something far more important. So, when will we know what that was, or is?

On 4 March 2012 – the day of the Russian Federation presidential election – *The Sunday Telegraph* carried a piece datelined Moscow from its correspondent Tom Parfitt about a 26-year-old blonde Russian girl who was going to act as an official observer in that day's election for the Russian presidency. Her newsworthiness was due to having *not* been expelled from Britain for spying. A few months earlier, just about everyone was familiar with the unforgettable name Katya Zatuliveter, whose ex-lover, 65-year-old Liberal Democrat MP Mike Hancock, served on the parliamentary defence select committee while employing her as his parliamentary researcher. To appoint a known Russian citizen to work in an office where classified documents were kept, was bizarre. To appoint a young woman with almost photographic memory to do the job and then have a four-year sexual relationship with her was, to put it mildly, verging on the insane. Afterwards, Mr Hancock did say that to have an attractive girl of much less than half his age wanting to go to bed with him should have rung an alarm bell. So he's on the learning curve.

At the Special Immigration Appeals Commission hearing in November 2011, MI5 officers demanded the deportation of this graduate of Bradford University on the grounds that she had betrayed some of the secrets picked up in Mr Hancock's office to a known SVR agent code-named Boris, attached to the Russian Embassy in Kensington Palace Gardens. Several of her meetings with him were videotaped by MI5 watchers and presumably replayed to the members of the commission in closed session. Enjoying diplomatic status, 'Boris' had been allowed quietly to leave Britain. The hearing was held to decide what action to take over Ms Katuliveter's activities. Although she had apparently also had affairs with a senior NATO officer and a Dutch diplomat,[217] it dismissed any accusation of espionage and confirmed that she had the right to stay in Britain. Although the MI5 men and women had failed abysmally to prove their case, Oleg Gordievsky, one of the highest-ranking KGB defectors ever, considered that Ms Zatuliveter had caused Britain more damage than any other agent for the last thirty years.[218] As *The Economist* commented tongue-in-cheek, 'It is a fair bet that a young British woman in Moscow would not fare as well as Katya Zatuliveter did in London.'[219]

Cleared by the hearing, this young Russian woman who chose to sleep with a NATO officer,[220] a diplomat and an MP entrusted with classified documents during the five years she spent in Britain, decided to head back to Russia on hearing that Vladimir Putin and Dmitri Medvedev were in the process of fixing another presidential election of the Russian Federation, to give Putin a couple more terms as president. Although a factor in her decision was lack of a job, she claimed to be motivated principally by the desire to do something positive about the corruption in Russian politics. Her status as an electoral commission member at a polling station in northern Moscow would, she hoped, allow her to detect fraudulent voting, habitually used by Putin's One Russia party. She was quoted as saying, 'We need an independent judiciary, we need MPs for whom people actually voted, we need equality of opportunity, not favours for a privileged elite. Putin can't provide these things. His time is over, he's out of touch.'[221]

What did she think of Putin's opponents in the presidential election? According to Mr Parfitt's article, she was sceptical of the four candidates facing Putin, accusing them of being Kremlin-approved stooges, ultra nationalists or simply corrupt. So for whom would she vote? Her preference was for a Green politician called Yevgeniya Chirikova, who was not in the race.

Her reason? 'We could do with a woman president. Women don't take so many bribes.'[222]

The girl's name Katya is fairly common in Russia. Another time it hit headlines in the West was in October 2010, when *The Telegraph* reported that Ekaterina Gerasimova – also known as Katya or Moo-moo on Facebook – has piercing blue eyes, an innocent girl-next-door face, and likes to do a little amateur modelling. A model agency photo-shoot shows this attractive brunette posing in her underwear, with vivid pink nail varnish and an inviting smile. It seems that the Kremlin also uses female agents at home, where the star operator of the Russian Federation domestic security organisation Federalnaya Sluzhba Bezopasnosti – Federal Security Service – is indeed Ms Gerasimova. Her main business activity seems to be discrediting Mr Putin's political enemies by enticing them in honeytraps. According to the report, the tools used to entrap at least a half-dozen victims were sex and drugs 'from cocaine to marijuana'. Satirical journalist and scriptwriter Viktor Shenderovich, married with a daughter, was one man who fell for it – and forfeited his quiet married life when his wife saw the video. Another was Mikhail Fishman, editor of the Russian edition of *Newsweek*, video-recorded in his underpants chopping up what appeared to be cocaine, to snort after having sex with Ms Gerasimova.

In the videos of these encounters – deliberately made grainy and amateurish-looking although Shenderovich believes they were professionally recorded by FSB technicians – which are in circulation on Russian Internet sites, several other opposition players are recognisable. None of them realised they were all being set up by the same girl because she used different names and perhaps they did not look at her face. More astute was politician Ilya Yashin, who was invited to join Gerasimova and another girl in a threesome with various sex toys and drugs. At that point he asked whether they were being filmed and left. How many Gerasimova enticed is not known, but several public figures were reported to be nervous about one day seeing their 'performances' on the internet whenever they annoy the Kremlin. Among politicians of varied hues calling for an investigation of this new version of the old KGB honeytrap used on so many Western businessmen and diplomats are far-right anti-immigrant activist Alexander Potkin, arrested in 2014 for asset-laundering after a Kazakhstan banking scam, and ex-political prisoner and Franco–Russian novelist Eduard Limonov, the prematurely grey-haired founder of the National Bolshevik Party. They believe they may yet see themselves on the screen, starring in one of Ms Gerasimova's home movies.[223] In reporting all this, *Huffington Post* advised any readers chancing to meet the blue-eyed lady in a glitzy Moscow bar to down their drinks and swiftly walk away. That seems a good idea.

Epilogue

This book is written in homage to all the courageous women whose activities are recorded here, drawn from all levels of society and education, and who did what they did for the gamut of motivations from simple humanity through patriotism to a burning desire for worldwide revolution. It is also the tip of an iceberg and could have been ten times as long, or longer. At its present length it demonstrates just how diametrically wrong were their male colleagues, who judged these women less able than their fathers, husbands, lovers, brothers and sons to fight in the no-rules clandestine world.

Hamil Grant's 1915 history of espionage included his considered claim that 'woman as a rule fails as a secret service agent' because she acted only for reasons of love or revenge and was virtually incapable of experiencing the platonic patriotism that, he believed, drove men.[224] Even Constance Kell, wife of Vernon Kell, founder of MI5, claimed that 'women were occasionally used by the Germans [in that war] as agents if they were possessed of a ready wit … but their usefulness was somewhat limited.'[225] Compared with what, one wonders.

Historian Tammy Proctor did identify just one tiny shortcoming of her sex in this field. The British postal censors of the First World War depended on chemical reagents revealing secret writing and it was suggested that semen could be used because it did not show up with the usual reagents.[226] For female agents working alone, procuring the semen might have been a problem, but knowledge of their dedication and resourcefulness suggests they would have found a way around it, had the theory been proven.

One hundred years after Hamil Grant and Constance Kell made their biased observations we have had a female head of MI5 in Stella Rimington, who noted that the agency recruited men 'as what were called "officers" [while] women had their own [lower level] career structure' even in her day. On the other side of the Atlantic, during the 1990s several female CIA officers sued that agency for gender discrimination and sexual harassment in the workplace and station chief Janine Brookner won a $400,000 settlement after suffering what was described as 'institutionalised discrimination' at Langley.[227]

Acknowledgements

Although even the Cold War is long past, many people did not wish to have their contributions attributed and their privacy has been respected. However, I can thank Marge Ben-Tovim for permission to use extracts from *A Long Journey*, the unpublished memoirs of Frieda Truhar Brewster. Patrick Hilliard introduced me to Daphne Maines' adventure in Prague. Anne Denney, née Kappius, generously sent material and photographs of Aenne Kappius. Dvorah Netzer helped with research in Israel, as did Tuvia Amit, who first put me on the trail of Sarah Arenson. Chanah Netzer-Cohen, no mean photographer herself, helped with photographic research. The Corrie Ten Boom Museum in Haarlem was a marvellous source for material and gave permission to use photographs. Patrick Gerassi threaded a path through the Spanish Civil War.

At The History Press, I should like to thank my commissioning editor Mark Beynon and project editor Lauren Newby.

Notes

1. All translations are by the author, unless otherwise attributed.
2. All photographs are from the author's collection.
3. Reasonable steps have been taken to establish copyright. In the case of any infringement, please communicate with the author, care of the publisher.

Notes and Sources

Introduction

1   www.publications.parliament.uk/pa/ld201011/ldhansard/text/110606.
     htm (abridged)

1. The Perfect Cover for the Perfect Spy

2   C. Pincher *Too Secret too long* London, Sidgwick & Jackson 1998, p. 12
3   M.H. Mahoney *Women in Espionage* Santa Barbara, ABC-CLIO 1993, p.
     80
4   Spelt 'Sonja' in the German fashion.
5   J. Haynes & H. Klehr *In Denial: Historians, Communism and Espionage* New
     York, Encounter 2005, pp. 149–50
6   Pincher, p. 70
7   He also used several other names in his clandestine work.
8   Mahoney, p. 138
9   *Ibid.*, p. 139
10   Pincher, pp. 54, 86
11   *Ibid.*, p. 84
12   *Ibid.*, p. 58
13   N. Moss *Klaus Fuchs, The Man who Stole the Atom Bomb* London, Grafton
     1989, pp. 53, 55
14   Moss, p. 63

15 Pincher, p. 121
16 A comprehensive account of the creation of the GDR and its political
    system may be found in Boyd *Daughters of the KGB* Stroud, The History
    Press 2015, pp. 13–218.
17 Published in English as *Sonya's Report* London, Chatto & Windus 1991.
18 The second time was in 1969.
19 Her husband had been born with the name Nussbaum but changed it to
    Norwood.

2. Handmaidens of the Red God

20 B. Macintyre *A Spy Among Friends* London, Bloomsbury 2014. pp. 40–1
21 Deutsch was a mystery man. No one seems certain from where in Central
    Europe he originated, but his record as an educated and very clever
    Comintern agent and handler was undoubted.
22 Some sources say it was liver cancer.
23 Unpublished memoirs of Frieda Truhar-Brewster
24 *Ibid.*
25 A neologism to denote the few hundreds of people in the USSR of
    whom Stalin had heard and who could be appointed to key posts because
    he knew their names.
26 Truhar-Brewster memoirs
27 *Ibid.*
28 *Ibid.*
29 Quoted in *Potsdamer Frauen* ed. G. Schnell, Potsdam, Potsdamer
    Verlagsbuchhandlung 1993, p. 104
30 *Ibid.*, pp. 99–108
31 The name of the Soviet international assassination arm was an acronym
    of *schmert spionam*, meaning 'death to spies'.
32 Boyd *The Kremlin Conspiracy* Stroud, The History Press 2014, pp. 170–1

3. Born in Bessarabia, Buried in Beijing

33 P. Sudoplatov *Special Tasks* London, Little Brown 1994, p. 189; T. Sharo
    Stalin's American Spy London, Hurst 2014, pp. 61–2
34 Sudoplatov, p. 189
35 *Ibid.*, p. 189–90
36 *Ibid.*, p. 94
37 *Ibid.*, p. 192
38 *Ibid.*, pp. 190–1
39 *Ibid.*, p. 363

40   *Ibid.*, p. 424
41   Boyd *Kremlin* p. 140

4. The Women Who Did Not Talk About It

42   In Castillian, *Partido Obrero de Unificación Marxista*
43   *Journal of International Women's Studies*, Vol 10, Issue 4, Article 11,
      May 2009
44   Records in the Servicio Histórico Militar, Madrid, reference cabinet 4,
      SIPM file 240
45   Article by Ibón S. Rosales in www.lainformacion.com 18 July 2013
46   *Cante Jondo* Stockholm Norstedt 1937
47   http://elmundo.es/elmundo/2011/05/01/galicia/1304248966.html
48   She wrote a book about her experiences: *Spy-jacked – A Tale of Spain*
      Horsham, Gramercy 1991
49   *Journal of International Women's Studies*, Vol 10, Issue 4, Article 11,
      May 2009

5. Women Against Hitler

50   *The Labor Branch of the Office of Strategic Services* Doctoral thesis by D.M.
      Lynch submitted to Dept of History, Indiana Univ 2007, p. 36
51   The correct spelling is Änne or Aenne, a Scandinavian form of Anna.
52   Although Hermann Göring, in his capacity as Prussian Acting Interior
      Minister, inaugurated the camp system, Himmler swiftly added it to his
      empire.
53   P. Marquardt-Bigman *Amerikanische Geheimdienstanalysen über Deutschland
      1942–49* Berlin, Oldenbourg 1995, p. 113
54   J. Persico *Piercing the Reich* London, Michael Joseph 1979, pp. 75–6
55   Lynch p. 35 fn
56   Persico believed there were fifteen cell leaders.
57   Lynch, pp. 36–7
58   Persico, pp. 82–3
59   *Ibid.*, p. 85
60   K-D Henke *Die Amerikanische Besetzung Deutschlands* Berlin, Oldenbourg
      1995, pp. 645–6
61   The accounts of the ISK members rely heavily on extracts of original
      documents and photocopies supplied by Anne Denney, including
      Werner Link *Geschichte des Internationalen Jugend-Bundes (IJB) und des
      Internationalen Sozialistischen Kampf-Bundes (ISK)* Meisenheim am Glan,
      Anton Hain 1964, pp. 307–22.

62   She also used the cover names Hilde Olday, Selma Trier, Helen Harriman, Eva Schneider, H. Monte, Hilde Monte and Hilda Monte at various times.

63   Surviving script of the transmission

64   Lynch, p. 40

65   Persico, pp. 241–4

66   The complete letter may be found on the University of Wisconsin site using the link http://www.library.wisc.edu/archives/wp_content/uploads/sites/23/2015/06/letters_death_mildred_fs.jpg

67   The poem may be found on www.library.wisc.edu/archives

6. The Human Submarines

68   Incredibly, given the extremely high levels of security, successful escapes by 144 men and women are documented.

69   Thousands of prisoners suffered from dysentery, cholera and typhus and were too malnourished and weak to reach the filthy and inadequate toilets.

70   B. Lovenheim *Survival in the Shadows* London, Peter Owen 2002, p. 22

71   A play on words, *Rundfunk* being the German for broadcasting.

72   Sources vary on the rate of remuneration.

73   Quoted in Lovenheim, p. 67 (abridged)

74   There was later a French sector, carved out of the British sector.

75   Lovenheim, p. 198

76   Stella's story is documented in P. Wydon *Stella: One Woman's True Tale of Evil, Betrayal and Survival in Hitler's Germany* New York, Doubleday 1993. Wyden had been at school in Berlin with Stella.

7. When the Men are Away …

77   E. Fischer *Aimée and Jaguar* tr. E. McCown, London, Bloomsbury 1996, pp. 11, 17

78   Under the Nuremburg laws, there were degrees of Jewishness, depending on how many Jewish grandparents one had.

79   Fischer, p. 107

80   *Ibid.*, p. 35, p. 161

81   *Ibid.*, p. 166

82   Quoted in Fischer, p. 173 (abridged)

83   Quoted in Fischer, p. 175

84   Fischer, p. 177

85   *Ibid.*, p. 185

86   The twilight of the gods

87   Now Zmigród in south-western Poland

88 Quoted in Fischer pp. 246–7 (abridged)
89 Lovenheim, caption to photo of Lina Arendt's card
90 Quoted in Fischer, p. 260 (abridged)

8. SOE SOS

91 Le Service du Travail Obligatoire
92 D. Boyd *Blood in the Snow, Blood on the Grass: Treachery, Torture, Murder and Massacre, France 1944* Stroud, Spellmount 2012, pp. 23–4
93 S. Helm *A Life in Secrets* London, Abacus 2007, p. 22
94 Also spelled Devereux
95 E. Devereaux-Rochester *Full Moon to France* British edition London, Robert Hale 1978
96 Boyd *Blood in the Snow*, p. 73
97 For a full account, see Boyd *Blood in the Snow*, pp. 56–101.
98 *Ibid*., pp. 75–9 for the full account
99 *Ibid*., p. 78
100 They were sent in by SIS, the Gaullist BCRA, the American OSS and even, in two cases, on RAF flights, by the Soviet NKVD.
101 This account of the Bouchou/Faytout episode was a personal communication to the author by Cathérine Hestin, née Bouchou.
102 The full story, including the recent recovery of some of the hidden weapons, may be found in D. Boyd *Voices from the Dark Years*, Stroud, The History Press 2015, pp. 253–7.
103 P. Mignon *De Castillon à Sachsenhausen* Bordeaux, Publications Résistance Unie en Gironde 1990
104 Boyd *Blood in the Snow,* p. 24
105 Helm, p. 11
106 B. O'Connor *Churchill's Angels* Stroud, Amberley 2012, p. 103
107 Helm, pp. 13, 14
108 For the full story, see Boyd *Blood in the Snow*, pp. 24–8
109 Helm, pp. 33–4
110 Also spelled Natzweiller by German speakers
111 O'Connor, p. 63
112 Helm, pp. 199–200
113 *Ibid*., pp. 250–61

9. Heroine or Liar?

114 O'Connor, p. 201
115 D. Boyd *Blood in the Snow*, pp. 19–22
116 O'Connor, pp. 202–3

10. Rape as a Tool of War

117 B. Rey *Les Egorgeurs* Paris, Editions de Minuit 1961

118 B. Rey *Les Egorgeurs* Paris, Editions Libertaires 2012

119 *Ibid.*, p. 15 (abridged)

120 Transmission by Fr2 on 7 February 2002

121 Interview in *Envoyé Spécial* 7 February 2002

122 Sometimes misspelled 'Susini'

123 H. Pouillot *La Villa Sesini* Paris, Editions Tirésias 2001

124 Personal communication to the author

125 P. Aussarès *Services Spéciaux Algérie 1955–57* Paris, Perrin 2001

126 *Envoyé Spécial* 7 February 2002

127 Personal communication with the author. Name changed at her request.

128 *Ibid.*

129 H. Alleg *La Question* Paris, Les Editions de Minuit 2008, p. 39

130 See https://fr.wikipedia.org/wiki/Bataille_d%27Alger

131 *Envoyé Spécial* 7 February 2002

132 *Ibid.*

133 *Ibid.*

134 S. de Beauvoir and G. Halimi *Djamila Boupacha* Paris, Gallimard 1962

135 Article by S. de Beauvoir in *Le Monde* 2 June 1960

136 Article by C. Taraud on p. 64 of www.histoire.press.fr No 371 of January 2012

11. The Whore of the Republic

137 Article by K. Laske in *Libération* 6 April 1999

138 Quoted in Boyd *Dark Years,* p. 207

139 *Ibid.* (abridged)

140 P. Webster *Pétain's Crime* London, Pan 2001

12. Sayonara, SIS

141 W. Stephenson *A Man Called Intrepid* London, Macmillan 1976, p. 342

142 *Ibid.*, p. 343

143 A comprehensive account of the attack may be found in D. Boyd *De Gaulle: The Man Who Defied Six US Presidents* Stroud, The History Press 2013, pp. 53–7.

144 Stephenson, pp. 348–50

145 *Ibid.*, pp. 363–76

13. Two Daughters of Israel

146 A quotation from the book of Samuel 1:15:29
147 Sources vary.
148 Some sources say that Sarah was tortured to death by the Turks in Jaffa.
149 Unpublished material held at the Hannah Szenes Study Centre in Sdot
     Yam
150 *Ibid.*
151 *Ibid.*
152 T. Soros *Maskerado* Edinburgh, Canongate 2000, p. 231
153 *Ibid.*, p. 236
154 *Ibid.*
155 *Ibid.*, (edited)
156 *Ibid.*

14. The Pearl in the Lebanese Oyster

157 At the time of writing, 'Dvorah Meir-Dror' was still alive. Names in
     this chapter have been changed at her request, to protect her family;
     everything else is unchanged.
158 A. Golan & D. Pinkas *Code Name the Pearl* New York, Dell 1981, p. 45
159 The Mossad was not formally established until 13 December 1949
160 Golan & Pinkas, p. 345
161 *Ibid.*, pp. 383–4
162 *Ibid.*, pp. 405–6 (abridged)
163 It is now a medium-sized seaside resort.

15. Dutch Courage

164 Full title: Nederlandse Vereniging voor Vrouwenbelangen,
     Vrouwenarbeid en Gelijk Staatsburgerschap
165 *Spionne in het Derde Rijk* 2004
166 D. Vandekerchove *Fatale Opdracht* 2011
167 *Het Laatste Nieuws* 22 February 2015

16. Condemned for Mercy

168 Meaning 'frightfulness' or appalling behaviour
169 http://www.mairie-hautmont.fr/Decouvrir-Hautmont/
     Histoire-et-patrimoine/La-premiere-guerre-mondiale/
     Represailles-contre-les-civils

170 T. Proctor *Female Intelligence: Women and Espionage in the First World War* New York, New York University Press 2003, p. 173 fn

171 Thuliez, pp. 108–12

172 *Ibid.*, pp. 207–9 (abridged)

173 *Ibid.*, pp. 197–8

174 *Souvenirs de la Princesse Marie de Croy 1914–1918* Paris, Plon 1933

175 http://fondationprincessedecroy.org

176 *Marie de Croÿ*

17. Death Behind Bars

177 *RTBF info* 5 August 2014

178 Proctor, p. 119

179 *Ibid.*, pp. 93–3, 119

180 La Coupole, centre for history and memory in Nord-Pas-de-Calais region

181 Some sources have it that this was an Iron Cross and also that she received the French *Légion d'honneur*.

182 Republished as *Spionage!* in Stuttgart by Dieck in 1932. There was also a spin-off film.

18. Women in the Cold War

183 D. Boyd *Daughters of the KGB*, in the Introduction of which the author gives a brief account of his incarceration in a Stasi political prison

184 Sources: *Reading Eagle*, 15 December 1951; *Glasgow Herald*, 24 December 1951; *The Advertiser*, 3 January 1952; and other newspapers

185 For the full story, see Boyd *Daughters of the KGB*, pp. 165–7.

186 His official title was 'General Secretary'; Stalin was *Gensek* of the CPUSSR.

187 Boyd *Kremlin*, p. 167

188 So called because it compressed long transmissions so that they could be sent too fast for direction-finding

19. Women in the War Between the States

189 Introduction to her book

190 Published in London 1965 by Saunders Otley and Co, Belle Boyd's book is available in digital form at http://docsouth.unc.edu/fpn/boyd1.html by courtesy of the University of North Carolina, scanned with funding by the Library of Congress/Ameritech National Digital Library

Competition. The edited extracts used in this section are all taken from that edition.

191　Published London, Richard Bentley 1863
192　Published as *The Female Spy of the Union Army,* Boston, DeWolfe, Fiske, & Co. 1864, it was republished as *Nurse and Spy in the Union Army* and is now available as *Memoirs of a Soldier, Nurse and Spy: A Woman's Adventures in the Union Army* Dekalb, N. Illinois University Press 1999

20. 'Intrigues Best Conducted by Ladies'

193　The full story may be found in D. Jordan & M. Walsh *The King's Revenge* London, Abacus 2013.
194　http://legacy.fordham.edu/halsall/mod/women.asp
195　*Oxford Dictionary of National Biography*, article by I.J. Gentile: Chidley, Katherine
196　Some sources say five days; some say nine.
197　Some sources say nine or ten towers.
198　The MS may be seen on www.jimandellen.org/halkett/memoir.show. html. This extract is from pp. 19–24 of MS (abridged).
199　J. Fox *The King's Smuggler* Stroud, The History Press 2010, p. 88
200　Earl Clarendon *History of the Rebellion and Civil Wars in England*, 1702–04
201　Jordan and Walsh, p. 20
202　Fox, p. 20
203　*Ibid.*, p. 139
204　Quoted in Fox, p. 145
205　Saints, like royalty, had been banned, so it was then 'James' Palace'.
206　Jordan and Walsh, p. 315

21. Strange Ladies Indeed

207　*Los Angeles Times* 6 July 2009
208　There is an account at length of the affair in J. Wadler *Liaison: Real Story of the Affair that inspired M. Butterfly* New York, Bantam 1994.

22. Sex and the Secretary of State

209　It was later acquired by the National Portrait Gallery.
210　Obituary of Mandy Rice-Davies, *The Telegraph* 20 December 2014
211　Often misquoted as, 'Well, he would say that, wouldn't he?'
212　Y. Ivanov and G. Sokolov *The Naked Spy* London, Blake 1992

23. The KGB is Dead. Long Live the SVR!

213 *Sunday Express* 8 August 2010

214 Strategic Arms Limitation Treaty

215 Many Spanish-speakers have more than one surname. His full name was Juan José Lazaro Fuentes.

216 *The Guardian* 9 July 2010

217 *Daily Mail online* 25 October 2011

218 *Ibid.*

219 *The Economist* 3 December 2011

220 Her emails to him, intercepted by MI5, were described as 'cloying'.

221 *Sunday Telegraph* 4 March 2012

222 *Ibid.*

Epilogue

223 *Huffington Post* 25 May 2011

224 H. Grant *Spies and Secret Service: The Story of Espionage, its Main Systems and Chief Exponents* New York, Fredereick A. Stokes 1915, pp. 24–5, quoted in Proctor, p. 44

225 *Ibid.*

226 *Ibid.*, p. 45

227 *Ibid.*, p. 148

Index